Churning of the Heart: Volume Two
Memories of Maharajshri

Also Available from Sadhana Books

Churning of the Heart: Volume One
Introduction to Spiritual Life

Churning of the Heart: Volume Three
Union With the Infinite

Churning of the Heart: Volume Two
Memories of Maharajshri

❀   ❀   ❀

By Swami Shivom Tirth

SADHANA BOOKS
An Imprint of Berkeley Hills Books
Berkeley, California

Published by Sadhana Books
An Imprint of Berkeley Hills Books
P. O. Box 9877
Berkeley, California 94709
www.berkeleyhills.com
(888) 848-7303

This work was originally published in 2000 by the Devatma Shakti Society,
Thane, India, in Hindi, with the title *Hriday Manthan, Volume Two*.

Cover design by Elysium, San Francisco.
Cover photo of Swami Vishnu Tirth.
Printed in the United States of America.
Distributed by Publishers Group West.

I 3 5 7 9 IO 8 6 4 2

Library of Congress Cataloging-in-Publication Data

(Available from the publisher)

Contents

Foreword

The three-volume series, *Hriday Manthan*, was originally written in Hindi and thus its distribution has been restricted to readers of that language. Hindi readers have appreciated the trilogy greatly. Sadhana Books in Berkeley, California, USA, has accepted the responsibility of bringing the English translation of this series to readers under the title *Churning of the Heart*, for which I am grateful. I hope the English-reading audience will welcome this trilogy with the same enthusiasm and sentiment as the Hindi audience.

The three-part series is a compilation of the instructional speeches and spiritual activities of Swami Vishnu Tirth Maharaj, and the story of a disciple with a defective inner self. On the one hand, the aspirant is troubled with the desire-filled nature of his heart; on the other, he draws inspiration from the compassionate words and actual incidents and experiences of Maharajshri. The heart of the disciple lies in between and, churned with the rod of instruction and sadhana, keeps rising and falling. The above-mentioned state of contemplation, or churning of the heart, is imperative for every novice sadhak. The series is a presentation of this state.

I hope the English reading audience will like this series and be inspired to churn their hearts through these sermons.

Shivom
Indore (M.P.), India
July 9, 2001

Introduction

The memory of Maharajshri is like a fragrant garden of flowers filled with fresh floral perfume, joy and cool breeze. Every dew drop in this garden is shimmering with light. Every flower, branch and leaf is vibrant proof of the workings of chetana [consciousness]. It is pulsating with the intoxication of sadhan, tenderness of the heart, waves of emotion, and soaring experiences of spiritual knowledge in the inner sky. His style of presentation had a remarkably supernatural quality. The language was beautiful, easy and delightful to hear. The concepts were supported by personal experiences, appropriate references to context, and corroborated with examples from the scriptures. Each and every word of his directly struck the heart of the listener. The methods were appropriate to the level of a sadhak [disciple] — the listener. Display of scholarship was never the purpose of his speech.

His heart was so generous that followers of every caste, religion and spiritual practice used to find a place in it. He did not see any path, principle or way of worship moving in the opposite direction from God. The whole world is a child of God. To find his Supreme Father an aspirant can take any path. All have the same ardent desire; He alone is everybody's goal. The emotion, faith and belief of each aspirant can be different. Diversity is this world. The day all ideologies become one there will be no world.

It was his opinion that the awakening of Shakti [energy] is a river that must be crossed to advance on the spiritual journey. There may be different expressions for this awakening of Shakti, but all have accepted it in one form or another. In this the country, path, sect or principles do not matter. Spirituality is much higher than sects. No devout follower of any sect is closer to God than a spiritual person. In spirituality, all sects cease to exist.

Part One of *Hriday Manthan* was welcomed with such enthusiasm and feeling that a second edition had to be printed within four or five months. Meanwhile there were demands from readers that the author give details about himself. Some even said there should have been more description of the states of other aspirants. The only response I would like to give readers is that this is not my autobiography. The only purpose of this has been to bring to light the personality of Maharajshri and to compile and publish his teachings. It was not for me to look at the states-of-mind of other disciples. Yes, here and there observations are made about the group mentality of the aspirant community. If someone is discussed in the context of some incident, his or her name is not mentioned. To illustrate the impact of Maharajshri's teachings on disciples, I have been the representative of all the disciples. It is, in fact, very difficult to understand the inner state and dilemmas in the mind of someone else, and if someone else had been discussed they might feel bad. This could cause unnecessary complications. It is not within the capacity of a common person to fathom the depth of the words of great beings. However, due to his ego, everyone believes that he has understood everything.

The thoughts and sentiments described in this book are only Maharajshri's. I am only a messenger. I have tried to remain a messenger and not to add anything from my side to the teachings, except when there is a description of natural beauty and the churning of my own heart. Along with me, my style of expression has also borne the responsibility of being only a messenger. It has only done the job of bringing the thoughts and sentiments of Maharajshri to readers.

Just as in Part One, in this second part there are only two characters, Maharajshri and myself. If ever the name of another is mentioned, it is only of someone who is not with us now. The only exception to this is Shri Narayan Tirthji Maharaj — it would have been improper not to mention his name. I understand that readers will appreciate my feelings and respect that.

Hardly anyone knew that Maharajshri had contact with many invisible, great beings because Maharajshri never talked about it to anyone.

Only a few knew some thing about Agasha. If Maharajshri had not talked to me about it I also would not have known anything. Maharajshri instructed me to not talk about it during his lifetime. I followed Maharajshri's instructions fully, and not only during his lifetime, but also during my own, I have not spoken to anyone about this until now. Now, when I see the evening of my life, I have the good fortune to compile the teachings of Maharajshri. I could not resist the temptation to unveil this part of Maharajshri's life.

Maharajshri never praised his siddhis [spiritual powers] with his own voice. Although the spiritual height of a great being cannot be measured by his siddhis, many talk about his miracles. For instance, when he was in Rishikesh and Shri Yoganand Vijnaniji Maharaj, his Guru, was living in Swargashram, Maharajshri crossed the Ganges River walking on the water while having an upsurge of Shakti. When I tried to discuss this with Maharajshri he just smiled. Therefore I cannot say whether it is true or false. Even if Guru Maharaj had siddhis, he never exhibited them.

Maharajshri never propagated his experiences during sadhan. If he had to explain something to someone regarding sadhan, he would always explain it on the basis of scriptures. In his books also, he never referred to his own sadhan. He used to say that experiences in sadhan were not for publicity. By doing that ego can arise in the mind, which is an obstacle in spiritual progress. I have written a book on Maharajshri, entitled *Sadhan Diary*, which is based on the diary kept by Maharajshri, and which was somehow preserved. I did know about the diary for quite some time, and the book was written only after he had merged with Bramha [cosmic consciousness].

I have never seen so modest a personality as his, in spite of his enfolding such a vast treasure of knowledge and experiences within: simple like a child, affectionate like a devotee, disciplined like a yogi, and even-minded like a jnani [a person of spiritual knowledge]; always adorned with simplicity, always absorbed in devotion, always under the rein of self-control, and always balanced with equanimity. Someone once expressed that Maharajshri was not proud of being such a great person. It is true. How can someone be great if he is proud?

A morning walk was Maharajshri's daily routine, no matter what the weather, however busy he might be. Whether he was in Dewas or somewhere else, at five in the morning he would invariably be found on his walk. After waking up in the morning and after his nap in the afternoon he used to drink some water, routinely. If someone were sitting with him while he was eating he would never forget to offer some food to that person. He used to say that no matter how sattvic your food might be, if you eat it alone while among people it becomes tamasic [inert] in nature.

Whether Maharajshri was being affectionate or explaining something, there would be a rare kind of joyful experience in everything. But I felt happiest when he would scold because at that time a sense of belonging, affection and blessing for the best used to radiate most. His anger was like sacred blessings. The difficulty was that he rarely used to scold. He used to say that he never scolded anyone with anger. "Only when there is too much love does one hear me reprimand."

One day, in the library, a book named *Pratyabhijnahridayam* came to my hand. Abhinav Gupta, the famous Tantra master, had written it. I could not grasp anything upon reading it. I asked, "What is this *Pratyabhijnahridayam?*"

Maharajshri had a distinctive way of explaining. He would say things very precisely and with such profoundness that it would penetrate to the listener's heart. He answered, "You met someone, but you forgot. This is ignorance [ajnana]. After a long time you see the same person again. You cannot recognize him; you are certain that you have seen him somewhere, but cannot remember who he is. This is knowledge [jnana]. Then you try to remember him and you start asking people that are around him. This is called, abhijnana — proceeding toward knowledge. Then you remember or someone reminds you who he is and you recognize him. This is called pratyabhijnana.

"This can also be applied to spirituality in the following manner. There was a time when the jiva, the individual soul, directly knew the Atma [soul], but now the jiva has forgotten him. This is his ignorance.

When he reads scriptures, listens to discourses, does satsang, he has some idea about God, but cannot directly experience God. This is knowledge [jnana]. To experience God he does sadhana, looks for a Guru. This is called abhijnana, meaning 'proceeding towards knowledge.' When he has a direct experience of the Parmatma, the absolute Self or the Atma, the soul, and recognizes it, that is pratyabhijnana. The scripture in which this particular subject is illustrated is called *Pratyabhijnahridayam."*

Thus Maharajshri's style was very simple, yet appealing to the heart. The subject would immediately be accessible and clear. Maharajshri used to say that the person who explains has to come to the level of the person who is trying to understand and only then explain. If one could learn from books alone then what was the need for schools, colleges and teachers? If the lecturer goes on expounding his knowledge and listeners do not understand anything then what is the use of such scholarship? Following this, Maharajshri wrote a brief commentary on the book *Pratyabhijnahridayam.*

I cannot say what the impact was on others or what others grasped from Maharajshri, but each and every word and each and every action compelled me to look within. Many vices and shortcomings that were fully present in me, to which I had been indifferent so far, started to come to my attention. My real personality started to come to light. Often my soul would shiver looking at my own vices. I realized that I had sunk into a deep well of illusion and that I had been totally unaware of that fact. Maharajshri turned my attention inward.

The whole world is filled with sinful, hideous feelings and thoughts, but the ego of a living being does not let him see the real state of his chitta [mind-stuff]. Then where does the question of accepting one's own faults or courageously admitting them before society arise? If someone displays such courage, society measures that also on the scale of ego. But once the attention is turned inward, one becomes indifferent to the world. No matter what one does and the manner in which one does it, the world is going to point fingers in every situation because pointing fingers is the world's job. Seeing these ways of the world, an aspirant does not give up his path. Any attempt to look good or bad is nothing but false ego. Maharajshri used to alert us against this. He used to say that everyone wants to look good but no one wants to become good. The difficulty with a human being is that even though he sees nothing but darkness within him, he is unable to get out of that darkness. First, there is the darkness; second, he is blindfolded. Also he does not have a walking stick to explore the path. To top all of that, there is the intoxication of Maya [illusion]. His steps falter and he falls again and again. Guru Maharaj is the only support. He dispels the darkness, removes the blindfold, and provides a walking stick. He makes us aware of Maya, too.

Who is not troubled by his mind? Saints such as Tulsidas, Tukaram and Surdas all have resolutely blamed their mind. They have cried to God about the mind. They have warned sadhaks and bhaktas, devotees, about the unruly and thankless mind. When Nanak said, "I am lowest of the lowly," he did not have a desire to gain status either as a great author, orator, devotee or social reformer. He did not have any concern about the opinions of the world. Only a businessman would make efforts to attract the world, but not a devotee or a spiritual aspirant.

A person for whom writing is not sadhana, but a supportive part of sadhana, does not chase the world to earn fame as a writer. He does not write to entertain the world. Rather he writes to convince his own mind. His writing holds the screams of his heart. His separation from God and awareness of the futility of the world are contained in his writing. Our ancient sages were spiritual beings first and then they were writers. They wrote for inner satisfaction. With the same perspective they used to take the support of music. They were not known as musicians but as devotees or yogis. All the fine arts were the same. Artwork used to have a special appeal because it was an outburst from the heart. Whether it be prose or poetry, it can be a source of inner benefit only when it is dominated by spirituality. That is when it can touch the heart and soul of readers and listeners.

I mentioned that all living beings are enveloped in the attraction of Maya. Pride stops one from really looking within. But all are naked under their clothes. No one is worthy of criticizing anyone else. If someone does criticize then it is nothing else but pride.

The essence of Maharajshri's teachings is in grasping this secret. Even after starting on the spiritual path, one can be lost if this fundamental fact is missed. Even while the sun is shining he is unable to remove his blindfold. If he has any interest in any specific art form, he remains lost in the art only. Art is a means to untangle the knots of the heart. When the window of the heart opens art flows out from within. At first the knowledge of language takes place in the intellect. Along with the study and recitation of scripture the heart must be affected. When feelings of the heart are expressed naturally, know that the knot of the heart has begun to open. Then the writer does not consider what the world expects from him. He writes only what he wants to offer to the world. Those who like it may accept it, and those who do not like it may leave it.

In the introduction to the first part of *Churning of the Heart* I wrote that this book was written more for myself and less for others. The teachings of Maharajshri are equally beneficial to all, but real benefits depend upon whose heart is churned in the light of his teachings. I know about my own heart. As the teachings started to enter me, my mind became restless to leave the darkness and enter the light. The natural state of the chitta kept on unfolding.

Now I have greater eye problems and I am not sure whether I will be able to write the third part or not. I hurried through this second part so that I could finish it before my eyesight became worse. There is no guarantee for the body. Who knows how long the body will keep us company? I will always regret that having attained a human body, having found a Guru like Maharajshri, I did not reap the benefits to the extent possible. I have heard that a Guru is like a philosopher's stone, which turns iron into gold by a mere touch, but I have remained iron only.

Someone asked me whether I tried, while praising Maharajshri highly, to find any vices or faults in him. It is not correct that I never tried to see any vices, but whenever I did try, his virtues kept coming before me and I was lost in awe. Hence I could never see whether he had any faults or not.

Memories of Maharajshri keep returning, but while writing this book his presence was experienced constantly — the same style, the same smile and the same love. Now he is free from the confines of the physical body and has become a part of cosmic consciousness. At least that is our belief. Therefore he has become enormously more powerful and potent than before. He is very much more capable than before. I have faith that by his grace, one day or another, difficulties will definitely be alleviated. My efforts will be worthwhile if even one spiritual seeker follows the right path with the help of this book. With the best wishes of the readers, one day my boat, too, will certainly reach the shore.

I end this with a prayer;

May Guru-Shakti be beneficial to all of you.

Swami Shivom Tirth.
Indore, Madhya Pradesh, India
January 1, 2000

Churning of the Heart: Volume Two
Memories of Maharajshri

1. Churning of the Heart

January 19, 1961. In the morning at eight o'clock, after getting relief from the pain of sciatica in Ahmedabad, I stepped down from the train at Dewas railway station. In front of me a hill was visible, standing with its head lifted before the clear sky. Visible in front was Narayan Kuti, shining at a distance in the cold sunshine of winter. On reaching the ashram, that very day, Maharajshri gave me Bramhacharya diksha [initiation into celibacy, on the path to Bramha — ultimate reality]. I had worn white clothes until then, but now I started wearing saffron clothes; only my loincloth remained white. The right to wear a saffron loincloth is received only after sanyas, renunciation. I started wearing saffron clothes, but I was not used to it yet. When I went to the market to shop I would feel shy. When people stared at me I would look down or turn my face away and look somewhere else. Sometimes visitors at the ashram would ask me when I had started wearing saffron and I would only smile.

On the one hand I was shy; on the other ego had begun to sprout. Now I began to consider myself different from ordinary people. What was the difference? I did not know then. So far, the difference was limited only to the color of my clothes. In the market, if someone bowed to me looking at my saffron clothes I would feel happy. Those who bowed to me became good in my opinion; my ego was on the rise. Slowly my mental state became such that if someone approached me I would expect him or her to bow. If he passed by without bowing I would feel disappointed.

Even in the ashram I began to feel that I was someone special in contrast to others. In place of feelings of service, I began to feel that I had special rights. There was no difference in the work I was doing but there was a difference in my attitude. Thus Bramhacharya diksha had an adverse effect on me in the beginning. This was not really due to Bramhacharya diksha but to the saffron clothes. One day, upon introspection,

I found that I was on the way to a downfall. Pride and display were growing in me. The feeling of being someone special in comparison to others was arising in me. I had come to expect a show of respect. Observing this state of my mind I became frightened. I was better off before getting Bramhacharya diksha. My mind was already polluted, and now was added a heightened ego. Who knew where it would take me? I was shaken. I decided to present the whole situation to Maharajshri.

At the time of our morning walk I presented the situation to Maharajshri. I described my mental state and lamented my regression. Maharajshri became serious and said, "Bramhacharya diksha means that you are now entering upon the life of a tapasvi — an ascetic. You are well familiar with the meaning of tapa: It means lighting a fire under you, burning the tendencies and impressions, destroying your mind and ego. With a peaceful chitta and tolerance, go through life and put an end to your destiny. It means controlling the senses and burning the jiva bhava, the individual identity, to ashes. Very often people doing austerities develop pride about them, whereas the purpose of austerities is to annihilate the ego. You have not even started austerities. You have simply pledged to live an austere life. Because of this your pride has begun to increase. This means that you still lack discrimination. You will have to make an effort to clearly understand and grasp the purpose. Only after understanding the intent [of diksha] does the question of implementation arise.

"Your problem is due to lack of discrimination, but there is another factor here. The source of your ego is your saffron clothes. You have not understood their significance and implications. The saffron color is a symbol of fire and fire reflects austerities. The way in which anything thrown into fire turns to ashes, similarly whatever you throw into the fire of austerities — all desires, memories, defects, impressions, and destiny — are consumed. There is a defect in the austerities of an aspirant whose ego or anger increases due to austerities. That person who puts on a saffron robe but does not live an austere life is deceiving people. The defects of his mind never get burned away. In the fire-pit of his chitta, the fire of austerity is not yet ablaze.

"There is one more thing to be understood about the saffron color. Geru [the soil used for dying saffron clothes] is a special kind of silt. Its saffron color symbolizes the fire of austerities, and also indicates that, ultimately, all is going to be one with the earth. For this reason Bramhacharis and sanyasis [renunciates] wear it while they are still alive. This is to remind them that if they are ultimately going to be one with the Earth then why have an ego? After this analysis you need to look at yourself carefully. After wearing geru, which should remind you of the fire of penance and ultimate merging with the Earth, you have instead given rise to pride. In this way you have not only insulted geru, but you have also exemplified your ignorance."

This advice pierced through my heart like a sharp arrow. On the one hand I was ashamed of myself and hated myself; on the other I was enthused to receive the appropriate guidance. It was natural for me to resolve to fight with my ego. I touched Maharajshri's feet there on the road and accepted that this was really my own mistake. "I should have started on the path of austerities after Bramhacharya diksha. Instead, because of my ignorance, I turned towards egoism. Now please tell me whether one can walk on the path of austerities without formal initiation into Bramhacharya?"

Maharajshri replied, "Formal initiation is not just a mere act of performing the external ceremony. It should influence the mind. If the external ceremony were a necessity then householders would have no authority to perform austerities. There are householders who conduct their married life according to the scriptures and live like ascetics. Most of the ancient rishis [sages] were householders. Each phase of life has its own rules and regulations. By following those rules one can live a life of an ascetic."

We had returned to the ashram and my mind was filled with a constant stream of thoughts. I had lived like a voluntary servant and I must continue to do the same. A servant does not have anger, pride or narcissism. A servant does not demand anything. He does not demand any authority. His only authority is to serve. Then how come I felt that I was someone special? A year earlier I had made the decision to serve my

Guru. Then why were my feelings opposing my decision? My mind was filled with remorse. I kept on thinking that I could not fulfill the duties of a servant. Ego, anger and selfless service cannot co-exist. My heart sank frequently and I kept on trying to lift it. Finally I decided that as long as I lived in the ashram I would remain a servant. I would neither expect any special authority, nor expect to be respected.

2.   The Answer for Freedom from Vices

Churning the heart is a subject that most people try to avoid. Humans are most frightened of their own limitations. People are not interested in studying their own selves because when they look within they discover a jungle of vices and perversions. When one looks into one's own mind, ego rises up and stands in the way and immediately attention shifts outward, while our own bad qualities remain unchanged. In fact, they may even get stronger due to ego. The main reason why the sense of individuality remains in this world is the inability to examine one's own self.

I had many defects but, by the grace of the Guru, it became my nature to continually examine myself. When I tried to search within and shake my mind I would find an army of vices and faults ready to do battle. For the previous few years I had been trying to somehow get rid of my faults, but sadly, I had no success in defeating even a single warrior from this army. Ravana was not even talking about dying. If Rama chopped off one head another would grow in no time. This was the condition of Ravana in the form of my aberrations and faults. Sometimes I would feel that certain weaknesses were gone but in no time they would reappear. After being totally disappointed because of this I surrendered at the Guru's feet. I had heard and read about the glory of the Guru for some time but never took it seriously. So far I had more faith in my own efforts. I was tired of my own efforts. Now I was disappointed and sad and realized the need for a Guru's grace.

Once when Guruji came to Nangal, during a discourse, he said that many people read the scriptures but do not receive their grace. When the desire for finding a Guru arises, then it may be known that the scriptures are benevolent. The grace of scriptures turns you toward the grace of a Guru. My condition was similar. I was studying scriptures a lot but had not yet attained their grace. Finally, when I was disappointed with my own efforts, the grace of the scriptures manifested. I landed in Dewas.

I expressed my grief to Maharajshri. "I know I have many faults. There must be many more that I am not even aware of. I have been making colossal efforts to fight these faults but I have not succeeded in removing a single weakness. What should I do?"

Maharajshri replied, "The defects will not go away that easily. The basic reason for all these weaknesses, defects, vices and tendencies are samskaras, accumulated impressions. These weaknesses will not leave you until impressions are struck down. If you rid your mind of one defect the samskaras will revive it and bring it back. People mostly fight with their faults and leave the accumulated impressions untouched. You are probably making the same mistake and, as a result, you have not yet succeeded.

"It is also true that a person makes efforts and does not succeed because his efforts are made with ego, thus he cannot free himself from weaknesses. Because of the presence of ego, he can fill the mind with defects but he cannot free it. One needs God's grace for this. Freedom from weaknesses depends upon grace. By the grace of the Divine the fire of knowledge and the fire of yoga are ignited within. This is known as the awakening of the Kundalini, Allhadini or Pratyak chetana. This is the experience of prajnana described in Vedanta. Along with the weaknesses and tendencies, this fire also burns the root cause of these weaknesses, the accumulated impressions. Efforts by the individual are of no help. The more effort one makes the stronger the ego becomes.

"This does not mean that one should not make efforts. One must. Then when nothing is attained by effort the person will accept defeat and decide from experience that nothing can be done. He will surrender to God and pray and be eager to receive the grace of a Guru. A sense of surrender will develop within him naturally. By the mercy of God and the Guru he will experience the power of grace. It does not mean that after receiving grace the aspirant does not have any responsibility. As long as there is even a trace of ego how can responsibility be finished? But his responsibility is to make efforts to merge his ego in the awakened

Shakti, to retain a sense of surrender, and to take refuge only under Guru-Shakti."

With these thoughts in mind, I asked, "Maharajji, usually people of the world do not even want to imagine that they have faults. They believe that they are virtuous, intelligent, knowledgeable and capable. According to them, others have all the faults. What will happen to them?"

Maharajshri replied, "This is their ego. There is no one who does not have virtues as well as vices. Mostly there are vices. Is it not a vice to look for faults in others? Isn't it a vice to overlook ones own faults? Isn't it a vice to have pride about one's virtues? Are not attachments and aversions, jealousy and vengeance vices? You asked what would happen to them. As long as they are not aware they will continue to be crushed between the grinding stones of Maya, the grand illusion. Until the habit of introspection develops, vices will not be apparent."

Question: "Is it enough to see one's faults in order to eliminate them?"

Answer: "No. To see faults, to understand their causes, is only the beginning of their destruction. Next comes the feeling of disgust to-wards these faults, and efforts to be free from them. But it is not enough to free one's self from them, because freedom is not dependent on one's efforts but on the kriyas of the Shakti [the spontaneous activities of awakened Shakti]. It is the duty of an aspirant to be very alert when such kriyas happen. Under the influence of such kriyas he must not make the mistake of accumulating new impressions. A feeling of hatred toward faults helps maintain purity in practical life, which is directly related to destiny."

Question: "Worldly activities today depend on human weaknesses. If everyone is free of them then how will these worldly activities occur?"

Answer: On hearing this question Maharajshri laughed loudly and said, "Why do you worry about the activities of the world? First of all, everyone's chitta [psyche] is not going to be purified. It is more than enough if even a few people become pure. Did all have a pure mind in the kingdom of Lord Rama? If that were the case why did Sita have to suffer exile in the jungle? If we assume that some day all will be free of weaknesses, the world and the activities of the world will still go on. Yes, in that world there will be no place for deceit, cheating, selfishness or falsehood."

Question: "Maharajji, what most of us call virtues are defects from the point of view of spirituality. But you are talking about removing defects and not about removing virtues."

Answer: " 'Defects' means rajo guna [disturbing qualities] and tamo guna [the quality of inertia or inactivity]. 'Virtues' means sattva guna [harmonious qualities]. All these are within Maya and they should all be abandoned. However defects are unholy tendencies and virtues are holy tendencies. Unholy tendencies never subside; even if they are silenced, they arise again. But holy tendencies subside spontaneously after self-realization. This is the reason why we have reiterated the subject of eliminating defects or vices. Vices are always for worldly affairs. If virtues are dominated by ego then they are also vices, even if they are harmonious in nature. Virtues that are free from ego are real virtues. These real virtues are inclined towards the soul. These are the holy tendencies that subside upon attainment of the Self."

3. The Way to Retreat from Action

It was now a year and a half since I had come to the ashram. Initially I had thought of staying and serving at the ashram for only one year. That time was over. I was concerned about what people might be thinking. Perhaps some were gossiping. It is true that I had been able to adjust myself, to some extent, to circumstances. Perhaps I was also feeling a desire to be in solitude. Whatever it was, I was yearning for solitude. But I was not able to muster enough courage to talk about this to Maharajshri. Much of the ashram responsibility had come to rest on my shoulders. This, in my belief, was the grace of Maharajshri — that he considered me to be worthy and accepted my services. By now I had also succeeded in suppressing my ego to quite an extent. Occasionally problems emerged, but by the grace of the Guru they would be resolved. There was no problem due to the ashram, rather it was mainly due to my state of mind. Even while serving in the ashram my mental development was not suitable for the ashram. I had come to live the life of an ascetic, thinking about renunciation and total solitude. This thought would not leave my mind. Often the banks of the Sutlej River and the attractive ranges of the lush, green mountains of Himachal Pradesh would float in front of my eyes. Memories of the time spent amid that beauty would come alive in my heart. But how could I talk about this to Guru Maharaj?

One afternoon Maharajshri was sitting alone in his room. Thinking that the time was appropriate, I started the conversation. "Maharajji, the last time I spoke of going away you told me to stay for a few more days. I decided then to reap the benefits of staying at your feet for one year. Now the year is over. Therefore I request your permission to go. Whenever I am needed, I will return."

Maharajshri sat quietly for some time and then said, "The Guru should not be selfish. To stop you from going because you are serving me would be selfish. I have no problem if you want to go somewhere for spiritual benefit, but in my opinion it is beneficial for you now to stay here. You will go from here and build a hut on the banks of the Sutlej River and live there in solitude. Your detachment is not ripe yet. Neither do you have the experience of this life, nor do you have complete spiritual discrimination. If you remain in solitude with unripe detachment, you will not be able to survive for long. Therefore it is best for you to get personal and practical experience of the selfish and illusory nature of the world. The world is sweet on the surface and very bitter inside. People have one thing in their heart and they say something else. When you experience the futility of the world, then your detachment will be firmly grounded. Then you will learn about its futility with certainty. Mere intellectual detachment is not sufficient. It must be accompanied by experience. You will not get this experience in the solitude of Himachal Pradesh. Without indisputable detachment, spiritual attainment is like a daydream. For this reason it is best that you stay here. Do not have a time limit. Along with meditation, experience Maya [illusion] and the futility of the world. However, I will not force you into anything."

I was in a dilemma after listening to Maharajshri's viewpoint. His point was logical, and besides it was from a pure heart and for my benefit. Thus, for me, Maharajshri's wish was my command. All these factors forced me to reconsider. For me it was improper to even ask for time to think it over. That would mean that I had the power to make a decision. It would be contrary to a disciple's duty, as well as that of a servant. Thus I ought to have said immediately, "Very well, Maharajji. I will do as you say." But instead my mouth remained shut due to ego. I became absorbed in my thoughts. Maharajji also became quiet after saying what he had wanted to say. I did not say anything and went out and sat in the verandah.

As I sat on the verandah I was jolted as if by a strong electric shock. I suddenly became very conscious, as if awakened from a deep sleep. What had I done? When Maharajshri gave his clear opinion what right did I have to think it over? "You are guilty of disrespecting Guru Maharajshri by leaving him without giving an answer. You are good for nothing. Your desire to serve is worthless." I berated myself.

I got up at once and went straight inside, grabbed Maharajshri's feet, placed my head on them and started weeping heavily. Maharajshri asked, "What is the matter? I did not say anything to upset you. If you want to go then go merrily. I am happy if you are happy."

On hearing these words I began to cry even more and said, "I will not go anywhere. I made a big mistake — even after knowing your views clearly. I took so long to say, 'All right.' What is the value of my thought against your views?"

Generally Maharajshri was not affected by such events. Many disciples came and went. He never asked anyone to come or go, nor did he stop anyone from leaving. Had I left, it would not have affected his mind in any way. He simply said whatever was good for me. Listening to me, his jovial nature came alive. He said, "Good. Make me a cup of coffee. I will have a cup of coffee now."

It needs to be noted here that he used to drink coffee only once a day, at three in the morning.

4. Discourses on the Gita: Chapter Twelve

Maharajshri began to take me out with him occasionally. Other celibates, bramhacharis who were senior to me, would usually go with Maharajshri in his service. Sometimes, if they were not available, I would have an opportunity to go. Every year, in Ujjain, a meditation retreat used to be arranged where Maharajshri was invited. This time I was in attendance. In this three-day program, Maharajshri would give a discourse at five o' clock in the morning. In the evening program he rarely spoke. The subject of the discourse was the twelfth chapter of the Gita. The essence of the discourse was as follows:

(1) All those who praise God believe that they are devotees. But there is a big difference between a devotee and a favorite devotee, a devotee who is dear to God. A devotee walks holding God's hand and sometimes his hand can slip. God holds the hands of his favorite devotee. A devotee tries to climb the wall of devotion through self-effort. God extends his hands and pulls his favorite devotee over it. A devotee takes pride in his devotion, but a devotee dear to God has a sense of surrender. A devotee walks the path of life carefully. God carries his favorite devotee in his own arms.

(2) A beloved devotee experiences the grace of God within him, which is known as the activation of Allhadini in the path of bhakti, or devotion. Direct support is available to the devotee only after this. Until such time he takes the help of some symbol or another and continues to speculate on an emotional plane. A devotee can become a beloved devotee only after the experience of active Allhadini. Active Allhadini is saguna bhakti [devotion with awareness of the qualities of God]. That which is commonly propagated as saguna bhakti is actually idol worship.

(3) God is omnipresent. In some places he is saguna, with attributes, and in others he is nirguna, without any attributes or qualities. In the

chitta of devotees the nature of God is qualitative because it manifests depending upon their samskaras. This revelation of God's Shakti takes place within the realm of the gunas, or qualities. True saguna bhakti occurs only after the awakening and activation of the Allhadini Shakti.

(4) Those aspirants who start a spiritual practice without understanding its relevance are wasting their time. Meditation starts by renouncing the fruits of action. Jnana, or spiritual knowledge, comes with meditation, and spiritual practice is conducted with that spiritual knowledge. This implies that spiritual practice includes meditation, knowledge and detachment from the fruits of action. How can the spiritual practices of a person who does not give up attachment to the fruits of action bear fruit? Also, efforts are wasted if practices are done without meditation and spiritual knowledge.

(5) Bhakti, or devotion, as described by Lord Krishna, develops the mind, intellect and heart, and keeps one untouched by the negative influences of the world. It holds the mind and senses in restraint. It includes Karma Yoga [the yoga of action] and knowledge. It also teaches us to remain joyful in this world. This bhakti starts with action and extinguishes the effects of that action. It gives rise to a balanced state of mind.

(6) If a person attains authority, wealth or fame he becomes egoistic. Ego is the root cause of all defects. Where there is ego, lust, anger, greed, hatred, jealousy and vengeance follow one after the other. A living being does not understand that and keeps on accumulating bad impressions. But a devotee knows this and even if he attains some authority, etc., he does not become conceited. This is the natural state of his mind. Hence a devotee always remains balanced whether he is in the middle of loss or gain, fame or defamation, praise or insult.

(7) It is extremely important that the mind of a devotee, or spiritual aspirant, not be perturbed by the good or bad behavior of the world. A devotee is tested in favorable, as well as in unfavorable, conditions. Neither should ego arise, nor should his mind get agitated. Besides, his behavior must be so kind, gentle and sweet that nobody should have any excuse to be troubled by him. This is an important aspect of spiritual

practice, but it is unfortunate that most remain indifferent towards this. Consequently their minds become restless and they cause distress to others.

(8) In the twelfth chapter of the Gita, on Bhakti Yoga, the state of mind of a real devotee is described, in which he is neither affected by the events of the world, nor by the behavior of others towards him. This is elaborated at length as the characteristics of a devotee. This is a distinct state of the mind of a devotee. This is called devotion. If someone prays a lot or recites the sacred texts but his state of mind is not so, then he cannot be considered a devotee.

(9) There is no mention of prayers, recitations, spiritual practices or devotional songs in the path of Bhakti Yoga described by Lord Krishna for attaining the mental state of a devotee. However he emphasizes action without attachment. According to the Lord the progressive stages in action are as follows:

(a) Only Bhakti Yoga is the highest state, in which a devotee remains absorbed in devotion and meditates on God all the time with a steady mind. As a result of this he attains a place in the abode of the Lord. In this state he does not need to perform any action. In states lower than that, action is essential to varying degrees. It must be remembered that when the Lord refers to action, he implies action that is free from desires, or action compelled by a sense of service and duty.

(b) To remain steady in this highest state is possible only for a rare and fortunate person. Otherwise the mind is fickle. It is the duty of those who are unable to stay in this state to relinquish the fruits of their actions, and gain the support of knowledge through study, thinking and contemplation. The support of meditation and abhyasa is also necessary in this process. According to *Yoga Darshan*, the effort to stabilize the mind in a steady state is called abhyasa, or practice. This effort to steady the mind should go on while doing worldly activities as well as while meditating. Then only will mental tendencies and accumulated impressions become weak, and a state of constant steadfastness be achieved.

(c) On the surface this solution looks very easy, but it is extremely difficult to accomplish. Hence, the Lord steps one level lower and depicts another state. If some one finds himself incapable of following the path of abhyasa yoga then that person should perform all actions for God and for pleasing God, and continue to offer the fruits of his actions to God. At the time of doing work the only goal should be to gain the grace and love of God. This way the person will remain free from the bondage of action while performing the action. Over time he will attain a steady state of Bhakti Yoga by keeping God's love as his goal.

(d) For an average person even this is difficult. His ego makes him involved and attached to the outcome of every action. Instead of offering the fruit of his action to God he becomes happy or unhappy due to the results of his actions. Therefore the Lord recommends that the aspirant make efforts to keep the mind in control and to try and remain unaffected by the outcome of action. Consequently your mind will gradually become inclined towards spirituality.

This view can also be understood in another simple way. In the Gita, the way to perform action is presented in a descending order. First of all, the highest state is described, and then, one after another, gradually lower states are presented. We will now climb the opposite way. We will describe the lowest state first.

An average person is full of attachment. Not only is he is definitely attached to the body, but he is also attached to the actions that can be performed with the body and their results. He gives rise to a false ego of doership by maintaining a sense of ownership towards the Shakti active within him. The ego identity within the individual takes the form of pride and spreads throughout the world and attachment escalates. An individual has to start on the spiritual path from this state. The progressive states are as follows:

(i) The power, action and fruits of the actions of an individual soul belong to him. He is the doer, but whenever his actions bear fruit he offers them to God. When his intellect tells him that only good actions should be offered to God, at that time the results of bad actions remain with him to endure. Hence, gradually, he stops performing bad actions.

(ii) Actions belong to an individual; the doer is the individual and the fruits of his actions belong to him, but God is the giver of these fruits. Hence, it is his duty to endure peacefully whatever God deems appropriate by treating it as his divine grace.

(iii) He thinks that the energy is his but all the work belongs to God. It is his duty to carry out his work. The results of his actions are not in his control but in God's, but he is not concerned about this. Whatever the outcome may be — that belongs to God. He is simply the performer of his duties.

(iv) Thus far the aspirant has been walking on a path with personal feelings, but once Shakti awakens, he is made to realize that he is separate from the Shakti. When the aspirant finds out that his belief that the Shakti, or power, belonged to him was false, at that time his attitude begins to change. Shakti belongs to God. All his responsibilities also belong to God. It is his duty to use the divine power to perform the work of God.

This way the aspirant progresses in the direction of action without expectations. All the events that occur in the world and all the actions of all beings are the activities of the divine Shakti, but due to his ego, an individual soul considers them as his own. Thus he gets entangled in his own web. This sense of doership is not eliminated until he has experienced prajnana, or Chaitanya, [the state where one realizes it is the Shakti that gives conciousness to the sense organs]. Only after this awareness will his destiny and accumulated impressions start thinning out. Prior to this an individual remains sunk in ego.

5. My First Lecture

Today was the last day of the meditation camp at Ujjain. This evening Maharajshri was scheduled to give a speech. During the day Maharajshri said to the organizer, "Doctor Saheb, kindly give our Bramhachari an opportunity to speak." The organizer told Maharajshri that it would be arranged.

I went and met Doctor Saheb separately and told him, "I have no experience in public speaking, so please do not take Maharajshri's request seriously. I do not know in what mood he asked you." Doctor Saheb asked me not to worry.

In his evening sermon Maharajshri said, "Think a thousand times before stepping on the path of spiritual practice and devotion. This path is full of thorns and steep slopes, and slippery all over. Those teachers who say that the path of devotion is easy are doing so only to establish your faith. On the contrary, there are obstacles at every step. The ego must be given up on this path, for which the mind is not ready. On this path detachment is essential but the individual soul does not wish to give up attachment. It is a must to be compassionate, whereas a common man continues to burn in the fire of revenge. On this path one needs to love his enemies and opponents, and also to wish them well. The world is unable to understand these beliefs of a devotee and keeps on opposing him. The expression of love is considered a weakness, a trick or ostentation. A devotee has to swallow many insults. The mind jumps outward but one has to control it. All of these are not easy tasks. Hence I tell you to weigh the idea in your mind thoroughly before embarking on this journey.

"It is said that spiritual practice becomes very easy after Shaktipat because an aspirant does not have to do anything of his own accord after that. I do not agree with that. The kind of surrender that is required after Shaktipat is not observed in any aspirant. Practical difficulties remain the same in this path as in others, but because of the fast depletion of samskaras more difficulties are encountered. After Shaktipat there is a greater need for tolerance, generosity and compassion. Can you say this is easy?

"Before starting to climb the slope of spirituality, understand that you can be free only after enduring your destiny. Instead of enduring our destiny we are still busy creating a new destiny. In order to wipe out destiny through endurance, a specific state of the chitta is necessary. First and foremost it must be clearly understood that the cause of happiness and misery is not the world but your own destiny. Due to a lack of this understanding the cause of insult, loss and misery is thought to be a specific person or circumstance and man is motivated towards revenge. He continues to burn with anger within and keeps on strengthening his samskaras. The destiny of a person who is full of revenge can never be thinned out. A traveler on the path of spirituality or devotion considers the world to be only the medium, not the cause. By presenting miseries and difficulties in front of the aspirant the world does him a great favor; it opens up the path to reduce destiny. A devotee or an aspirant is neither afraid of miseries, nor shaken by them. If you can do this then march in the direction of devotion, otherwise go with the flow of the current era.

"The present era is an era dominated by intellect. The thinking prowess of a human has evolved along with the advancement of science, but this development is progressing in a reverse direction. Deceit, fraud, ostentation, secrecy, devious means of getting work done — these are the directions followed in today's world. Coercion is not used in spirituality but is used for getting work done. The dominance of intelligence has pushed the heart to a secondary place. Today an attempt is made to understand even the emotion of the heart with logic, whereas devotion is mainly related to the heart. I am not against intellectual advancement, but for spirituality you need both — discerning intellect as well as devotion. An emotion without discretion, and prudence without emotion are both useless. An aspirant, a devotee, has to give proper direction to his intellectual discrimination while kindling devotion for God in his heart. This is not easy task.

"In the present era the circumstances are adverse for performing spiritual practices, but spirituality blossoms best in adverse circumstances. Actual sadhan is possible when there is not even a single grain available to eat. In a life endowed with all kinds of amenities there is a lot of ostentation, and pride continues to increase. Was there a shortage of poverty for Kabir? Was there a lack of dearth for Tukaram and Jnaneshwar? What comforts and wealth did Nanak have in his pocket? Didn't Meera give up all kinds of royal comforts? It is not possible to do sadhan while having a bank balance and relying upon the interest. Dependence on any person, a bank balance, or any other such arrangement does not allow one to fully depend on God. Without dependence on God one cannot have total surrender and without surrender sadhan is not possible. Do not sit and wait for suitable circumstances. Whatever circumstance God has given is certainly suitable for sadhan. The feeling of favorable and unfavorable is only from a worldly perspective, not a spiritual one.

"Performing spiritual practice is like walking bare-footed on the edge of a sword. The path leading to God is very narrow. It is not possible to take any person or any worldly belonging with you. Even subtle elements like the mind, intellect, tendencies and samskaras cannot go along. This is a path of renunciation, not accumulation. The more you are able to give up the farther you will be able to go. Renunciation is a subject of the mind. A life devoid of attachment is true renunciation."

Now I do not remember what else Maharajshri said in his one-hour sermon, but his speech was very logical, based on experience and filled with concern. I do not know how others were influenced, but I listened to the discourse, steadfast like a statue. Who knows where all my thoughts of the world disappeared to? Maharajshri spoke with an uninterrupted flow; it seemed as if words and feelings were spontaneously flowing through his voice. At that time his face had a strange divine glow.

After completing his sermon Maharajshri stepped down from the stage and sat down in the audience. The atmosphere was still and solemn. In the meantime the voice of Doctor Saheb resonated on the loud speaker. He had announced my name. On the one hand I was out of sorts due to the influence of Maharajshri's discourse, and on the other I had never given a talk. How could I talk in such a situation? There was no subject before me to talk about. My condition was similar to a person who did not know how to swim but had been thrown into the water. I was helpless because it seemed improper to say, "No," in front of the audience. I took a seat on the stage. The stage was very small, just enough to seat the speaker. Maharajshri was sitting in front of me, down among the audience. I was feeling very ashamed that I was settled on the stage. I was accustomed to sitting at the feet of Guru Maharajshri and today it was reversed. I had been staying in the shelter of his feet, and I had always been around him with my head bowed. Today I was sitting higher than that very image of my honorable Guru. For three to four minutes not a single word came out of my mouth. My mind was in a state of shock. My mind wished to step down from the stage at once, run somewhere and hide my face. But that would be a spectacle. Somehow I managed to gather my wits. I was glad that there was a stand in front of me so people could not see that my legs were trembling.

Just imagine: You have no experience, there is no context in front of you, and you have to give a speech! That, too, in the presence of Guru Maharaj. I started to talk. I do not know what I said or how I spoke. I was speaking with anxiety. I was embarrassed to see Maharajshri sitting below in the front. But at the same time I was getting inspiration from him. As I stepped down from the stage I was drenched with perspiration. This was the first lecture of my life. I do not know what came over Maharajshri so that he put me through this. A few days earlier he had opened my door for writing in the same way. When I came back to his room and tried to say something to Maharajshri he said, "This is how you learn. Who is born learned? As you have accepted the life of an ascetic, people will be eager to listen to you. How will you react at that time?"

6. Bramhachari Vishwanath Prakash

A disciple of Swami Shankar Purushottam Tirthji Maharaj of Siddha Yoga Ashram in Varanasi, Bramhachari Vishwanath Prakash Maharaj, lived on the banks of the Narmada River. He had great faith in Maharajshri. He used to come frequently to Narayan Kuti and stay for a few days. Once when he came I had a chance to see him. He narrated memories of Maharajshri:

(I) "The first time I saw Swamiji Maharaj was in Rishikesh, Vijnan Bhavan, in 1944. At that time he lived in the company of the late Shri Yoganandji and Bramhachari Prabhakar Prakash [known as Swami Pranavanand Aranya after he was initiated in sanyas]. I was in Dandivada. I had known Bramhachari Prabhakar Prakash earlier. I came to know through conversation that Bramhachari Prabhakar Prakash was staying at Vijnana Bhavan. I went to see him and had an opportunity to meet Swami Vishnu Tirthji Maharaj and Bramhachari Yoganandji. I began to go there every day. I received love and goodwill, and our relationship kept getting stronger."

"It so happened that Swamiji Maharaj came to stay at Triveni Ghat, in an empty building belonging to a devotee. Prabhakar Prakash was with him. He asked me to stay with him also. After that, for about three months, I got a chance to observe Swamiji very closely. He mostly stayed in a meditative state and spoke very rarely.

"Swamiji Maharaj was very simple, good-natured, very amiable and a man of few words. Swamiji Maharaj had translated a Bengali book, *Shaktopadesh* by Shankar Purushottam Tirthji, into Hindi while staying at this place. Maharajshri's mother tongue was Hindi, so when there was difficulty in translation Prabhakar Prakashji would help.

"Once we went to Garud Chatti with Maharajshri. Four other people were with us. We saw the Shilodaka Falls there. Swamiji told us that the special feature of this waterfall was that if anything fell in it — be it

cloth, wood, leaf, paper, etc. — it turned into stone. That is why it is
called Shilodaka. [Shila means rock, and udaka means water.]

"As we were returning in the evening Swamiji came down with a
high fever. His condition became so bad that he was not even able to
walk. His face turned red, his body was very hot and his feet were shaky.
In those days no vehicles were available to take us back to Rishikesh. A
big problem had arisen. Where to stay on the way? There was jungle all
around. We gathered courage and, somehow supporting him and even
lifting him at times, we came back to our destination. God brought us
back safely. After five or six days his health improved. This is when we
got a chance to see Swamiji's courage, patience, endurance and humility."

(2) "In May of 1945 I used to live at Ganganath, a holy place on
the bank of the Narmada River. One day, unexpectedly, Swamiji came
from Ahmedabad. Swamiji wrote a letter and invited Swami Krishnanand
Tirth Maharaj [Shri D. D. Swami] who lived to be 128 years of age. I
had been in Ganganath for quite some time and was ready to move, but
Swamiji kept me there. 'If you stayed it would be more pleasant.' I accepted and stayed on. This time I benefited from Swamiji Maharaj's
association for three months.

"Shri D. D. Swami was a great scholar of Sanskrit. Maharajshri was
also very knowledgeable. There were philosophical discussions. They
explained the Bramha Sutras, the Upanishads, and Vedic mantras. Very
often the interpretation given by D. D. Swami was different from
Maharajshri's. D. D. Swami was accustomed to using very strong words.
Hot debates used to take place. Books were closed when a controversy
would get heated and a discussion would take place. But strife between
saints is like lines drawn on water. In the evening the same thing would
happen: They would bathe, go for a walk, and then discuss. The following day, after the morning routines, discussions on the Vedic mantras
would begin again, followed by arguments and again books would close.
I learned so much while staying with them.

"In 1945 D. D. Swami and Maharajshri went to Kashmir. They
stayed at a devotee's house in Srinagar. From there Swamiji Maharaj
came to Ganganath by way of Ahmedabad and D. D. Swami came by

way of Varanasi. After staying in Ganganath for four months they went to Bhavnagar."

(3) "My third meeting with Maharajshri took place in 1950, at Indore. The people who organized the meditation program in Ujjain also arranged a two-day program in Indore. Maharajshri wrote a letter to me and invited me to Indore. Lots of discussions regarding work took place. People used to listen to Maharajshri's lectures on Hatha Yoga very attentively."

(4) "The fourth meeting took place in Nemavar. Maharajshri had come there with devotees. In those days I used to live in the Siddhnath temple. In the compound of the temple a tent was set up for Maharajshri's stay. He stayed there for three days. This was in the year 1953."

(5) "I met him for the fifth time in February of 1955 [the Indian lunar calendar date of Magh Sudi 12 Samvat 2011] at Narayan Kuti. A statue of Vidyeshwar Mahadev was to be installed with elaborate rituals and festivities. D. D. Swami, Sadanandji, Narayan Swami, Amaranandji, and many other saints and devotees had come from far places. On that occasion I stayed in Dewas for many days."

I was very impressed with the humility of Bramhachari Vishwanath Prakashji. Every time he came to Dewas I used to take advantage of his satsang.

How pleasant are memories of meeting saints! How happy Bramhachariji must have been to meet Maharajshri! I was also lost in memories of my time spent in the company of Maharajshri, at first in Ghaziabad and later in Nangal. There were tremendous emotions and enthusiasm among all the disciples. I remembered Maharajshri's child-like simplicity and forthrightness. Even after staying so close at his feet my mind could not be like his. The reason for that, I understood, was that my proximity was only physical. I had not yet succeeded in connecting my mind to his honorable feet. That is why my mind was not yet colored by Guruji's personality. Even now my mind was dry, curt, strict and egoistic. The exalted, highly-developed love visible in Maharajshri was not in me. Bramhachari Vishwanath was quite similar to Maharajshri; possibly he had attached his mind to Maharajshri's.

7. The Agasha Incident

Very frequently I heard Maharajshri talk about a great saint, Agasha. This saint lived about 7,000 years ago in Egypt. Now Egypt is primarily a desert. God alone knows what it was like in those days because the geography of places does not remain the same forever. According to Agasha, he roams around invisibly on the subtle planes even today. Some people experience his entering into them just as a deity descends into a selected medium. Usually when people experience a subtle spirit who has entered into them other people ask them questions related to worldly desires, difficulties and problems. During the descent of Agasha nothing like that takes place. He only discusses pure spiritual knowledge. Knowledge imparted by him is very consistent with the principles and spiritual practices of Shaktipat. Agasha has frequently talked about Maharajshri through his mediums, although the mediums themselves had never previously heard about Maharajshri. Most of these people never visited India, yet, surprisingly, they knew a great deal about Maharajshri and his ashram. Some of his followers even used to have visions of Maharajshri.

According to the mediums of Agasha, when Agasha lived in Egypt 7,000 years ago he had 273 companions. One of them living today is Swami Vishnu Tirth. As his companions started to give up their physical bodies they started to dwell and move around on extremely subtle planes.

Agasha has said, "From these subtle regions, we help those spiritual aspirants who are earnestly absorbed in spiritual practices. The way in which I give guidance and conciliate doubts of aspirants, by subtle entry into the medium, is the same way Swami Vishnu Tirth, dwelling in a physical body, tries to show the path of supreme benefit to spiritual aspirants through the medium of Shaktipat. The only difference is that I am doing the work while remaining invisible, but Swami Vishnu Tirth is doing it while in a visible body. After some time Swami Vishnu Tirth will become invisible and at the appropriate moment one of our companions will manifest. In this manner the task of the well-being of the world will continue on both the subtle and physical levels. This task is conducted according to the divine command. God wishes that all living beings created by him be free from fear, sorrow and perversity, and glide in the world of bliss. But individual souls are so attached to this world that they do not even like to hear about liberation. There are only a few who can embrace the holy path."

Some of the sacred teachings given by Agasha to his followers during his weekly gathering are presented here. Agasha used to enter into a man named Richard Zenor. Based on this, a book named *Telephone Between Worlds* [by James Crenshaw] was written. Maharajshri had a copy of that book, but then it was lost and no one knows who took it. Richard Zenor founded the Agasha Temple of Wisdom in America, in the city of Los Angeles, California, in order to disseminate the principles and the ways of spiritual practice given by Agasha. Here he trained many spiritual aspirants who became mediums for the manifestation of Agasha and also became teachers. Many disciples had visions of Agasha. An average individual is unable to understand to what extent, or in what form, or what activities are being carried out by Agasha, Swami Vishnu Tirth Maharaj and their companions because he can only experience that which is within the scope of his physical senses. In the Temple of Agasha people used to assemble once a week at eight o'clock in the evening. At that time Agasha used to manifest through a medium and give discourses.

(1) Monday, January 9,1956, evening session. "I endeavor to live in the illumined regions of God because I know that God is in me. Whomever I meet, I fill them with love, light and peace. He is the Illumined One and I, too, am the Illumined One. He is engaged in making efforts and I am also striving. The way in which I shower light and divine peace on human beings who are eager to struggle — in the same way he also bestows upon me light and peace."

Meaning: The meaning of the word "meet" above does not mean meeting on the physical level. It is a union of two chittas — psyches. This is Shaktipat. With this union the aspirant receives the support of a master teacher's chitta, or psyche. The peace, love and luminescence in the mind of the spiritual master starts to enter into the mind of the aspirant. The fire of union with God that is ablaze in the master is also kindled within the aspirant and his inner consciousness is awakened inwardly. Here the union of two psyches implies the meeting of the psychic power of the master with the psychic power of the aspirant. This process influences the inner power, as a result of which there is a change in the state of the chitta of the aspirant; also samskaras and mental tendencies start to burn. On the one hand the aspirant benefits; on the other the saint also gains. First, by initiating someone on a spiritual path peace is achieved. Second, at the cosmic level, the layer of Maya [illusion] gets slightly thinner. Third, experiences that a master can have cannot be had during his own meditation but only by this process.

The saint and aspirant both are forms of light. The only difference is that the light of the saint can be experienced while the light in the aspirant is under a cover. The saint and the aspirant both worship Shiva, the Great Consciousness present within them. To experience the inner light the aspirant needs a person who has had the experience of the inner light himself, and also has the ability to impart such an experience. If the saint is afflicted with greed, delusion or the desire for fame then the attainment of the goal becomes impossible. On the contrary this can degrade the saint.

(2) Monday evening, July 9, 1956. "I am firmly established on the sacred path. I am patient with myself. I will make every attempt to reach my kingdom. I am the path. I am the light. I am everything, and I am the bedrock of everything that has ever manifested. The power that takes care of my physical body is the Absolute Self, God. That God is the root consciousness. It can have any name. We say that it is in every being. It is an all-pervading power. I strive to attain the maximum possible in my life. If I am patient, I will achieve everything that is necessary for me to achieve."

Meaning: "I" is used here to signify the firm determination of an aspirant. Whether to give and when to give is in the hands of God, but it is essential that an aspirant possess strong determination and patience. Without patience, there is a fear that the resolve and sadhana may be broken. "Kingdom" means the state in which one is firmly established in his own self-awareness. When will I reach it? God alone knows. But I, from my side, will make enormous efforts in the way of full vigilance, efforts full of surrender and sadhana. In reality, consciousness is my nature. An attempt to remain steady in that consciousness is called "sadhana."

In other words, I am the path. Consciousness is the light and the world is illuminated by consciousness. It is consciousness that makes the organs of acquiring knowledge capable of acquiring knowledge, and the organs of work capable of performing work. It is consciousness that brings the tendencies, thoughts, resolutions and defects to the forefront. Due to my ego I have put layers on my true nature. But I shall embark on the path of consciousness, and with the grace of God I shall attain the state of pure consciousness. This is my firm resolve.

Everything that has occurred in the world so far, everything that exists now, whatever substances, things, scenery and circumstances may arise in the future — all of them are the result of the vibrations of consciousness. Everything is the activity of consciousness. It is the cornerstone for everything and the same consciousness is my true self. Consciousness grants liveliness and experiences to the physical body. Blood flowing in the veins, the digestion of food, the experience of joy and sorrow, enduring destiny — all this is possible due to consciousness. The accumulation of impressions, the rise and fall of modifications in the mind and the fruits of destiny all depend on consciousness. God is consciousness. The entire visible universe is a specific state of the same consciousness.

There could be diverse names and forms of God, but it is one and the same in its governing power. An individual names God according to his faith, feelings and experiences, and then, holding on to that name, he argues with others. God does not have any form, but all forms are His because without his power no form is possible. He dwells in all movable and immovable aspects of the world. He is omnipresent. Even the tiniest space is not devoid of Him. A human being does not have to find Him. To find God is only a formal expression. Something could be found only if it is lost. Due to the ego of the individual God has become invisible. One has to simply experience his illumination by removing the cover. I hope I can achieve the most in this life. Whatever wealth, luxury and abundance I have acquired so far is absolutely insignificant compared to finding God.

For this an aspirant needs patience, enthusiasm and firm resolve. Continuous sadhana and good karma are essential. This is the teaching of Agasha, which he has been imparting for the past 7,000 years while remaining invisible. For this he chooses someone as a medium and puts him in a trance. He grants direct support of the divine consciousness to aspirants. It is possible that, intermittently, he completely unites himself with God when he becomes disinterested in the world. However, after some time, he again immerses himself in activities that benefit the world.

No individual brings spiritual benediction to another; only Shakti, or consciousness, does. The physical Guru is only an instrument. If a Guru feels proud of being a Guru then it is false pride because, in reality, he is not a Guru. Perhaps this is the reason why there is a decree that the position of the Guru is bestowed through a lineage or tradition. There is a rule therein that the Paramguru [ultimate and original Guru] is the real Guru, so that a Guru considers all his responsibilities as a Guru to be service to his Guru, and this will not make him proud of himself being a Guru.

(3) Friday evening, May 25, 1956. "A suggestion for meditation."

"Tell yourself that, whatever work you are doing, you should do it more efficiently. After that pray for your health. Then request the fulfillment of your financial needs. Tell yourself that you should become more tolerant and patient. Wish that you might be spared from criticism. Wish that your behavior should not be negative. Ask that you be able to destroy hatred and evil. Desire that you may rise above jealousy, hate and enmity. You should ask of yourself, you should wish for yourself, that your soul be directly visible to you. You should wish that your soul become your supporter and a teacher to you, just like your friend. Finally, wish that you may always be compassionate."

Meaning: Here Agasha suggests affirmations before starting meditation. Meditation will be what it will be, but praying to God prior to that to subdue your weaknesses adds sanctity to the sadhan. The first prayer that is suggested is that, whatever work we are engaged in — that is, the meditation we are doing— we should be absorbed in it with total concentration. Whatever tasks we perform with a sense of service, let us do them more efficiently. We should become more successful in the service of the downtrodden. Whatever chanting, worship and puja we do, let us continue to remain engaged in that. After that a wish is expressed for good health. In *Yoga Darshan* physical ailments are considered the first and foremost obstacle. If, for some reason, one's health is not good then the mind should be so healthy that the physical discomfort is endured well.

Pray for the fulfillment of our financial needs. Seva [service] and prayer are possible only if there is food in the stomach. Here wealth is not for pleasure and luxuries, but has been requested for fulfilling basic needs.

Patience and tolerance are essential constituents of spiritual practice. There is nothing wrong if you ask these of God. Whatever may be written on the value of tolerance, it is inadequate. Tolerance is responsible for contentment in the mind. It keeps the chitta in equilibrium in the midst of joys and sorrows and the mind remains peaceful. All these are beneficial for progress in sadhana. Next, the recommendation is to stay clear from criticism. The mind of a critic is restless. The person who is criticized may or may not have flaws, but with the passage of time the critic himself will definitely develop those flaws. To criticize implies that one accepts that the world is real. Thus protecting one's self from criticism is the path to sadhana. Drive away evil, likes, dislikes and hatred. Be eager and inquisitive to establish yourself with the Self.

In the end, one has asked to maintain compassion in the heart. Compassion is tenderness of the heart. The heart will remain like a stone until it becomes tender. A stony heart is unfit to attain God. Love for God can grow only in a tender heart.

These are some samples of the teachings of Agasha. As was said earlier, Agasha does not talk about worldly matters. He only discusses spirituality and love for God. He is industrious towards liberation from the bondage of the world. He talks about giving up attachments. He engages us in sadhan and service. He awakens discrimination [of good from bad] in the intellect and tenderness in the heart.

Maharajshri used to talk about Agasha occasionally. A spiritual aspirant from the Agasha Temple of Wisdom, Mrs. Betty Sapaugh, used to go regularly to the programs of the temple. She used to write letters to Maharajshri. Once Maharajshri showed me some letters he had received from Mrs. Sapaugh, and also his replies to her. He said, "There were many more letters but I do not know where the rest have gone." There were eight letters written by Betty, of which two were New Year greeting cards. There were four letters from Maharajshri. In one letter Betty wrote:

"For the last three months, and especially for the last few weeks, Master Agasha has discussed you, your ashram, and the work that you are carrying out. Even an ascended master from Atlantis talked about you. What an amazing person you are, and how difficult is the endeavor that you are carrying out in your beautiful ashram! Agasha's colleague, Donna, also talked about your beautiful ashram. At the end of last week Agasha took us on a spiritual journey to your ashram along with Donna and other Gurus. I do not know whether you were aware of our presence or not.

"Last Monday, in the weekly gathering, Agasha talked elaborately about your ashram. He said that you were one of his 273 companions 7,000 years ago. He has detailed knowledge of the work you are accomplishing. You are walking with a miraculous goal.

"I am not talking about these esoteric things to impress and please you. Our Guru, Agasha, has emphasized that all these things are holy and respectable. Last night Agasha and Donna said that we would spend a week in your ashram. It will be a matter of great honor.

"You are so important to Agasha that he has made many trips to your ashram recently. The way he talks about you it seems that you know all about this. Agasha has told us that you know all about our group and you have written a great deal.

"The teachings you impart are the same as were given by Agasha 7,000 years ago. It is a matter of great joy for me that I am working as a medium between you and Agasha."

Commentary: As I have written, Agasha is an invisible great being. His trips to Dewas must have been in an invisible form. It is possible that Maharajshri was aware of his arrival. There were indications that Maharajshri was in contact with some other invisible masters, too. Live "Gurus" of Agasha means those who were benefited with Agasha's energy entering in them to give guidance to others. Donna was one such Guru. It is very mystifying that Agasha knew all about Swami Vishnu Tirth Maharaj and used to inform his disciples about this through a medium. It is very difficult to fathom the depth of the heart of great beings. Maharajshri used to talk about Agasha, but it is possible that he did not say everything. Perhaps he did not consider us worthy.

Betty wrote in one letter, "The year 1955 is going to be over very soon. The most important incident in my life is that I got in touch with you and was a medium between you and Agasha. This is so miraculous for me because it is beautiful and alive.

"Agasha talks about you quite frequently in the class. Recently he told us that your teachings and his teachings were the same. Your ashram is a happy ashram because one experiences anand [joy] there. He also said that he had come to Dewas in a subtle form to see you on January 26. You were very engrossed in reading. He stood behind you and saw that you were reading a Sanskrit scripture. He continued to watch you for some time and noticed that you were reading something that Agasha himself had written 7,000 years ago."

In another letter she wrote, "I showed your letter to my teacher, Moffetti, and he was very interested in your letter. On Friday, May 20, Agasha's teacher, Koman Coban, who attained the Buddha-state many thousands of years ago, told us that at thirty minutes past eight you had come to our class. I do not know what your experience was like. I feel that some day we may be able to listen to you lecture."

In one letter Betty wrote, "In your last letter you told me to ask Swami Agasha whether he could come and visit you in the night instead of the afternoon. When I asked he replied, saying, 'Yes, it will definitely be according to your convenience.'

"On Sunday evening an amazing master emanated. He lived in India thousands of years ago. He told us that he is in touch with many masters in India. One of them has a very charming ashram. He also said that he is recording teachings of Agasha in writing. Some time ago Agasha and Donna manifested in front of that master. I am so happy to know this. The Indian master also said that Swamiji has a closed wooden box, which will be brought here very soon, and that Swamiji will manifest in a subtle form and talk. All this will be possible through some disciples working here."

Commentary: Maharajshri used to talk about Agasha in general. He never talked in public about meeting with Agasha, or going to the Temple of Wisdom in a subtle form, or about any other subtle experiences. Perhaps he talked about it with a special deserving person. In the night, from 9:30 to 3:30 in the morning, he used to be alone in his room. During the day also he would be in a deep meditative state sitting on his chair. Who knows where he used to go at that time, what he used to do, or what he saw within?

A question arises here: Why did he ask Betty, through a letter, to ask Agasha something when he was in direct contact with Agasha and could have asked him directly? Perhaps he did this to give respect to Betty. Perhaps the request that Agasha visit him during the night instead of the afternoon was made because he used to be alone at night.

In one letter, Betty wrote expressing her confidence that someday Maharajshri himself would come to witness the phenomenon of the manifestation of the deity Agasha and other heavenly beings. "Deity Agasha says that on this path the main thing is to walk with patience and to constantly develop your awareness."

Commentary: The question naturally arises, Why must one go to Los Angeles to see the manifestation of Agasha? Since Agasha used to come to visit in Dewas he could have manifested through any medium in Dewas. The answer to that is that Swami Vishnu Tirth Maharaj was doing the same work as Agasha in Dewas in the way of Shaktipat. Spontaneous workings of consciousness used to occur and purify the mind. The relationship between Agasha and Maharajshri was very deep. How, where and what they were doing is known only to them.

Betty kept on writing one thing or another about Agasha to Maharajshri. Once she wrote, "You have written in your letter that you are not very keen about contacts with these great invisible beings. I am also experiencing something similar. Our Swami, Agasha, says that touching and seeing gratifies our materialistic side, but from a spiritual perspective it is insignificant. Twice Agasha told me that when he visited you, you remembered me. I am very thankful for that."

Commentary: It is indicated in this letter that Maharajshri was not drawn to invisible holy beings that helped aspirants. Help is often needed by aspirants because they are still at a level of sadhana where they have many difficulties and obstacles. These obstacles stand in the path of spiritual progress. Maharajshri had already gone beyond this painful state of sadhana. There was no problem or obstacle in his sadhana, so he had no need for any such help. Nevertheless he used to have occasional contact with these invisible holy beings. These holy beings used to come to meet him and see him. The area of Dewas is also a home for many invisible great beings. Some fortunate people have visions of them. Maharajshri was in touch with some of them, but he never expected any spiritual help from them. If they met sometimes, it was okay. If not, that was okay, too.

This forced me to reflect that my mind was so impure, so full of problems, obstacles and discontent. I definitely needed help, but had not received any grace from any invisible holy being. I was disappointed many times. Suddenly someone shook me up from this deep sleep. When a real and visible Maharajshri has his hand of grace on my head why should I have even curiosity about the vision and grace of an invisible holy being?

Another thing that shook me was the statement made by Agasha that to touch and to see can gratify our materialistic side, but its spiritual significance is minimal. I was still lost in touching and seeing. What will happen to me? How will I get out of this trap? To touch and to see are the basic physical functions through which the world is reflected in the mind. This is how we know the world. Knowledge of the world is the cause of bondage. My senses are fully functional and keep on pushing knowledge of the world inwards. Only Guru Maharaj can protect me.

Betty's letters had a kind of personal touch, a child-like innocence and honesty. Now we will have the joy of seeing the tenderness and benevolence in the letters written by Maharajshri.

Maharajshri wrote in a letter, "Dear Betty, hearty thanks for sending me the book by James Crenshaw, *Telephone Between the Worlds*. I am an unrelenting follower of the Hindu religion and believer of the Upanishads and Gita, based upon thoughts, teachings and experiences of the ancient rishis [seers of truth] of India. I think that, after 7,000 years, the philosophy and teachings of Agasha are echoing similar tunes. According to ancient chronology, the Vedas and Upanishads were written even before the teachings of the Gita were given by Lord Krishna to Arjuna 5,000 years ago on the battlefield of Kurukshetra. By reading the book sent by you, I was pleased to know that the time has come for the whole world, in spite of its diversity, to accept that the teachings of the ancient rishis are the root of all religions, having one and the same goal.

"We Hindus believe in reincarnation, and that for self-realization we accept a new body. We also believe in the existence of other worlds besides Earth, including six astral regions above us enveloping the earth. There names are: Bhoo [Earth], Bhuvaha [the intervening skies], Swaha [heaven], Maha [the higher regions of the masters], Janah, Tapah, and Satya. The last three are 'Bramha lokas' [regions of Bramhan], cosmic worlds where liberated souls reside. Literally, 'Bramha' means the great universal creative consciousness of God. All individual souls are nothing but individualized specks of the same divine cosmic consciousness.

"The philosophies of the Upanishads are known as 'Vedanta,' meaning the ultimate knowledge. In the Upanishads it is conveyed that each individual soul is similar to Bramha. They are one with Him but appear separated from Him due to their egos in consciousness, which is the root of their being. The five senses, the world composed of things, experiences of the world through the mind and intellect — all are reflections of that initial universal consciousness.

"Different lokas [regions or abodes] where the souls reside also represent different levels of development of the consciousness embedded in objects, and these many levels of consciousness start with vegetative life.

"Is this not, in a nutshell, the philosophy of Agasha? Please forgive me if I wish to pronounce the word 'Agasha' as the Sanskrit word 'Akasha.' This word is formed from the root word 'kasha' in Sanskrit and a prefix 'Aa' is attached to that. This means 'luminous, to shine.'

"According to the Upanishads, akasha is the body of God. Today the word 'akasha' is interpreted in the gross sense as 'vacuum,' and on a subtle plane as 'inner space' or 'chittakasha.' Reverend Master Agasha has appropriately called himself 'luminous,' and established in universal cosmic consciousness.

"I am very impressed by the prophecy in the book. Here, in a village near Gwalior, a master used to manifest through a young man. Some of my friends who are still living had the opportunity to see this phenomenon. There are many similarities in his prophecies and the prophecies given in your book. This master did not disclose his name, but through the young man who was the medium many prophecies were conveyed. This medium never became unconscious. He also used to give a commentary afterwards. He used to see his master directly in front of his eyes, whereas the master was invisible to others. He was able to clearly hear his master's speech, but no one else could. Whenever the medium wanted the master used to come to him. This young man passed away around 1942 or 1943. He had predicted that the British would leave and India would be freed without any bloodshed. Princely states of local kings would be terminated.

"In this case the master used to manifest in full form. Why did that not happen with Richard Zenor? I think it should have been possible. If that were to happen, that would be an enormous help toward spiritual progress. Your teacher may think over this suggestion and request guidance from the master. I wish that Richard Zenor could remain conscious to whatever is being conveyed through him. It is essential that he become the live telephone.

"Many spirits come to a son of one of my friends in Dewas. His father is worried about the son's health. I will ask them to contact your institute."

In another letter Maharajshri wrote, "I read your letter with great interest. Residents of the ashram who were present were also asked to read it. Everyone showed interest in the things you wrote. This ashram of ours is a center for the hidden knowledge (in our words 'knowledge of yoga'). Here I initiate men and women for spiritual development. When aspirants sit for meditation with me, their dormant energy gets awakened. I am a sanyasi. A sanyasi is a person who has renounced his family and worldly relations. A sanyasi is a monk. 'Sanyas' means renunciation. It is natural that my associates and myself have interest in spiritual activities all over the world.

"Appropriate attention has been given to the concepts you presented. The prayers you do at the beginning of your class are very similar to our ideas. Our scriptures command us to perform similar affirmations at the beginning of meditation, etc. 'I am Bramha. I am light. I am knowledge. I am all joy. I am peace.' etc. This is nothing new for us. In meditation we empty our minds of all kinds of worldly and social thoughts. And we transform our individual consciousness into subtle consciousness beyond time, place and all materialism."

In another letter Maharajshri wrote to Betty, "Whatever the holy soul of Master Agasha, who is equal to God in my understanding, has said about me is far beyond my own understanding and knowledge. The work that is being done through me is so small that I feel shy of the high adjectives used for me. I am pleased to know that you have come here on a subtle spiritual journey with Agasha and Donna. I do remember that one time, at midnight, when I was in bed, I did feel your presence for half an hour.

"Possibly you know that in everyone another person is present. This other person is a spiritual companion of the human being. The average person, when his dormant Shakti is awakened, meets his ever-present companion. At this time he is awakened in the spiritual sense of the term and he becomes one with God. It is written in the Vedas that the soul of a person resides in his heart, and that the soul is like God. In my gross consciousness I am not aware of the things told by Agasha about me, but the soul within me knows it all and tells me what is relevant. It does not reveal my past and future to me, and the reason for that is also well known to the soul. Perhaps it is solely for my benefit.

"The news of your coming was given to me by the same soul within me. I am thinking that Agasha can throw more light on this because I am certain that when he meets me he must rendezvous with the inner soul. With the help of the inner soul I awaken Shakti, to an extent, of the aspirants. The aspirants have to give further speed to the Shakti with their own efforts.

"As far as Richard Zenor is concerned, I am told that the work that he is doing is to be done only by him and his work can develop more when he reaches higher spiritual states. I am told that you are a very highly evolved soul.

"One aspirant from our ashram was saying that a week ago, in the afternoon, he felt the presence of two male souls. After reading your letter it seems that they may be from your circle. Is this true?"

Commentary: Although Maharajshri rarely discussed anything about Agasha, his institute, and subjects related to him, this letter gives some indication about that. Maharajshri has accepted in this letter that Agasha and his companions used to come to Dewas and Maharajshri felt their arrival. He also used to know how long they stayed there. On the other side, Agasha's disciples mentioned a few times that Maharajshri was present at the Temple of Wisdom in Los Angeles. One aspirant from California, Jack Malott, also wrote in a letter that many times Agasha had given information about the presence of Maharajshri in the Temple of Wisdom. This way both of these great beings used to visit each other's places in subtle form. The only difference was that Agasha used to inform his disciples about this, while Maharajshri used to remain silent on the matter. Sometimes Agasha used to bring other people with him, whereas Maharajshri always went to Los Angeles alone. However Maharajshri never went to America physically. Once there was a serious discussion about Maharajshri visiting the United States, but Maharajshri expressed a lack of desire and ended the topic.

One day he told me that he had no inclination for anything. He said, "For me, America is wherever I am now. I am also getting old. You must complete the task of going to America." His coming and going were taking place on a subtle level. Maharajshri did not reveal this to anyone, whereas Agasha talked about it. Why was this so? This was known only to the two great beings.

Maharajshri writes that he was informed about Richard Zenor and Betty but he does not say who told him. Possibly it was the voice of his inner self or of active Kriya-Shakti. Maharajshri used to say that Kriya-Shakti talks to aspirants. An aspirant should consider himself advanced only when Kriya-Shakti starts to talk to him. This implies that Kriya-Shakti must have told Maharajshri.

Although the treasure of infinite knowledge is within, a human being has a very limited intellect. He has no knowledge of his past or future, but this lack of knowledge is limited only to the gross consciousness. Knowledge of the past, present and future — all exist within the inner self. Because the individual soul is extrovert it sees the world and cannot see the soul within. One's knowledge of the world is also limited by the reach of the senses. Very often that knowledge is also illusory and, in reality, that knowledge turns out to be ignorance. This is what Maharajshri writes to Betty: "I do not know with my gross intellect. Whenever Agasha meets me his contact must be with my inner self. Therefore only he can tell you what is in my inner self."

The chapter of Agasha illustrates how long the spiritual journey is, how far the destination is, and how much sadhana is required. If we compare an ordinary person with Agasha and Maharajshri then we realize where we stand and how far we must travel. The individual is trapped in the world and his inner journey has not even commenced. People considering themselves to be spiritual aspirants are not even ready to detach from the world and turn inward. Even now pleasures of the world attract them and they burst with anger even for insignificant matters. Even a trivial event influences their mind. Deep lines of likes and dislikes are fixed in their mind as if chiseled in stone. Spirituality is not a subject of intellectual art. Deceit, showmanship and trickery do not work in spirituality. The world is very shrewd at proving truth to be false and vice-versa. The aspirant has to complete his journey while living in a world filled with selfishness, delusion and pretentiousness. Generally, aspirants cannot endure the games of the world and get lost on the path.

Agasha and Maharajshri are ideals for aspirants. It is easy to climb an incline while keeping high peaks in mind as a goal. It does not matter that we are standing below now. If we start to walk and climb then one day we will arrive. We will get up and walk again if we fall. If we get lost we will find the path again. If a big rock falls in the way then we will move it and go to the other side. How many aspirants can do all this earnestly? Most are controlled by their anger and egoism. Agasha asks us to pray to God for compassion in the heart, but usually people push those who are falling. All are busy watching the faults of others. If they do sadhana, it lacks the solemnity expected from an aspirant.

Agasha asks that we be more patient and tolerant. Be free from gossip. Pray to God that your behavior not remain negative. Ask to eradicate hate and harmful actions. Wish that we may rise above jealousy, hate and enmity. This is the path for receiving spiritual benefits. All efforts for spiritual progress are futile if these aspects are ignored. But this is what goes on in the world. When I examine my own mental state, I realize how lost I am. My mind becomes all the sadder when my attention goes to this fact of being lost. When will I attain a peaceful state of mind? When will perversions of my mind leave me? There is no chance of an inner journey if I am all tangled up in worldly affairs.

How can there be sadhana if there is no love for God. Sadhana with love is the only sadhana. Vices in the mind of a devotee are burned to ashes in the fire of love. When will love of God awaken in me? When will I be uneasy due to my separation from God? When will my heart give up qualities of the world and acquire qualities of God?

When attention turns towards the peaceful and loving personality of Maharajshri, then the mind becomes hopeful. The destination and goals become clearly visible. We have found the same path by the grace of Maharajshri that took Maharajshri to such a state. Why can we not walk on this path? Maharajshri is our ideal, goal and strength.

8.   Yogic Siddhis

It must be the grace of Maharajshri that my mind was never inclined towards attaining siddhis, or supernatural powers. It is also true that my mental state was never conducive to attaining siddhis. Before attaining yogic siddhis one must reach a state of pratyahara — withdrawal of the senses from external objects — whereas my mind was very active and restless. In such a condition, even if I hoped for siddhis it would be like seeing a dream in broad daylight. I was anxious to attain the siddhi of a pure mind. I was definitely interested in the siddhi of serving the Guru, but from time to time defects would come to the forefront of my mind and create havoc. My mind kept on swinging between hope and despair.

Maharajshri's thoughts on siddhis have already been enumerated in *Churning of the Heart, Volume One*. However, today one aspirant came and again raised the same question. This aspirant was quite serious and advanced. Maharajshri's comments here are very different from those given in *Volume One*.

Maharajshri said, "What are siddhis? They are the manifestation of the divine power of God within the framework of Maya [illusion]. Divine power has three aspects: wish, action and knowledge. All three aspects can manifest through the medium of siddhis. As such, a wish also contains an action and knowledge. Similarly, an action contains a wish and knowledge, and knowledge, too, has a wish and an action. Siddhis are named according to the predominance of one of these three aspects. For example, in the siddhi of distant vision knowledge is predominant; the siddhi of attaining things just by wishing is dominated by wish; and in astral travel action is the main power. In reality all these siddhis are natural for every human being. But they are lost under the illusory covers of ego and extrovert tendencies. The power of God is present in every living being, therefore its qualities and powers are present in all living beings. Birds manifest the siddhi of flying, and aquatic creatures display the siddhi of living in water. Many animals, birds and insects have a forewarning of impending weather changes. Humans have a natural siddhi of intellectual development, and if one desires he can further develop that. If a baby animal is thrown into the water he spontaneously starts to swim. In a nutshell, all siddhis are present in each and everyone because God dwells in everyone. This means that siddhis do not come from outside, they manifest from within.

"A human being sees birds flying in the sky every day, but for him this is not due to any siddhi that the birds possess, nor is it a miracle. The physical anatomy of birds is such that they can fly. Now imagine if someone sees a human flying — then he will immediately accept it as a siddhi, or a miracle. His eyes depend upon physical evidence only. However if a bird dies then, in spite of having the same body, it will not be able to fly because the power to fly has been rendered useless. Then again, a balloon does not have any wings but it can fly. Its flight does not depend upon wings. It rises into the air because it is light. But all such concepts are on a physical level. The root cause of all siddhis is beyond matter. This root cause is only experienced, or manifest, in these physical phenomena."

Maharajshri divided siddhis into two categories. The first type is siddhis attained through samadhi. Here we are refering to samprajnat samadhi [samadhi with a seed, or conscious concentration]. Asamprajnat samadhi [seedless samadhi] is possible only when all siddhis, accompanied by all knowledge and activities of the chitta, dissolve into the soul. Nothing remains. The sense of individuality, the sense of an observer, and even the sense of surrender disappear. Only the pure soul remains. Thus, in that state, one cannot even imagine any siddhis. For siddhis ego is essential. Without ego and the activities of the chitta there is no foundation for siddhis to manifest. To attain siddhis one has to perform spiritual practices, but a true spiritual aspirant does not perform spiritual practices for attaining siddhis. Instead he does sadhana to remove the obstacles to siddhis.

Prior to attaining samprajnat samadhi an aspirant has to do many things. Without pratyahara, in other words without turning the mind and senses inward, disciplines such as concentration, meditation and samadhi are not possible. Without that control samprajnat is not possible, and without samprajnat, siddhis or supernatural powers cannot manifest. The essence here is that yogic siddhis are attained along the spiritual journey; when an aspirant attains siddhis he has gained victory over the mind and senses. He views siddhis as a milestone on the spiritual path. But it is possible that, when supernatural powers, or siddhis, are attained the aspirant may get attached to them. Therefore *Yoga Darshan* considers them as obstacles on the spiritual path and cautions aspirants.

Other siddhis are attained through japa [repetition of a mantra] and they are different from yogic siddhis. In japa, also, the mind and the senses have to be withdrawn. Without turning inward the mind cannot concentrate, and without concentration the deity of the mantra will not manifest and grant power. In essence all siddhis are the activities of the power of the conscious-self. The power that operates within the siddhi is called the "deity" of that siddhi, or power. In ancient times all branches of knowledge were developed on a supernatural level. Ayurveda [the science of longevity], music, astrology — all of them had the supernatural as their basis. In other words, all these were expressions of the divine energy. According to Mantra-Shastra, the science of mantra, all siddhis are the energy of a mantra and can be awakened through japa. Therefore to attain expertise in any field one has to serve the Guru, control the mind and senses, and perform japa and spiritual practice.

From another perspective siddhis can, again, be divided into two categories. Siddhis attained through personal effort and those granted by a great being. For siddhis attained by one's own effort one has to do sadhana. In the second kind a saint can shower his grace and grant a specific siddhi, just as the sage Vishwamitra gave weapons to Lord Rama. To be able to grant a siddhi to another person is also a siddhi.

Kalpita and akalpita are two further distinctions in understanding siddhis. Kalpita is the kind of siddhi that is attained through spiritual practice done with a resolution in mind to attain the siddhi. These siddhis are short-lived. They are lost with time. Kalpita siddhis are not of much use because if one has a desire for attaining a siddhi he will naturally develop attachment to the siddhi and ego arises on its attainment. One also feels like showing off these kalpita siddhis, which can further inflate attachment and ego. The path of the kalpita siddhi is not a spiritual path. Akalpita siddhis manifest spontaneously. The aspirant is not busy in making an effort to attain these siddhis, but rather he is absorbed in a spiritual pursuit and the siddhis emerge along the way. An aspirant must remain indifferent to these siddhis.

Yoga Darshan shows five causes of siddhis. They are: birth, herbs, mantra, austerities and meditation. Among these, siddhis due to meditation are known as yogic siddhis and those through mantra are known as mantra siddhis. Austerity also is a kind of yoga; the only difference is that it emphasizes austerities instead of self-control. In today's age we cannot find siddhis through herbs. Possibly, with the passage of time, such herbs may have vanished. Perhaps the knowledge of such herbs is lost. However we do find reference to these siddhis in books. In a siddhi acquired from birth, sadhana is unnecessary. Siddhis attained with spiritual practices in the previous life manifest effortlessly in this life.

Siddhis of the spirits, in which ghosts and invisible spirits are brought under control and miracles are performed with their help, are tamasic siddhis. Practitioners of such techniques ultimately meet with an undesirable fate.

A spiritual aspirant has only one goal: the attainment of the Self, which will permanently free him from worldly miseries. All other siddhis are roadblocks in the attainment of the Self, hence a real spiritual seeker does not get involved in those.

A self-realized spiritual master can utilize siddhis for the benefit of the world. They do not become egoistic by the use of siddhis.

9. Sevak Dharma: Duties of a Sevak

By now I was fairly well established in the ashram. No one mistook me for a servant because I was wearing saffron robes. My work of serving the ashram went on as usual. I tried to follow the rules of a sevak [an attendant] as before. In spite of all this the impurities of the mind did not leave me alone Even now my anger continued. On feeling bad about something, I just suppressed it in my mind. I understood that I should not feel bad about anything, but I would recognize it whenever my mind was affected.

I realized that the life of an ascetic was very difficult only after living with Maharajshri. People used to be preoccupied by their own affairs and would remember Maharajshri only during their spare time. Someone would be free at one time and others at another time. Everyone expected that Maharajshri would be available whenever they came to the ashram. If someone tried to tell them differently then they had bad feelings towards that person. I tried to explain this to some and they would be upset. They would respond, "Maharajshri does not say this. You are making it up yourself."

Another problem was that of space. Whenever there was a special occasion or festival and many people would come, each person would want the best room. This was not possible. Some would not even get a room. They would have to be content with staying in the hall. Some would understand the limitations, but others would be ready to fight and, being displeased, eagerly await an opportunity to seek revenge and release their anger. They did not understand that this was the place of a Guru. No one had special privileges here. No one could say anything to Maharajshri so I would end up being the scapegoat.

A third problem was that of water. There was a shortage of water. There was a well, but who was going to draw water from the well? Everyone wanted to take a bath in the bathroom because it had running water. And everyone wanted to wash clothes in the bathroom. People who did not get a chance to use the bathroom would complain because they would have to draw water from the well to bathe and wash their clothes. I realized that it was extremely difficult to maintain a sense of service.

To Maharajshri all the disciples were equal. I also made an attempt to always treat everyone the same, as far as possible. Some reasonable people would say, "We have all the amenities and luxuries at home. We have not come here to enjoy comforts. We have come here to be with Maharajshri." But such people were few in number. Most of the people preferred comfort. During festivals many people would settle in my room, and in the night I had to search for a place to sleep. But who had the time to notice this inconvenience?

In this world it is extremely easy to criticize someone. Prejudice is a weapon that can be used against anyone. This weapon of prejudice was severely used on me as well. It is natural for someone to like certain people, but even with such feelings I always ensured that I was free from bias. However, the strange thing is that I was accused of taking the side of people for whom I did not have any special affinity. When a human being gets fixated on a point, then he does not abandon it and does not want to let go. Sometimes he realizes that his point is baseless, but he does not give it up, making it an issue of pride and honor. As a result the sevak or attendant of the ashram is the one who suffers. He is helpless because in every situation and circumstance he has to serve the people. He has to love, even if those people are going to blame him for something. The sevak does not want any respect or a medal. Even if someone disrespects him he continues to serve that person.

This world is merely a stage for a human being to bear the fruits of his actions. This world does not disturb him. By refreshing his memories of old and new faults, the world alerts him toward the future. But a human being becomes sad because of this. A living being makes mistakes, but he does not like to remember them. If anyone reminds him of his mistakes he gets angry; that is why he becomes happy and sad in this world. He declares that this world is a house of miseries and thinks of running away from it. When he reaps the rewards of good actions he feels very happy, but when inauspicious samskaras manifest their demonic forms he starts to scream. This is the problem of a human being. This is his destiny.

My condition was no different. The mind is very strong and tricky. Many intellectuals have been rendered helpless by the mind. I understood very clearly that the world is like a cinema screen on which scenes of joy and sorrow keep manifesting. The world is not the cause of these scenes. But this knowledge would disappear when someone would say something good or bad, or when there would be an incident of some kind. My mind used to drag me into difficult terrain where I would lose my way. Believing that the world is everything, I would try and find the cause of my problem in the world. At that time anyone's misconduct used to take on a very scary appearance and stand before me. I used to get disturbed. This was the weakness of my mind, and I was unable to control it.

In such times I used to remember Gurudev and other spiritual masters. I would try to establish a connection with their minds, and also remember saints like Mirabai, Kabir and Tukaram. My mind would become quiet for sometime, but after a few moments it would again take the demonic form and create havoc. I was placing the entire blame on the world and was indifferent to my own mental state. I kept on suffering in my own mind.

One day I talked about my mental state to Maharajshri. He replied, "Bramhacharya initiation is a ceremony for entering the life of austerities. This internal suffering, burning of the mind, getting disturbed — this is the process of austerity. But the feeling of sadness causes insufficiency in the level of austerity. The fact that you are becoming miserable means that your sense of attachment is quite strong. You may say that you do not want respect for the work you are doing, but when you are disrespected you get unhappy. This means that the seed of desire for respect is not yet destroyed. You are simply pretending that you do not want respect. Make an effort to endure respect and disrespect both with a balanced mind, without becoming happy or unhappy. This will be your austerity. To endure mental attacks with a calm mind is austerity.

"It is extremely difficult to remain in the service of a Guru. When mental blows are inflicted, even the strong ones run away. If there is the slightest desire to attain respect then it becomes very difficult to bear the mental torment. But the austerities that can be done while serving the Guru cannot be done in any other way. The street of Guru-seva [service to the Guru] is so narrow that if you walk even a little bit forward, the inner faults and other companions leave your company. By the time an aspirant reaches the destination of love for the Guru he becomes totally alone. Only the sentiment of service to the Guru remains.

"Mental torments do not come from the world; they come from within. The source of thoughts, tendencies and feelings is within, and they accumulate in the chitta in the form of samskaras, or impressions. The meaning of the assault of thoughts and torments of the mind is that the accumulated impressions are arising and coming to the surface. Sometimes the accumulated impressions rise without any external factor. You must have had direct experience of this at the time of sadhan, or meditation, when there is no external stimulus, yet feelings of anger, shame, joy, and so forth, manifest. By enduring them peacefully — that is, through austerity — the force of samskaras is stopped; they lose strength.

"The joy and misery that you experience, and the mental shocks and obstacles you have to bear, are not caused by the world but by your own mental state. Without understanding this, the color of austerities does not become fully radiant. Even after understanding this completely, mental tendencies do not allow you to go on the straight path; for that you need discerning intellect and self-control. Every aspirant has to go through a mental struggle in the beginning. The aspirant falls down frequently. But he who does not struggle will not know what it is to fall and to rise up.

"Bramhacharya initiation does not mean that once you are initiated your impressions and tendencies are cleared. This initiation is only a resolve to practice austerities. It is not true that everyone who is initiated gets absorbed in austerities. Most are stuck at the initial stage of initiation. If, with patience in your mind and enthusiasm in your heart, you get involved in austerities then perhaps your problem will be solved.

"Even if a human being is aware of his faults and weaknesses, it is extremely difficult to repel them. He might be restless inside, he might be suffering, he tries to protect himself, but when the force of his weaknesses becomes strong he surrenders to them. An aspirant is in the same condition as someone who is in strong chains and unwilling to budge, but who is forced to move by fear of the whip. You do not know the mental condition of the aspirant who has caused inconvenience to you. It is possible that they are burning in the fire of repentance. They might also be going through an internal struggle. They may be falling and getting up. Aspirants must give support to each other and go further. They have to tolerate and help each other. If someone is falling and one thinks of making him fall further, it will be damaging for both. Help is only possible with mutual cooperation. Tolerance is essential for this.

"If you do not receive cooperation from the other party and continue to face misconduct, you should still maintain your ascetic perspective. This will help in the purification of your own chitta. If you do consider yourself a servant then your responsibility is greater than that of others. Others will escape this responsibility by being worldly, but the goal of a servant is service. The task of serving is not limited to making arrangements for food and lodging. To be part of the people's spiritual upliftment is also included in service. For this you will have to be big-hearted and tolerant. An aggressive attitude is an obstacle in spirituality. By aggression someone can be defeated from a worldly perspective, but that is not spiritually beneficial for either the aggressor or the aggrieved."

I said, "But Maharajji, if you try to lift someone and they try to push you down then that is going to cause distress."

Maharajshri responded, "The common rule of the world is to throw down the ladder by which one has climbed to the top. The perception of such people is worldly, even if they claim that they are spiritually inclined. If a worldly person does not change his ways then why should a spiritual servant give up his ways? He must always strive for the upliftment of others, as well as his own.

"In this matter you are committing the same mistake. After doing good to others you are blaming them for bad behavior. You are not paying attention to your own thoughts. Generally aspirants make this mistake, and this is a big hindrance in the development of a spiritual attitude. Generally, feelings of anger, ego, likes and dislikes are very strong in aspirants. Even those who have great interest in sadhan have these faults. Pride increases with more sadhan. On thinking deeply, the reason for this seems to be their lack of desire to serve. A sense of service brings an understanding of surrender and adds radiance to sadhan."

10. The Right to Initiate

This incident took place in June of 1961. Some people were going to come from Nangal for initiation. Maharajshri had finalized an auspicious time through a letter. One day Maharajshri said, "I am thinking that you should give initiation to the people coming from Nangal."

I was surprised to hear this unexpected thought from Maharajshri. I said, "Maharajshri, I have not even become a complete disciple. How then can I be a Guru?"

He replied, "Yes, you do have some limitations, but why do you think that you are becoming a Guru? The way in which you are doing all these services, such as sweeping the floor, washing the dishes, washing clothes — in the same way give initiation: as a service to the Guru. The greatest obstacle that stands in the way of being a Guru is the ego of being a Guru. If this problem is not solved by the Guru, he goes deep into the abyss of egoism. Since there is no room for a sense of service in his life he cannot establish himself in this frame of mind.

"The position of a Guru is achieved in two ways: by attaining that state as a result of continuous ongoing sadhan, or by the Guru's command. Even if such a state is attained through spiritual practice, a Guru's instruction is considered essential to save one from egoism. The humbling sense of being the Guru's servant can be easily maintained while doing the work of initiation under the Guru's command. In fact, what is effective here is the Guru's resolve, while the disciple does this work as part of his Guru-seva, his service to the Guru."

I said, "But in front of the disciples my personality will be perceived as a Guru's. How can I present to them this hollow personality of mine? I never imagined that you would ask me for something like this. Please, let me become a disciple first. To do a Guru's work many more deserving people are available. I am content with the happiness that I find in serving you at your feet."

Perhaps Maharajshri did not think it appropriate to talk any more at that time. He became silent. The next day, during our morning walk, the topic of discussion was initiation. Maharajshri said, "Initiation is a science known to very few people. It is passed on through the Guru-disciple lineage. It begins when someone comes to the Guru with a request for initiation. Not only is a future disciple tested with discrimination, but the Guru, from his experiences, must know whether the disciple is worthy of initiation or not."

Maharajshri described this experience elaborately and said, "At the time of initiation, when the Guru-Shakti returns after contact with the disciple's Chitta-Shakti, it can return with good and bad karma of the disciple." Then he talked about the experience of knowing whether the karma is good or bad. If the karma is good then there is no problem. But if it is bad then he explained how the Guru should protect himself. Sometimes the force of a kriya becomes very strong and starts to affect the situation. He explained how to control that excessive force. He mentioned a few other things that indicated how deep his knowledge regarding Shaktipat was. A disciple may make a mistake, but Maharajshri never stopped his kriya as a form of punishment. However, he described how to halt the kriyas of a disciple.

I asked Maharajshri, "How do you know all these things? Do you know this through your own experience, or did Guruji [Shri Yoganandji Maharaj] tell you all this?"

He said, "At first Guruji introduced me to all this, and later it was confirmed and strengthened through personal experience. The knowledge of the science of initiation is preserved through the Guru tradition. To attain this knowledge through personal experience would take one's whole life. One would also not know what knowledge has to be acquired. The only way is through the Guru lineage and tradition. But now the tradition of this science is becoming extinct. Once the kriyas of a particular gentleman went out of control. His Guru was unable to control them. He was sent to me, and by the grace of the Guru his kriyas were controlled."

I asked, "Do all Gurus know this science well?"

Maharajshri said, "I do not know who knows and who does not, but I can definitely say that all do not possess this knowledge." Maharajshri said that there are some experiences that only a Guru can have and he described some of these experiences. I am not explaining all this extensively here because this knowledge is only for the Guru and is received through a lineage. For three days during our morning walk this was the subject. By then the people from Nangal had arrived.

Maharajshri told the people that he was thinking that Bramhachariji should initiate them. Although they were my old friends, their faces became dull. Superficially they said, "Okay. As Maharajshri wishes. Whether you give initiation yourself or through the medium of Bramhachariji, in reality you are the one initiating so it does not make any difference."

I went to their room and asked them not to worry. "Maharajshri himself will initiate you. How is it that I have already become a Guru?"

Then I also made a request of Maharajshri, saying, "These people have come with a desire to get initiation from you. How can they then be told that someone else will initiate them? Please grace them yourself." Maharajshri remained silent.

In the morning at three, before the initiations, I made arrangements for Maharajshri's bath and requested that he take one. Maharajshri asked, "Will you take the bath or should I take it?" [Prior to the initiation ceremony the Guru must take a bath.] I requested that he take the bath.

This shows the generosity of Maharajshri. First of all, getting my book *Sadhan Path* published, then encouraging me to speak at the meditation program, and now asking me to give initiation showed how eager he was to stay in the background and bring his disciples forward.

11. The World Is Filled With Virtues And Vices

Maharajshri used to say that everyone has vices as well as virtues, no one has only vices or only virtues. However, there is usually a difference in the proportion of the two. Some have more virtues and others have more faults, but all have both. If someone is sinful in this life, perhaps he has been a holy person in many other past lives. Sattvic samskaras from those times exist in his mind. Who knows from which life samskaras came forward and made him sinful? In everyone's mind the three gunas [qualities] remain in imbalance and the balance keeps on changing. Sometimes one guna predominates, and at other times another. Only saints are close to a balanced state of the three gunas. A perfect balance of the three gunas means that the world will be dissolved [for that person]. The body is also a part of the world. He who nurtures the pride of being a great soul — God alone knows what kind of life he will have in the future or in births that follow. Maharajshri used to say that a spiritual aspirant must continuously look within his own self. He does not have time to look into the minds of others. Besides, someone who cannot look within his own mind is not in a position to look into someone else's mind. He assumes faults in others, judges them, and in doing that he makes a mistake. If he looks within himself he will realize that he is full of vices. Kriyas take place while doing sadhan. One gets happy that he has kriyas, but what is that? It is nothing but an outburst of the pollution of the mind. Samskaras turn into kriyas. If you want to speculate, think in this way: "If I have so many kriyas then how many samskaras must be stuffed within me!"

I had no shortage of impurities and faults. There were so many faults in me that I had become a fault incarnate, but with the grace of the Guru some virtues were emerging. To nurture those virtues and to develop them was a hard task for me. Weaknesses of the mind often dominated and struck at the newly-developing virtues, shaking their foundation. Sometimes I used to get so shaken up that my only option was to accept my defeat. This struggle continued to go on within. Others thought I was very quiet. Only I knew the condition of my mind.

One day Maharajshri said, "People who come here come to see me. Your behavior with them should be such that it does not affect their relationship with me. If you consider yourself a servant then your duty is to cooperate with me and help me in my work. Whether they are good or bad is for me to decide. How to behave with them is also my decision. If you take this decision into your own hands, it will be an impediment to my work. It will be difficult for you to stay here as well."

Maharajshri's words became a subject for me to ponder. I cared about these things even prior to hearing what Maharajji had just said. I tried never to be an obstacle between Maharajshri and his visitors. Yes, sometimes someone would come to the ashram toward whom I would be compelled to behave coldly. If Maharajshri said this, there must be a reason. I surmised that Maharajshri expected greater tolerance.

Maharajshri had a unique way of teaching forbearance. He would sometimes scold knowing fully well that a person had not made a mistake. He would ask a person to seek forgiveness even if he was not at fault. It seemed that he would often strike at the ego and give training in tolerance. Some might say that they did not have this experience, but I am only narrating my own. How can I say anything about anyone else? Maharajshri would say that without tolerance, sadhan is only a facade.

Yes, so I was mentioning Maharajshri's manner with visitors. During the morning walk I raised the subject. I asked, "Maharajshri, did I make a mistake in my behavior that made you tell me what you told me yesterday? I am trying to be very sensitive, but sometimes a sadhak comes along and it is very difficult for me not to be terse with him. Besides, people do not know when you are in what state, which causes some inconvenience."

Maharajshri said, "I do not say things like this to everyone. Upon my speaking so, if someone flares up and reacts negatively, I do not say anything to them ever again. My only intention was to warn you, not to make you feel that you had made a mistake. An aspirant must know his goal very clearly."

12. The Sequence of Creation

Today an old disciple came to the ashram. The subject of Maharajshri's discussion with him was new to me. I was listening with great curiosity. Maharajshri said, "Pashu, meaning living beings in bondage, the noose of bondage, and the Lord of the Pashus, meaning Shiva — the awareness and understanding of these three is called jnana, knowledge. The process by which purification takes place, in six ways, and that same process remaining in the control of the Guru, is called kriya. There are three ways to remove obstacles of multiplicity [known with different names] and three ways to remove obstacles of form. Thus there are six limbs of sadhan to free the individual soul in the form of an animal.

At the beginning of creation, through the resolve of Lord Bramha, sound, or resonance, was created, and from that sound arose the name, or word. From this resolve came vibration or movement, and from the vibration came agitation, and from agitation manifested the form. There are two categories of the creation: mobile and immobile. Both have names and forms." Maharajshri narrated the sequence of their manifestation, and then stated that Shaktipat was the means to retract this expansion, which exists in the form of the world:

When the universe was created nothing existed. Neither light, nor darkness. Neither white, nor black. Neither beauty, nor ugliness. Neither man, nor woman. Neither city, nor wilderness. The sun, moon and stars — nothing existed, because all of them are a part of the creation. Before creation how could anything else exist? The Shakti, whose vibrations and sound caused creation, was contained within its causal Bramha. Also the ego, the visible universe, kriya, or happenings, sound, and so forth — all were in the unified, or dissolved, state. If there was no ego how could there be a visible universe? And when there is no visible universe how can there be ego? At that time the Bramha was totally established within his own self. No witness. Nothing to be witnessed! There was no one to talk and no one to listen. Rishis, seers, saw this in meditation and wrote accordingly in the scriptures. This can be experienced only by rising above the human level. It is impossible for humans to even imagine this. Humans can know the world only with the help of the senses, which function with the help of the intellect, which again is only one of the activities of Shakti manifesting through the chitta or psyche. This knowledge attained through the senses is very limited and erroneous. This knowledge, in fact, is ignorance. Experiences beyond this universe begin when the activity of the Shakti in the form of intellect ceases.

A resolve at the subtlest of the subtle level took place in Bramha. It was beyond the limits of subtlety because nothing like subtle or gross existed. Call it a resolve or call it play, in reality it was not a sankalp [resolve]. Then what was it? It cannot be verbalized because humans do not have a word for it; but it is called a resolve. The resolve of Bramha and the resolve of an individual soul are totally different, because Bramha does not have samskaras, illusion and vasana, which exist within an individual soul. Jnana, or knowledge, also was hidden within at that time. It cannot be called knowledge because nothing like knowledge or ignorance existed.

Bramha resolved, "I am one, let me be many." This clarifies a few things: 1) The creator is Bramha. 2) The creation is within Bramha. 3) The creation is Bramha. 4) The creation appears to be multifold, but in its original form it is one and the same. 5) The creation is not separate from the creator, Bramha.

As soon as a sankalp, resolve, arose the first spandan, vibration or change, occurred. Due to this, Shakti, or power, was awakened within Bramha. Shakti of Bramha is not separate from Bramha and it is one and the same as Bramha. If Bramha is the bearer then Shakti is the newborn. Shakti sometimes is latent within Bramha and sometimes awakened, but it is never annihilated. This awakening of Shakti was within Bramha, it was not manifest and separate, and only Bramha knew about this. Bramha did wake up but his eyes were still closed. Then the second spandan or vibration took place and Shakti became discernible, as if it opened its eyes the same way a sleeping person wakes up and opens his eyes.

Bramhavastha is Shivavastha, in which the ego exists but in the seed form. In the absence of creation the ego remains dormant. After the first vibration, because Shakti is awake, it is called the Shakti Avastha [state] or Shakti Tattva. In this state the Shakti is awake but has not yet manifested. Shiva and Shakti still remain merged together. The spandan, vibration or change, that follows [the third spandan or vibration] causes the Shakti to manifest, even though it is still merged or unified with Shiva. This form is exemplified by the authors of the scriptures as the Ardhanarinateshwar, in which half the body is a woman and half a man [Lord of the Dancers, i.e. Shiva]. This form of Bramha is one step closer to the creation. Prior to creating the universe, Bramha must manifest his Shakti in the fullest form, because without Shakti no action is ever possible and there is no greater event than the cosmic creation. That is why this state is named Shiva-Shakti or Sadashiva [everlasting Shiva]. In other words, just as Shiva existed prior to the manifestation of Shakti, similarly Shiva also exists after the manifestation of Shakti. On the basis of Shiva alone, his Shakti sometimes manifests and sometimes assimilates back. There is no change in Shiva or in the Shakti. Maharajshri gave an example of this state: A garbanzo bean has a skin covering two parts of the bean. When the bean is planted in the ground, the skin tears off and, from the union of the two parts, a new plant sprouts. If the two parts are separated and then planted no new plant will sprout. Similarly, Sadashiva is like two parts of a seed; wherein Shiva and Shakti both are present. Creation is not possible without Shiva and nothing can be born without Shakti. In the universe, wherever Shakti is present, its basis, Shiva, is always present. Even at the gross visible level this unity prevails, hence the name Sadashiva [ever-present Shiva]. Aham, "I" [the Creator], and Idam, "This" [the Creation], the seer and the sight, both coexist like two parts of a seed.

In the next vibration [the fourth principle] the skin is torn off. The "I" takes the form of Ishwara [God] and "This" takes the form of Shakti, his Power. Here Bramha, having taken the form of Ishwara, becomes cognizant of the work of creation in unison with his Shakti. This state [the fifth vibration] of the Shakti is called Shuddha Vidya, or pure knowledge. Shiva and Shakti are in such a state that peace, stillness or turmoil — nothing exists. So what exists? Only saints on whom God bestows his grace know and experience what exists then. That is why Shiva and Shakti are called Shantyatita [Transcending Peace]. Sadashiva, Ishwara, and Shuddha Vidya are all pure elements, but to show that these are on a separate level, below the Shiva-Shakti level, they are included in the phase named Shanti [Peace]. So far the universe has not been created. Impurity exists in creation, which is the result of a vibration in Shakti. But there is no impurity or disturbance in Shakti.

In the subsequent vibrations, Bramha, in the form of Ishwara, along with Shakti, gets ready to create the universes. First his Shuddha Vidya is transformed into Ashuddha Vidya, or impure knowledge. Although Shakti is Shuddha Vidya, because it faces Maya [i.e., the illusionary knowledge of limitation of the Self; the grand illusion] it descends to the level of vidya [cognizance], and while remaining integral to the phase of cognizance it manifests as Maya, time, kala [phases], niyati [order], vidya [cognizance], raga [attachment] and purusha [an individualized Soul]. The size or shape of the moon does not change, but it appears to wax and wane; these changes in the moon are referred to as its phases. In the same way there is no change in Shiva or Shakti, but, due to the vibration, it seems as if there are changes. These phases, meaning the appearance of changes, continuously go on in the cosmic universe. Vidya [cognizance] takes the form of Maya and causes illusion. Time gives the sense of duration; phases shows changes. Vidya, or cognizance, gives us the knowledge of the universe. Niyati, or order, takes the form of destiny through samskara-aashay [the stockpile of impressions]; raga causes attachment; and purusha, the soul who is God himself, gets enveloped in these layers and becomes a jivatma — an individualized soul, a soul with a separate ego identity.

There are infinite universes. They keep on flying around like fireflies in the Mahakasha [Great Sky]. One universe dissolves while another one is created. It is an extremely beautiful and enchanting show. Like fireworks the emergence and collapse of the universes go on. Bramha enjoys watching it. The individual souls, enveloped in sheaths, keep on playing different roles like different characters in the drama. Each universe functions like a stage. Ishwara has put out seven different sheaths: of Maya, time, phases, niyati [destiny], vidya [cognizance], raga [attachment] and jivatva [the sense of individuality]. The jiva, the individual soul, enveloped in these layers, keeps on wandering under the illusion in the world. In other words, Shiva himself becomes subjected to Maya and becomes a jiva when attired with the five layers of time, phases, cognizance, destiny, and attachment.

As the jiva, the individual being, establishes himself in Maya and adorns the garb of jivatva, the sense of individuality, the following phase is named pratishtha [establishment]. In this phase there are twenty-three principles, including avyakta, the unmanifested form, or the hidden prakriti [aboriginal nature; the creative principle], mahat [the first manifestation of the creative principle], ahamkar [consciousness, or ego], mind, the five senses of perception, the five organs of action, the five states of matter, and akasha [ether], air, fire, water. The twenty-forth principle is earth, but it is included under the phase called Nivritti because even after this, the spandan, or vibrations, of the Shakti continues without interruption. However it abstains from creating any new tattva, principle. This is the sequence of the manifestation and evolution of creation. Prakriti, the creative principle, has two categories: inert and active. In the inert prakriti, five elements and the visible world are included, and in the active prakriti, those five physical senses are included on the basis of which the chetana, or consciousness, works. At the root of the inert, as well as of the active, creative principle is the same power of consciousness, called cosmic or universal consciousness. In the active aspect of the creative principle the same power is working in every living being at the individual level, which is called individual consciousness.

It became clear to me that spirituality is not a subject of words or scriptural knowledge alone. Long-term sadhana in line with the Guru's instructions, along with faith, is essential for that. Just as Shakti, after it starts to pulsate, turns external and remains active in the world, in the same way until and unless the reverse sequence of its upward and inward journey is experienced the knowledge of Bramha, the Absolute Truth, cannot be acquired. The order in which the tattvas, the principles, have been developed — their dissolution must be experienced in the exact reverse order. These activities are known as kriyas based on the tattvas [principles]. But before one can have kriyas based on the principles, one has to go through a very long and arduous journey of kriyas based on samskaras [accumulated impressions] that must be completed. Samskaras and vasanas [mental tendencies] have created a unique world within the mind. First, the destruction of this so-called world must take place. After the Shakti awakens, that is what it does first. It becomes active to destroy samskaras and vasanas. Those samskaras that have taken the form of destiny [prarabdha] are even more complicated to destroy. The jiva has to helplessly endure the fruits of his destiny. According to the statements of Maharajshri, through logic and tricks one comes to know the cause of creation and knows Bramha, the ultimate reality, indirectly. Then, after purification of the mind, one gets direct and personal experiential knowledge of that. In other words, if, with sadhana, one succeeds in destroying samskaras and vasanas then the path to direct and personal experience, or realization, of Bramha is opened.

Maharajshri said that the world is either symbolized with name or with form. Although the whole universe is the result of the vibrations of the sovereign cosmic consciousness, it appears to be multiple due to different names, forms and functions. Whether the soil in the farm is used for growing fruits, vegetables, grains or flowers, its name is farm and it is in the form of soil. When the same soil is used for making a pot, its name and form both are changed to a pot. Even though the soil is the same, there is great dissimilarity. Similarly, the whole creation being originally the same Shakti, even so, somewhere it is solid, somewhere it is liquid, and somewhere hot. Everything appears different in form, name and function. The jiva gets entangled in the multitude of names and forms. For those established in the Self, names and forms are secondary and Shakti is foremost.

A jiva [individual soul] faces many complexities after getting entangled in multiple names and forms. He believes names and forms are everything. He finds some things good and other things bad. He is attached to some things and despises other things. Desirable things give rise to greed and discomfort gives rise to anger. The jiva gets tied into many different desires. Then destiny does its work and, with the accumulation of samskaras, destiny starts to form. Once the wheel of destiny starts to move, the jiva spins in it like a top. The root cause of this wheel of destiny is the entanglement in names and forms, meaning avidya or ignorance of the ultimate reality. In *Yoga Darshan*, the root cause of all miseries is said to be avidya.

Not only is Shakti separate from the world, but it is also the creator, and it is the material cause of creation as well. To create the universes it did not need to go anywhere to get the raw material. Shakti itself is the raw material. This means that whatever is visible in this cosmos, all things in different shapes and forms, are the same divine Shakti. God is a very unique sculptor. He makes all, becomes all, nurtures all, and then absorbs and blends all within himself. The jiva does not know the artist. He gets entrapped in the world made by him and gets attached. The jiva becoming attached in the world is also the artistry of the artist. How bizarre is the world and how astute is the artist!

The universes keep on lighting and extinguishing like fireflies. In other words, Ishwara [God] manifests them sometimes, and at other times submerges them within himself. Manifesting is called creation, and submerging within is called Pralaya, dissolution of manifestation. During creation Shakti goes on manifesting in the form of tattvas, or principles, one after another, and during annihilation the principles go on retreating back, one into the other, and finally all are absorbed into Shakti. The emergence and collapse of the universe happens at the cosmic level. After due thought one will realize that the process of dissolution is different at the individual level. The universe remains as it was, but dissolution occurs at a specific state at an individual level and the individual is liberated. By doing the sadhan given by the Guru, the gross or physical principles, in reverse order, fold their qualities within and return to the Shakti. While returning to the origin at the individual level, Shakti gives many different experiences to the aspirant. These are called divine experiences. In reality, the creation of the cosmos and every event that occurs therein are the activities of the Shakti, hence they are all divine. They are not considered divine because the jiva has made them the cause of his attachment to the world. The inner experiences during sadhan are considered divine because they are the cause of liberation. Spirituality is not for the dissolution of the world, but for liberating an individual soul from the bondage of the world. Pralaya, dissolution, takes place at the individual level. *Yoga Darshan* also says that for average people the world remains as it is, but for those who are fulfilled the world dissolves. Lord Shiva is called "The Destroyer" because he brings about final destruction to the jiva and liberates him from bondage.

Guru Maharajshri used to say that speech is like the physical expression of knowledge. Just as all activities are done through the senses, in the same way knowledge is expressed through speech [sound or voice]. The orator gives a lecture through speech. At the para [transcendental, unmanifested] stage, speech is hidden in seed form. At the pashyanti [the finest impulse of sound, the first manifested consciousness, the seat of all knowledge] stage, speech sprouts. At the madhyama [mental speech; ideas and thoughts] stage, it takes the form of words. It is expressed at the vaikhari [audible or vocal speech, the grossest level] stage. Speech brings all the knowledge of the world to light. It is the main connecting thread between the "I" and the world. When it turns introvert, it starts to open the seams of the mind and starts a reverse process. Vaikhari folds into madhyama, and madhyama into pashyanti, and finally pashyanti merges into para. The extrovert process is towards the world and the introvert process is towards the soul. Speech is also a kriya of the Shakti, thus discipline and control of speech open the pathway to a direct experience of Shakti. Maharajshri also presented the subject here with the help of speech. When Maharajshri talked it felt as if he had vak-siddhi [the power of spoken words to make reality].

Repetition of a mantra [japa] is equally accepted by all paths as an important part of spiritual practice. Japa hits every breath like a hammer and directly strikes the mind and prana, the life-force. Japa is regarded as the main means for awakening Shakti. On the other hand, in scriptures and the writings of saints, the grace of the Guru is said to be the main factor and the knowledge of Shaktipat depends on the grace of a Guru. As far as anavi [individual] practices are concerned, mantra-japa and pranayaam are the two primary practices. In today's age, the right environment for pranayaam is very hard to find, but everyone can do mantra-japa, thus it is said to be the primary practice. In the path of Shaktipat also, the Guru gives Shaktipat through a mantra [sound].

Mantra is related to philology, the science of language, and it has three limbs. Varna means the basic alphabet. By joining letters words are formed. By combining words a mantra is formed. Some mantras are called "beeja" mantras, or "seed" mantras. In a beeja mantra each letter is a mantra. In other words, in each seed, or letter, a word and a mantra are included. A sadhan of japa is a pathway to go from a lower to a higher level, or to go inward from outward. In other words, this is the path from materialism to spirituality, starting with language, which is a part of this world and also a part of physically-expressed speech. The purification of letters, words and mantra inspire purification of the mind. Meanings and sentiments in the mantra strike the mind and enthuse it to awaken. Some aspirants start to have spontaneous pranayaam by doing japa, which is a sign of awakening.

These three components of speech have a direct relationship with the three parts of the visible world: kalaa, or phases; tattva, or principle; and bhuvan, or place. As mentioned earlier the meaning of phase is the transformative quality. Phases sometimes grow and sometimes fade. These changes are illusory. The moon remains the same but it appears to be changing. Shakti does not grow or diminish, yet it appears as if there has been a change in Shakti. This is due to intense vibrations of the Shakti. Vibrations cause waves in the water, yet the water remains water; only the shape of water is called a wave. Due to the same changeability and vibrations, one after another, the tattvas, or principles, seem to manifest, just as the same water may become snowflakes or steam. Then the principles [the five physical principles] — form, qualities, function, nature and condition — start to appear distinct. Bhuvan means the place where the principles exist or become. It is clear that they reside in the great vacuum of the sky. The scriptures describe these places of becoming for the five elements in detail, but here, this much understanding is enough for readers.

In reality, if one observes at the individual level, every moment phases are waxing or waning in the body. The wheel of changes keeps on turning. Sometimes the individual is a child or an old man, sometimes a healthy and sometimes a sick man. No one's body remains the same. The state of mind also keeps on changing. Sometimes happy and at other times unhappy, sometimes lusty, sometimes angry, sometimes contented, sometimes dissatisfied. The state of the psyche also does not remain the same. The body is a symbol of the world. The body also, like the world, resides and moves within the sky. It is also made of the same five physical elements [ether, air, fire, water and earth].

The pathway for the inner journey opens up upon purification of the three parts of mantra japa: feeling, thought and action. Feeling, thought and action become impure due to samskaras and vasanas. An aspirant has to wear these away with spontaneous kriyas after the inward awakening of the divine Kundalini-Shakti. With the weakening of samskaras and vasanas, feeling, thought and action are purified. One's attachment to the world is then greatly reduced. This is achieved through Shaktipat. Then one rises above the changeable world made of the five elements and rises above the body. Both of them exist in the sky. This way kalaa, tattva and bhuvan are purified.

As I reached this point in the discussion, I was lost in the churning of my heart. I had lost my way. Where did I want to go and where was I going? The spiritual journey is so long and life so short! The majority of the time of this short life had been wasted. I was drowning in ego when I had nothing else but a sense of individuality. And even that sense of individuality was simply a feeling, a feeling of being small, with a sense of doership, a feeling of happiness and miseries, helplessness, lack of energy. How big my ego was! Nobody was more intelligent, strong and artistic than I. My whole life had been wasted in this false ego. Now, with the sight of the lotus feet of my Guru, some sense had returned. At least now I was aware that I was lost.

The next day, during the morning walk, I asked Maharajshri, "Are

kriyas of sound and light based on accumulated impressions or the principles?"

His reply was, "Both. If samskaras, accumulated impressions, of
past lives are rising and kriyas are taking place due to that then they are
samskara-based. If these experiences are happening after samskaras are
destroyed then they are due to the tattvas, principles. Along with the
process of dissolution of the principles, these experiences continue to
take place."

Question: "Kriyas of sound and light take place during the dissolution of the tattvas, after all accumulated impressions have been destroyed, but where do the accumulated impressions of sadhana done in a
past birth come from?"

Answer: "When someone does sadhana with a certain imagination,
then, after long-term sadhana, this imagination starts to take a form and
experiences start to take place. The impressions of that begin to accumulate. With the passage of time, when the Shakti is awakened, then
those samskaras come out in the form of kriyas."

Question: "Aren't the impressions of kriyas happening due to tattvas accumulated?"

Answer: "Kriyas based on tattva, principles, take place only after
the chitta is purified, meaning when samskaras are destroyed. At that
stage tattvas are busy ending their so-called existence. In those kriyas
there is no place for individual identity as a jiva. There is no surrender
either. Then surrender also has finished its job. The sense of individuality is on the way to dissolving itself into the soul."

Question: "Purification of the six limbs, or parts, as explained by
you did not include anything about light and sound."

Answer: "After the process of the creation of the universe there
was only a description of the awakening of the Shakti through the purification of the limbs, and not of the activities following that. There was
no discussion about kriyas based either on samskaras or on tattva."

Question: "Does that mean that Shakti cannot be awakened without purification?"

Answer: "It can be awakened but it should not be. As long as the disciple is not worthy, Shaktipat cannot be fruitful. The disciple cannot get benefits of Shaktipat. All kinds of impurities in the mind — lust, anger, greed, and so forth — drag the mind toward the world and sadhan gets broken. It is best for the aspirant to look within himself and decide whether he is worthy or not for initiation. After that he can make his request of the Guru. Then the Guru may examine the disciple's worthiness and, based on his own strength and experience, decide whether the aspirant is deserving or not."

Question: "Maharajshri, I had not even heard about the purification of the six parts, yet you graced me by giving me initiation. How come?"

Answer: "You may have heard or not heard about that, but you used to do some japa, dhyan [meditation], study scriptures, sing spiritual songs, and so forth. This made you worthy. When I saw you the first time in Ghaziabad I felt that you were ready for initiation. At that time we had not even talked much."

Question: "This means that, in addition to the purification of the six parts, there are some other techniques?"

Answer: "What did I say? After some philosophical discussions I shed some light on forms of mantra-japa, its effects and awakening. For clarity on the background of the subject, I explained the sequence of the development of creation. By japa, pranayaam, bhakti, yoga, knowledge, karma without attachment, and so forth, the mind can be made worthy for initiation."

Question: "The qualities of deserving disciples given in the scriptures may hardly be visible in any aspirant, including myself. Does that mean we are all unworthy? The person who has those qualities would be a great being. Why then would he need to go in search of a Guru?"

Answer: "Yes, you are right. By efforts of sadhana, the psyche does not get fully purified. That is the job of Kriya-Shakti. It brings up samskaras and converts them to kriyas. But prior to diksha [initiation] one must have the desire to be free from samskaras and impurities. If, with sadhana before initiation, one can attain this, it is sufficient. After diksha, with sadhan and Guru-seva, annihilation of samskaras, purification of the chitta and destruction of the mind are received from divine Shakti in the form of alms. Scriptures describe the qualities of a deserving disciple, but they do not say that all the qualities should be in one person. It is impossible to have all those in one person. It is the Guru's duty to see whether Shakti will be received or not, whether the disciple will experience the effect of Shakti or not."

13. Tolerance

It was the monsoon season, 1962. There was a bramhachari in the ashram. Whenever he came he served Maharajshri with great diligence.

He had much love for me, also. Whenever I was in his company time passed very well. He wanted to go on a pilgrimage to Badrinath and Kedarnath and he asked me to accompany him. I did not have a single penny. After coming to the ashram I had followed the principle of not accepting money, nor keeping money. It was the third year since my arrival at the ashram and I did feel like going somewhere, but I had nothing to spend. And then if both of us went away on a pilgrimage, who would serve Maharajshri? That also required thought. Perhaps Bramhachariji understood my dilemma. He said, "Are you worried because you have no money for the pilgrimage? Whatever I have is yours. Yes, the question of serving Maharajshri remains. In any case, before we decide to go we have to get Maharajshri's permission. At that time everything will be sorted out."

When the proposal of the pilgrimage to Badri-Kedar was placed before Maharajshri he was very pleased. He said, "Good. You may go. With this plan you will also have a vacation. One gets weary staying in the same place for long. A worldly person, on getting weary, seeks methods of entertainment while an aspirant goes on a pilgrimage. But you must understand that the pilgrimage takes place inside, not outside. The external pilgrimage is merely a rehearsal for the internal pilgrimage. During a pilgrimage one has to face many difficulties, bear insults, face failures, and still continue courageously with a serene mind. In one place one sees mountain ranges, in another a vast ocean, somewhere a desert appears and elsewhere greenery. During a pilgrimage one sees variety. All this is nothing but a glimpse of the internal journey. The inner pilgrimage is very difficult. Extreme courage, enthusiasm, focus, firm resolve to move ahead, strong desire to see God and endurance are essential. During the inner journey one sees numerous sights and has many different experiences. There is a possibility of getting attached to them, but one must keep moving forward. The external pilgrimage is for learning all this, but today it takes the form of comfortable tourism; the sense of austerity toward the internal pilgrimage has disappeared. The main purpose of pilgrimage is made secondary by roads, railways, good places for lodging and boarding, money in the pocket, and the accumulation of things for comfort. When there is no real external pilgrimage, how can even there be the beginning of an internal pilgrimage?

"We did our first pilgrimage to Uttarakhand [in north India] in 1934. At that time perhaps a bus went up to Dev Prayag, but we started walking on foot from Rishikesh. Whenever we came across huts and ashrams of ascetics and saints we stopped for a meeting and spiritual conversation. We never broke our routine of chanting, meditation, and so forth. Going up and down in the mountains, we would enjoy the natural beauty, spend time in spiritual conversations, cook our own food, never buy cooked food from the market, endure comforts and discomforts, recite mantras even while walking and keep on going forward. Those were very inexpensive times, but still Guruji [Shri Yoganandji Maharaj] had given me some money. With this blessing of the Guru, the pilgrimage was completed.

"I still remember one incident from this pilgrimage. I was climbing the incline above Gauri Kund, on the way to Kedarnath, and someone was coming down after visiting the temple. As he walked by me I sensed that he was a follower of the same spiritual path. Possibly he also felt the same. After walking ahead a little I looked back and realized that the gentleman had also stopped and was looking at me. Spontaneously my feet went in his direction. He also came toward me. We were standing in front of each other and looking at each other. He broke the silence saying, 'I am Gulavani.' [A famous saint from Pune, a disciple of Maharajshri's sanyas Guru-brother, Lokanath Tirth Maharaj.]

"I introduced myself saying, 'I am a disciple of Yoganandji Maharaj.' Thus mine and Gulavani Maharaj's first meeting took place on the inaccessible heights of the Himalayas. In the inner journey, also, an aspirant meets spiritual adepts, deities and sages, but one has to go through a long and hard pilgrimage for that, and has to bear oncoming hardships and miseries.

"I recollect another incident on the way to Gangotri. At night we were sleeping in a campground for pilgrims. It was on the banks of the Ganges. It was raining very heavily. One person came with a lamp in his hand shouting, 'Wake up! The waters of the Ganges are rising!' We all woke up and went to higher ground. In the morning we saw that the Ganges was flowing where we had been sleeping. In the same way, God warns you about calamities on an inner pilgrimage, but you have to go to a safe place on your own.

"There was another similar experience. I was returning from Yamunotri on the way to Gangotri. There was a small, hilly path by which one could go to Uttarkashi directly. I was tempted to take the shortcut and I started on that path. In the mountains paths are not clear; during those days there simply weren't any. Someone gave directions and I started walking. The temptation of shortcuts is very destructive on the spiritual path. I lost my way. I wandered in the middle of the high mountain peaks looking for the trail. I had thought I would reach Uttarkashi quickly by using the shortcut, but instead I was surrounded by darkness and still wandering. I started to worry a little. How will I spend the night in this desolate jungle? Hunger and thirst also started troubling me. In front of me the darkness of the night was quickly approaching when I saw an old sage with a long beard and a small water vessel in his hand approaching. As he came near I bowed, and before I could say anything he said, 'Are you lost? Why did you come this way? The straight road was much better, even though it would have taken a little longer. As it is, by taking this shortcut you have taken even longer'.

"When he learned that I wanted to go to Uttarkashi he asked me to follow him. I started to follow the mahatma. It must have been only fifteen minutes or so and the lights of Uttarkashi were visible. I was looking towards the village in surprise and, as I turned around to look at the mahatma, he had disappeared. Who was he? Where did he come from? God alone knows.

"Once on the journey we met a French couple. After travelling through many countries they had come to India. I asked, 'What did you see in India that you have not seen anywhere else?'

"They said, 'Nowhere else is there a river like the Ganges. It feels as if it is not a river, but a mother. The beauty of its banks, the peace, divine joy, and the flow of pure love at its sight are not experienced anywhere else.' This is about the external journey on the banks of the Ganges. When you play around the banks of the inner Ganga, the joy cannot be described.

"Oh! I was lost in old memories. I forgot that you are going on a pilgrimage. If you want to experience the real joy of the pilgrimage then go on foot. If you want to learn to endure difficulties and make an impression on the mind then go on foot. If you want to learn to bear insults and respect and want to see things up close then go on foot. It is the monsoon season; you will experience the real joy of going through difficulties. Go and take advantage of the holy shelter of ashrams on the way. Saints that are living are like real holy places. They purify the mind. Do not run after comforts. Stay for three days at Badrinath and Kedarnath. May God make your pilgrimage successful."

I submitted, saying, "I am hesitant to go because there is no one to serve you."

He said, "Why is there nobody? There are all these people. You go without any hesitation. There is no need to hurry back. Stay on for an extra day or two wherever you feel good. I am fine here. Do not worry about me."

14. The Rules of Pilgrimage

Maharajshri's analysis of the pilgrimage forced me to think about some things — the churning of my heart had already begun. When I left the ashram I was kind of lost. Maharajshri had expressed very relevant and critical thoughts on pilgrimage. In reality, the external pilgrimage is a part of the journey of life and can give a right direction to life. It can bring a life running recklessly on the wrong path back to the right path. Even then the external pilgrimage remains external. Life on a bad path does not let you even start on the internal journey, whereas the right path opens the doors for an inner pilgrimage. Pilgrimages have contributed enormously to bringing lives to the right path. Developing forbearance, making the heart generous, instilling the habit of continuous absorption in japa, contemplation and meditation are all contributions that a pilgrimage makes. My mind was engrossed in thinking about the subject of pilgrimage. I was lost in these thoughts until our train reached Rishikesh. Bramhachariji also did not talk much. I came to the following conclusions:

(I) In the daily flow of life we get angry over small issues. If we do not express our anger, we suffer mentally. During a pilgrimage we lose control during unexpected circumstances and uncomfortable situations. If we practice control over ourselves at least during this time then we may be able to control our anger to a great extent. It is weakness of the mind and a lack of control over the senses that makes one susceptible to external comforts and difficulties. In such a state our mind can neither go on an inner journey, nor can it concentrate on anything. We remain incapable of concentrating even on the kriyas of Shakti. The most direct proof of the influence of worldly happenings on our mind is anger. It arises in the mind but shows on the face. It is expressed with words, and it may create trouble with hands and feet. The person who gets angry burns in its fire; the person who is subjected to anger is also miserable.

Anger is a great enemy of spirituality. Therefore a pilgrim must embark with a rule that no matter what happens, at least during the pilgrimage, he will control his anger. The attempt should be to not let anger enter the mind.

(2) Generally, humans are busy collecting and enjoying comforts. One spends time and energy to earn money in order to accumulate comforts. As a result, whether he gets comforts or not, he definitely becomes attached to them. He does not develop a habit of enduring hardships and poverty. The truth is that everyone has to encounter hardships and poverty, but due to lack of endurance one becomes miserable. If, during a pilgrimage, one gives up the desire for comforts and luxuries, tries to accept hardships, and practices doing without things even when there is no shortage then the door to relief from that attachment can be opened.

(3) People have difficulty in maintaining continuity in sadhan and bhajan. To some extent it is laziness, and to some extent they consider worldly responsibilities to be more important than sadhan. Hence sadhan is interrupted from time to time. But if one so desires, he can maintain continuity of sadhan during a pilgrimage. He can learn how to do sadhan while doing work. For example, he can do japa while walking, cooking, bathing or washing clothes. This practice during a pilgrimage can be helpful during regular life with its routines. Avoiding involvement in useless talk while on a pilgrimage can help prevent the wasting of time and irregularity in sadhan. A pilgrim should talk only when something has to be said or requested, or someone asks him something. In this way the habits of an aspirant will be solidified, and he will become a mature aspirant.

(4) If a pilgrim is a householder then he must donate according to his capacity. If he is a renunciate then he should remain satisfied with whatever is available and consider it as a gift of God. If someone is wealthy then he must go on a pilgrimage only with money earned honestly. A pilgrimage with money earned dishonestly, or by force or fraud, is not a pilgrimage but becomes a pleasure trip. One must remember that a pilgrimage should be taken as a spiritual practice. Then only can it help the inner pilgrimage, otherwise it is a sightseeing trip.

(5) A pilgrim must make every effort to maintain regularity in sadhan during a pilgrimage. First thing in the morning he must do his daily worship, then do japa and study scriptures. He must do meditation whenever it is appropriate. If he has to prepare a meal, he must prepare it and eat it or take it along. Focus on japa while walking. He must walk only so much in a day that he is not tired upon reaching the next stop. On the way, if he arrives at the residence of a saint, he must stop and seek their company. Wherever he stops for the night, he must do his prayers, offerings, chanting, reading, and so forth. Cook dinner, eat it, and go to sleep while meditating or chanting.

(6) These recommendations are for people who take long pilgrimages, such as going around the holy River Narmada or Uttarakhand on foot. Pilgrimage is also a form of sadhan. When the mind is restless, then it is better to wander for God. Only the mind that is free of restlessness can begin the inner pilgrimage. Some people object to a pilgrimage, but it is not a waste of time for all. The intent must be pure, clean worldly behavior, a sense of the futility of the world, and love for God. The pilgrimage of those who have these feelings cannot be worthless. Those who have already gone beyond the fickleness of the mind — for them a pilgrimage is unnecessary.

After crossing Rishikesh, we stayed at the hut of a master. We told him that we were going on a pilgrimage to Badri-Kedar on foot. He also said a few similar things to us. "Whoever suggested that you go on foot has given you an excellent idea. You will be able to enjoy the journey more, and you will see the scenery more closely and clearly. You will be able to sit on the banks of streams and drink water, but the real benefit of this is the spiritual benefit. In a journey on foot one has to undergo many difficulties, such as austerities. The monsoon season has started. There are floods in the rivers and streams. Many insects will be out and there will be many difficulties. You will have the opportunity to do many austerities. By walking you will meet many local people, and your knowledge will be enriched. You will meet many monks and saints, which will purify your mind. You will run into situations where you can help people who are in a miserable condition, and that will enhance compassion in your heart. By enduring respect and insult your tolerance will grow. You will have time for sadhan and bhajan. For renunciates like you, pilgrimage on foot is the best. Pilgrimage using vehicles is for those who have less time, or somehow want to 'cut the grass' of a pilgrimage."

15. The Secrets of a Pilgrimage

The pilgrimage took two months. We went to Nangal after that. Bramhachariji left from there; I do not remember where he was going. I went to Himachal Pradesh to the place where I once lived in a cottage. I came back to Dewas from there.

Maharajshri was sitting in the verandah. After bowing I sat down and he said, "Was your pilgrimage a happy one?"

I said, "Yes."

He said, "Did you remember the things I told you when you were leaving? I hope you followed my instructions. People develop pride about their travel, from an external pilgrimage. They do not reap any spiritual benefits. They just talk about how the people were, how the scenery was, and how the food was. How strange different things were. Thus they want to impress others. Do not do all this. There is nothing to be proud of in a pilgrimage. The person who becomes proud has not gone on a pilgrimage at all. It is true that today is not the age for a pilgrimage on foot. There was a time when Bhagwan Shankaracharya went on a pilgrimage covering all of India on foot without any baggage or money. In those days there was no shortage of alms for a monk. Today, if a monk goes to a village, people first question whether he is real or a fraud or a thief.

"The pilgrimage that you did is incomplete for a renunciate such as yourself. There is a strong relationship between pilgrimage and seeking alms. Asking for alms while on a pilgrimage strikes straight at the ego. If you do not get donations of food then you may even have to sleep hungry. If someone who is hungry asks for food from you, you may have to give your food to the hungry person. There is a big difference between begging and receiving alms. To beg is a business of worldly people. But for an aspirant, bhiksha, or to ask for alms, is a sadhana — a spiritual practice. The background and the feelings between the two are as different as heaven and earth. Asking for alms, or bhiksha, enhances sadhana. For an aspirant, bhiksha is the highway to perfection, to become a siddha. An ascetic is incomplete without bhiksha. A renunciate's pilgrimage is never complete without receiving bhiksha. The experience of enduring respect and insult that you get in bhiksha can never be experienced simply by a pilgrimage.

"The inference here is that fulfilment in an aspirant's life is not from comforts and enjoyment, but in quiet acceptance of suffering. Therefore pilgrimage and bhiksha are recommended. People may prefer to have a comfortable and joyful pilgrimage, but that idea destroys the basic purpose of a pilgrimage."

I listened to this quietly. Then I said, "Maharajshri, during the pilgrimage I experienced that we can do japa and other spiritual practices, but it is very hard to do sadhana of Shaktipat. It is better to stay at one place and do sadhan regularly."

Maharajshri said, "It is the best, but it is not possible to do that. The accumulated impressions of fickleness make the mind restless, and to pacify that one has to go here and there. If you want to go somewhere then a pilgrimage is the best, if one follows the rules regarding pilgrimage given in the scriptures. Otherwise a pilgrimage becomes only a trip and there is no spiritual benefit. Those whose minds have become quiet and peaceful do not need to wander."

16.   A Change in Temperament

During the morning walk I asked Maharajshri, "Why is it so difficult to change our nature? Even after a million explanations a human being is not willing to give up his nature. If someone wants to change even then he cannot succeed. How helpless one is!"

Answer: "Nature is a ghost that, once it gets on your back, does not get off for life after life. This ghost does not know what death is. It comes alive again and again. It does not run away when chased, does not get scared when frightened, does not go away even by prayer. It does not understand explanations. It burns you within. It squeezes out all the energy in a living being. Even great souls are helpless in its hands. They can give up everything but their nature.

"What is nature? It is a specific state of the chitta, or psyche, in which some specific samskaras are predominant. Sometimes they are latent; sometimes they are active and cause waves in the psyche. When samskaras are latent, the disposition also remains suppressed, but when the samskaras come up to the surface the real temperament manifests. For example, if someone is hot-tempered, it means he has more samskaras of anger. When someone gets angry, it means that his samskaras of anger have arisen. If someone does not have samskaras of anger, how will he get angry? When he is provoked, only a person will get angry who has samskaras of anger.

"When the same type of samskaras continue to come up and create waves in the mind, and continue to have an impact on the person, he is compelled to behave accordingly. He accumulates additional samskaras of the same type and samskaras accumulated in the past become stronger. That becomes the person's nature.

"One's disposition is always unnatural. The natural form of a human being is the soul, which is unchangeable and pure, free from faults and untouched by any layers. Nature, or temperament, is the attribute of individuality. The soul itself does not have any disposition. The greater the number of samskaras in the chitta, the greater are the variations in the nature of a person. The same person can have, in his nature, longing, anger, jealousy, hatred, gossiping, and so forth. Whichever impression arises, that type of disposition will manifest. When samskaras change, the nature of a person also changes. When the samskaras of anger arise he will be angry, but the next moment, when samskaras change, he might become fearful. The outside world is only a medium to awaken the samskaras and bring out one's nature. Sometimes, without any help from the world, the samskaras can be awakened and bring out one's nature. In solitude, with eyes closed, the memory of past events can arouse one's nature of anger or jealousy.

"It is not true that the form of one's disposition is always bad and impure. Good and sattvic nature is also there. Everyone's nature has a mixture of good and bad. Some have worse characteristics and others have better characteristics. Sometimes good nature is displayed, and at other times a bad nature may rise. Someone may assume divinity, and the next moment be demonic. Some people are compassionate, forgiving and generous. For spiritual progress this type of disposition is definitely helpful.

"Can one's nature be changed? Yes, it can change, but it changes by itself. It does not change by being changed, rather it changes by itself. When samskaras change, then one's nature changes, too. As long as samskaras of a certain characteristic influence the mind, no matter how much you try, the nature will not change."

Question: "You said that once the ghost of nature is on your back, it does not leave you alone. But now you are saying that when samskaras change, one's nature also changes."

Answer: "What I said is correct. When samskaras change, the nature of a person does change. But when the samskaras awaken again, then the nature of the person changes again. These changes and suppressions of nature are all transient. As long as the samskaras are not destroyed from the root, the process of awakening and dormancy will go on and on. Destruction of samskaras is not easy. You can continue with your austerities, keep trying to awaken your power of discretion, do chanting for long hours, but the samskaras will not die and nature will not change from its root."

Question: "What is the way to get released from one's nature?"

Answer: "There is a way, but it is not in an individual's hands. It is in God's hands. When God's energy awakens, becomes active and destroys samskaras, you can be freed from your nature. That is when the root cause of nature is eliminated."

Question: "We see many aspirants whose Shakti is awakened. It is active for many years but their nature does not change. Does this mean that God's Shakti has not destroyed their samskaras?"

Answer: "Shakti does its work, but the sense of being an individual soul hinders the path. The surrender needed for spirituality usually is not present in the aspirant. Surrender provides the scope within which Shakti can do its work. Surrender makes one free from desires and expectations. It turns the attention inward. Otherwise the aspirant remains extrovert. He nurtures the pride of being a mahatma. His ego gets blown up with experiences of kriyas. As a result, instead of uprooting nature it gets strengthened.""

I was able to see many vices inside that had taken the form of nature. Now my life was passing as I fought with those vices. I had not been able to defeat even one. I was wondering whether life would end like this? "Will this life pass away just like this, sunken in the mud of vices?"

But the words of Maharajshri were reassuring. At least Goddess Kriya-Shakti is present for our help. The only thing required is surrender.

17. Past Memories

At the end of 1962 Maharajshri went to Raipur, Bilaspur, Jabalpur, Wardha, and other places. At the request of his devotees and disciples, Maharajshri used to visit them. Not everyone could come to Dewas. Some people would have financial limitations and others, perhaps, were old and unable to come to Dewas. Some would have difficulty getting leave and others would have family responsibilities. If Maharajshri visited them then they all had the benefit of meeting him. For the first time I had the opportunity to travel with Maharajshri. In Jabalpur Maharajshri's uncle was a railway guard. Maharajshri lived with him when he was a student. His primary schooling was completed. He showed me the school in which he used to study. Then we reached Bilaspur, where Maharajshri had his first job, as a school teacher. We stayed on the same street where Maharajshri used to live. He showed us the room in which he resided. A major portion of the building had collapsed. Maharajshri said, "Who knows where destiny takes someone? Who knows how destiny keeps him? My birth was in Haryana. My primary schooling was in Jabalpur, high school in Rewadi [Haryana], and college in Nagpur. My first job was in Bilaspur. After traveling throughout India, now I live in Dewas.

"When old memories come back the events of life play on the screen of the heart like a film: memories of childhood, family life, the life of a lawyer, and then my monastic life. Generally a person is lost in the memories of the past or the golden dreams of the future, but he lives in the present. Memories of the past are not for growing sad but for learning. What had to be suffered due to what mistake? From memories of the past one can understand to what depths one has fallen, or was saved from falling. The past has already gone, but one can learn lessons from that and take advantage of that. The value of the past grows as it recedes. The experiences that we have today are gifts of the past.

"What benefit is there in imagining the future? Nobody knows what is hidden there. An individual keeps on building houses of imagination, keeps on making plans, but nobody knows what is to come. Our imagination flies away in thin air. What manifests then? One does not know that in the present. How limited is one's knowledge. He does not even know what is going to happen in the next moment. But one rides in the airplane of ego and flies in the sky of imagination. When this directly visible world itself is false, then how can there be reality in the world of imagination? Our past has been lost in the depth of darkness and it has left some memories behind. The future is covered with uncertainty. What is going to happen is yet to be seen. The present is here, but who understands it? With the blink of an eye the present becomes the past. We are left holding on to it. It slips away from our hand and is submerged in the deep ocean of the past. How can one trust even the present? The life-span of the present is only one moment. The individual soul has reached such a state of ignorance that in the deep darkness of infinite emptiness he wanders without direction, without seeing anything, and with his hands extended. On the top of that he is intoxicated with egoism. To come out of this ignorance and progress towards omniscience is called spirituality.

"In the eleventh chapter of the Gita, Lord Krishna tells Arjuna to see the past, present and future all together in one place. How is that possible? If it were possible then what would the experience be like? How would the journey be from ignorance to an all-knowing state? An ignorant being cannot even imagine. Even after accumulating much knowledge from the scriptures he remains ignorant. By explaining things to others he increases his pride, but he cannot extricate himself from the ditch of ignorance. Lord Krishna shows the three times — past, present and future together — to Arjuna. An ignorant being cannot see even one of them. But it is possible to see the past, present, and future together.

"We are walking toward a mountain. We cannot see the other side of the mountain. The scenery behind us also is becoming invisible due to distance, trees, and so forth. But as soon as you reach the peak of the mountain you can clearly see the landscape around you. However this example is also incomplete, because you may be able to see the scenery only in front of you, not behind you. Lord Krishna talks about seeing all past, present and future, simultaneously, from the same place.

"The wheel of time is turning and we are moving with it. We do not even know that we are moving. We do not even know that we have become ignorant. We nurture an ego of being very intelligent and powerful. The path of spirituality is to bring the aspirant out of this wheel of time to his real Self, and to show him that the wheel of time is separate from him. As long as an individual is going round and round with the wheel of time he keeps on wandering, sometimes in the illusion of the past, sometimes the present and, at times, the future.

"When the wheel of time is seen as separate from the self, then the past, present and future are visible together at the same time. Such an adept knows the past and perceives the future. One sees all these as a play of time. It is not the goal of an aspirant to look into the three periods of time. It is like trees and fruits seen during a trip. It can also be said that when someone sees into all — the past, present and future — he has attained a state that is beyond time.

Yoga Darshan says, in the aphorisms regarding God, that the seed of omniscience is present in God. This is one difference between God and the individual soul. A living being knows very little and God knows everything. Wherever there is a presence of God, the seed of omniscience must also exist there. Whatever energy the individual soul possesses belongs to God. In him, too, omniscience is present in the form of a seed. The sprouting of that seed is called Shaktipat. This is the spiritual path. Everything prior to this is an effort to enter the spiritual path."

I said, "Maharajshri, our conversation went from where to where? It started with your memories of the past and reached Shaktipat. Now, please explain: What is the relationship between Shaktipat and omniscience. And how that can be attained with sadhan?"

Answer: "I have said this earlier, that the divine power is present in the Shakti — that is, Kundalini — and hence omniscience is present in the seed form. In the dormant state the Kundalini is dormant, hence the seed also is dormant. To awaken it and start the process of sprouting is

Shaktipat. Omniscience cannot manifest at the very inception of sprouting. Prior to evolving into the grand tree of omniscience, Shakti has to cross many difficulties, many delays and many obstacles. This is not a one-day job. For a long time continuous sadhan and service with conviction are necessary. It s like a gardener who does not forget the seed after it is planted. He regularly gives it water and fertilizers. He prunes the plant on a timely basis, and protects it from buffaloes and goats. He builds a fence, sprays insecticides and makes arrangements to protect it from too much rain and sun. In the same way, simply planting the seed is not enough for spirituality.

"In sadhan storms of desires arise within. Floods of samskaras come, and fires of impurities are ablaze, and there is a possibility that the plant of sadhana might be uprooted or burnt down. In addition, attractions of the world trouble the aspirant. Vices stop you at every step. Sometimes lust, anger and greed erupt, and sometimes attachment, hate and jealousy arise and bring calamity. A long, inner spiritual pilgrimage is essential in order to remove the layers of desires, samskaras and impurities that cover the seed, which needs to manifest in the form of the great Banyan tree of omniscience that already exists within.

"The seed of omniscience implies that a jiva, a living being, may cover himself with many layers of ignorance and illusion, but the ability to know all is always there in a seed form. A human with cannibal tendencies and an animal — both have an abundance of animal instincts, yet omniscience is present in seed form. The seed does not need to be planted because it is always there. For it to sprout, attention, awareness and continuous sadhan are required. To make the seed of omniscience turn toward sprouting is called Shaktipat. That is when the destruction of one's ignorance begins. Simultaneous with the seed moving forward to become a big tree sadness disappears, boundaries are broken, and omniscience starts to unfold within the individual. An aspirant has to remain mindful, surrender, and continually do sadhan and service. Very often aspirants cannot do this and therefore, even after being initiated into Shaktipat, they remain empty. On the contrary, they put on another layer of ego regarding their sadhan.

"Shaktipat is a spiritual technique that has the power to transform ignorance into omniscience. It opens the door to omniscience by activating the Kundalini towards the Self. Kriyas give proof that it is awakened, but the proof of progress is manifestation of omniscience. It is up to the aspirant how much benefit he reaps from the awakening."

Question: "Usually aspirants do not pay attention to omniscience. They remain engrossed with kriyas and are happy with that."

Answer: "Those who have strong kriyas need that. Due to excess rajo guna, strong kriyas take place. Those who have either excessive tamo guna or sattva guna will not have strong kriyas, nor do they need them. To believe that intense kriyas are a sign of good sadhan indicates a lack of understanding. On the contrary, strong kriyas take place more at the physical level. Less bliss is experienced if more kriyas are on the physical level. As the kriyas ascend from the physical level they will become gentle. But greater bliss is experienced. Attention will be more and more introverted. The aspirant will be closer to omniscience."

18. Cutting and Pruning

I was working in the garden. Maharajshri was sitting in the garden on a chair. I was clearing the ground under a tree. Maharajshri told me to trim a particular plant, since that would help its development.

I was amazed to hear this and looked at Maharajshri. He was asking me to cut the plant when he had been a strong opponent of cutting trees and plants. I remembered a time when an unfinished building next to the cave was in progress. There was a small tree bearing yellow flowers in one corner. If the tree were not cut down, the building could not be built straight. Maharajshri was unyielding. "The building may be crooked but the tree will not be cut." Finally the size of the corner room was reduced. There was a brick wall in front of the building near which the tree was growing. To save the plant, it was decided that we build terraced flower beds in front of it. The flower beds were built. The plant was saved; the corner of the building was lost.

It rained heavily that night. All the buildings started to leak. The rain did not spare the flowerbeds under the tree. In the morning we saw that, due to the pressure of the water, the black soil had expanded and all the flowerbeds were now turned into heaps of soil and had shifted down. The tree had toppled. Even its roots had come out of the ground or were broken. Finally, sadly, Maharajshri said, "We tried our best to save the tree, but this was its fate!" The tree was planted at another location and it started to grow there. Maharajshri was very happy. But today he was asking me to cut the plants. I did the cutting, but I was very confused within.

During the morning walk I expressed my confusion. He said, "In general terms it is called cutting, but in reality it is pruning. There is a big difference between cutting and pruning. To cut means to cut down the tree and throw it away. Pruning means to cut unnecessary branches that may stunt the growth of the tree or destroy its beauty. Pruning makes the tree more beautiful. You can shape it the way you want by pruning. What is sadhana? To cut out unnecessary branches, such as desires and impurities, which stunt the growth of life and destroy the beauty of life. If cutting is death then pruning is life. If cutting is the evening of life then pruning is a beautiful morning.

"I am not talking about worldly people. When an aspirant is pruning a plant, he also keeps his attention on his chitta. Just as I am trimming the unnecessary branches of this tree, in the same way unnecessary feelings, thoughts and impurities of the mind must be trimmed and thrown away. These unnecessary waves make the beautiful tree of mind very ugly. An aspirant may be working in the garden, but at that time he watches his inner vices and faults. He can see his spiritual path very clearly. Just as the tree has bigger and better flowers and fruits after pruning, in the same way the chitta blossoms like a big beautiful flower after trimming off the branches of desires from the chitta."

I replied, "My attention had never been drawn to the difference between cutting and pruning."

Maharajshri said, "Not only you, but very few people think about that. Gardeners are aware of it, but they are not spiritual seekers. They cannot compare this process with the mental process. God does the cutting when the time comes. But a person has to do the pruning himself. A bad part of the body is cut away with surgery. Upon becoming fat, excessive fat is trimmed with exercise. Vegetables are cooked after bad parts are trimmed away. If there is garbage in the home, it is swept away with a broom. Desires and impurities are trimmed with sadhana. Pruning must continue in life or else the time for cutting turns up without notice."

19. The Slippery World

One day Maharajshri said, "With age one gets experience of life, and by experience caution develops. If someone slips and falls down once then the next time he sees a slippery spot he is cautious. For progress in life, being cautious is as important as enthusiasm and patience. Some people become cautious by seeing someone else fall; others become cautious if they fall once. Most do not become cautious even after seeing someone else fall, or after they themselves fall.

"Some people not only become happy on seeing someone else fall, but they also instigate others so that they can enjoy seeing them fall, too. Some people warn others who are likely to fall.

"Some people slip and then save others from falling. Some make others fall while trying to save themselves. Some can neither save themselves from falling, nor do they let others save themselves. And there are some people who let themselves fall so that others do not.

"Some fall before they can get up. Others get up before they fall again. There are some who rise and keep on rising up. Others fall and keep on falling. Some people balance themselves while falling, and others fall while rising. Some people pull others down before they can get up. Some lift others before they can get up themselves. There are some that get up but do not let others get up. There are others who will rise only with their companions. There are some that try to get up but cannot, whereas there are others who try and succeed in getting up. Some never try to rise. They keep on looking at the summit from down below. Some people spend their life in lifting others up, and some waste their life in pulling others down. Some get up cautiously, some are cautious after they get up. Some fall to bring others down, and some rise up so that they can help others rise.

"The essence is that this world is multi-colored. Many different thoughts, perspectives and feelings exist. The entire world is neither someone's ally, nor someone's opponent. Some walk with you, some leave you, some go contrary to you, and some stand in your way to stop you. Therefore an aspirant has to be very careful in his spiritual journey. As such the path of spirituality is against the flow of the world. It is very difficult to stay in the world and be indifferent to the world. The world is incapable of understanding the feelings and thoughts of an aspirant and, on top of that, this is a very difficult journey. An aspirant has to battle on two fronts at the same time, to cope with the world, and to fight against inner desires and faults. For a long time, in the beginning, both problems exist and often the aspirant has to deal with both."

Question: "Isn't it possible to give up worldly affairs completely, retire totally, and be fully engaged in spiritual practices so that an aspirant does not have to fight the spiritual war on two fronts? Even the scriptures praise solitude very highly."

Answer: "First of all, this is not at all possible for an ordinary aspirant. The fickleness of his mind and his inner desires will not let him remain in solitude. Solitude cannot be forced. Solitude emerges in the mind first. Only after that one can live in solitude physically. As long as the mind is on the run solitude is not possible. Yes, in between, as and when time permits, the aspirant may go into seclusion. Yet in this state, too, one is not free from the world. On returning from seclusion immediately the world regains its place. Then both fronts will be present before the aspirant."

Question: "This is a very complex problem. Neither is it possible to be in the world, nor is it easy to give it up."

Answer: "This problem only exists for a spiritual seeker. Worldly people are flowing with the worldly current. Whether they are happy or unhappy, they do not want to leave the world. The aspirant wants go against the worldly flow but he cannot. The world mortifies him but he is compelled to love it. The world insults him but he respects it. He does not do harm to anyone but the world does not let him rest. He wants to show them the path to welfare but the selfish world does not understand his feelings. This brings difficulties for the aspirant.

"This does not imply that the whole world is engaged in placing obstacles before the aspirant. Some may be favorable toward him. The challenge for the aspirant is to love all alike. He wishes well for all, whether the person is favorable, a troublemaker or his critic. Even if favorable people understand him, the troublemakers remain busy with their pursuits. There is no other path in front of the aspirant but to tolerate this. An aspirant must understand these things very clearly in his mind:"

(1) "The world will go on the way it has been going on. One must try to correct it but it is not going to improve. The desire to improve the world is very crucial for improving one's own self. If we wish good for the world, it will be beneficial to ourselves."

(2) "The world is full of good and bad people, but selfishness prevails almost everywhere. Even good people are eclipsed by ego and selfishness to some extent. Hidden feelings in them can throw them onto the bad path at any time. Those who appear bad now also have good thoughts hidden in them. Those good values may turn them into a good person at any time. Thus, everyone is good as well as bad. All this is within the realm of individuality. The soul, which is the real form of every human being, is beyond good and bad."

(3) "The cause of the good and bad behavior of the world is prarabdha [destiny formed by one's past actions]. Whatever happiness and unhappiness one has to experience is due to prarabdha. The entire world is bound by prarabdha. We are compelled to act according to prarabdha. No one inflicts pain or gives happiness to others. No one can respect or insult anyone. Prarabdha instigates all these things. No one is at fault in this. Our own prarabdha is at fault. If the aspirant understands this then he can be saved from the mistake of thinking that the world is the cause of happiness and miseries. The world is merely a stage for the prarabdha of the individual to play itself out. If the aspirant wants to get rid of miseries and joy from the world, he will have to get rid of his prarabdha. No one can stop the play of prarabdha on the stage of the world."

(4) "Mother and father, brother and sister, friend and enemy — all are relations due to prarabdha. Only due to prarabdha are people bound to each other in the world. All our relations of attachment, hate and

infatuation depend on prarabdha. According to prarabdha, relations improve and deteriorate. The wheel of relations will go on turning as long as prarabdha exists."

(5) "The whole life of an aspirant depends upon prarabdha. The effort to put an end to this dependence is called sadhana. This dependence is finished when there is no residual prarabdha left. Even if one is able to gain control over the mind and does not feel joy and misery, happy and sad situations will keep coming depending on one's prarabdha. When there is no more prarabdha residue left, then only will its fruits stop maturing. It is unknown when prarabdha was created, but it very clear that we are in its grip right now."

(6) "Just as the aspirant is under the control of prarabdha, the whole world suffers in its fire. We are all going up and down in the ocean of prarabdha. Compelled by prarabdha, we meet and separate, fight and love, and try to enter the world or escape it. In reality, spirituality also rests on prarabdha."

(7) "The reason for prarabdha is ego, because ego gives rise to attachment and aversion and the sense of doership. Ego accumulates impressions that create prarabdha, destiny. Ego rotates the wheel of prarabdha. The ego [sense of I-ness] goes through joy and miseries and also accumulates impressions. Ego gives rise to impurities and desires in the mind and engages in new karma. The lowest form of I-ness is egoism, which is fully in error and turned towards the world. This ego makes one lazy when afflicted with tamo guna, makes one restless when influenced by rajo guna, and makes a person a holy being when affected by sattva guna. Thus life goes up and down among the three qualities depending on prarabdha."

(8) "The individual does not have any Shakti of his own. He only has the ego of having Shakti. First of all, an aspirant needs to experience that the Shakti [power] in which he takes pride is not his own power. The depletion of samskaras, ego and prarabdha is directly related to this experience. This experience gives a sadhak a real knowledge of the separate individual soul that he has become. He starts to feel God's active energy after this experience. Only subsequent to this experience does the

path to annihilation of both desires and the mind open up. Only this experience lifts the sadhak out of worldliness and takes him into spirituality."

(9) "When the individual soul does not have any power of its own, how can he do anything? Who is the doer? When one has this experience, one's sense of doership is shaken. The one who was a doer until yesterday is only a witness today. The senses that did things yesterday remain only as a medium of action for the doer. One's experience of activity after awakening opens a field of spirituality that, so far, was hidden. Similar to the world, his body now appears to him as a part of the world. Even after the awakening and [spontaneous] experience of the activity of Shakti, prarabdha [destiny], mental tendencies and ego do not leave the sadhak alone. They are still solidly rooted on the firm ground of samskaras [accumulated impressions]. For this reason, the sadhak needs to do sadhana and service for a long time. He needs the grace of the Guru, and needs to look within himself continuously."

(10) "Now the final point: Sadhan is not merely for showing off. It needs total honesty and seriousness — honesty towards one's self, towards the sadhan and the Guru, and towards the goal. Sadhan is not done to earn the applause of the world. Whether the world accepts you as a virtuous soul or not does not matter. You are what you are. Someone calling you good or bad does not make you so. You must drive out the faults from your chitta with the fullest sincerity. You must arouse love for God and your Guru. You must develop a sense of surrender to God. If all this is happening within you then you are making progress on the spiritual path. To get rid of your faults you will have to weep before God with an open heart, to obtain love you will need to implore at the Guru's feet. You will have to try to follow the path of duty according to your own conscience. Do not stray from your path by listening to the world. Be ready to offer yourself as a sacrifice. Only by destroying yourself [ego-self] can you find the real Self. Those who have attained the Self have attained it in this way only. No one has attained anything comfortably, without losing anything. So be ready to get robbed. Only then will the darkness dispel, the light shine; only then will everlasting joy and bliss be yours."

Question: "Maharajshri, this sounds very good but it is very difficult to implement, not only for an average person, but also for great
spiritual aspirants and ascetics. Do ego and anger spare anyone?"

Answer: "I never said that it is easy. I told you only those things to
which an aspirant needs to pay attention. Everyone knows that walking
on the spiritual path is not child's play. For this you need to 'keep your
head on your palm' [be ready even to give up life]. Such love must fill the
heart that there should be no place for likes or dislikes, and everything
should be offered to God. Sadhan should be such that nothing but sadhan
should come to mind. Surrender should be such that nothing should be
left to call one's own. Service should be such that ego and anger are
crushed. Only then can something be achieved. There is no other way."

Question: "You said a great deal about prarabdha, but you did not
refer to self-effort [purushartha]. Is that because self-effort has no place
in sadhan?'

Answer: "Yes, self-effort is important, but I referred to it using
some other words. What you consider self-effort is not so from the
point of view of spirituality. Effort toward [finding] the soul is real self-
effort in spirituality, and such an effort can be nothing other than surrender. Any effort done with desire can only be the cause of downfall
from the real Self. Surrender is the means to attain a steady state within
the Self."

Question: "Please, elaborate on this."

Answer: "The meaning of the word 'self-effort' [purushartha] has
changed a great deal in literary contexts. Effort in any way, in any sense,
is called self-effort. This same meaning is also applied in a religious
context, but that is not acceptable in spirituality. Only the effort for
attaining the soul [purusha] is self-effort. If action is performed with
attachment then it causes the accumulation of new impressions, which
will be the cause of a fall from the Self. What is commonly understood
to be self-effort is not, in fact, self-effort. Surrender is the only state
that, if formed in the heart, will destroy accumulated impressions and
tendencies, hence surrender is self-effort in spirituality. I have mentioned
self-effort in the form of surrender. Now the question is how should
one surrender? As long as the deity is not present before you, surrender

will only be sentimental and not real. After awakening, when Shakti is directly present before you, this problem is solved."

Question: "Do you mean to say that one's endeavor is not a matter of self-effort, but a specific level of sadhan once the deity being worshipped is realized?"

Answer: "Yes, it is a level. But to remain at that level the aspirant has to work at it. Thus self-effort is a level of sadhan, as well as one's endeavor. When surrender becomes natural, endeavor is gone and sadhan is filled with self-effort [surrender].

"Debates about self-effort and prarabdha go on, but this debate is in reference to one's desires. The subject of the debate is whether self-effort or prarabdha play the main role in obtaining one's goal. Spirituality is the path to rise above both — the desire to obtain, as well as prarabdha. Consequently this debate becomes irrelevant."

Now it was my turn to introspect. Maharajshri had explained that, as surrender grows, ego will diminish. But so far my ego was at a high point. How can surrender develop in such an impure mind? Even after starting on the path to omniscience I was still lost. The path was correct, but due to darkness nothing was visible. Despite having a cane in my hand for support I was stumbling and falling. Life was passing by very fast and I was still sitting in the dark, hoping for a ray of light. It cannot even be said that I was on the right path as long as surrender had not awakened in my mind. The ferociousness of ego had gripped me from all the four directions. If the grace of the Guru is there then nothing is impossible. Sometime or the other the path will become visible, the ray of light will be seen, and clouds of misery will disperse.

20. Love and Hate

Two aspirants were arguing about love and hate. One was saying that love is essential for sadhan, while the other was of the opinion that there is no relationship between love and sadhan. Finally, the subject was presented to Maharajshri. This is what Maharajshri had to say:

"Love is spirituality, whereas hate is the world. Love is harmony, whereas hate is discord. Love is fragrance, whereas hate is foul odor. Love teaches tolerance; hate teaches revenge. Love and hate are opposite poles. Love is the way to put an end to individuality, and hate is the way to solidify individuality. There is no place for hate in the mind that is filled with love. Where there is hate, love cannot even enter.

"What is love? In the hands of spiritual people love is a weapon that cuts the feelings of attachment and aversion. In love there is no attachment or aversion. You fall in love with all living beings. All belong to you, and all are the same to you. No one is your opponent or enemy. The lover imagines his Lord in one and all. If he is slightly advanced, he sees the divine power active within everyone. If he is even more advanced, he sees the Absolute Self in everyone. When his beloved is dwelling in everyone, who is a stranger?

"The lover does not ask anything of his beloved Lord. To ask is to doubt his all-knowing nature. Love is the path of giving and sacrificing, not of asking. It is the path in which you offer everything you have at the feet of the Lord. Finally the lover even merges his ego and himself in God. If the lover thinks he can merge himself in God, he thinks it is his own ego. How can he do that? God himself showers grace and merges his devotee within himself. The lover does not own anything. Everything belongs to God. The Lord can give him fame or insult; he experiences God's grace in everything. The devotee constantly remains intoxicated with God.

"The lover has generosity, a forgiving nature and tolerance. There is no trace of attachment and aversions. Love is another name for austerity. The element of love is the essence of existence. Love is the best medicine for those suffering from the disease of birth, death and rebirth. It is the cool shade of a banyan tree for those burning in the heat of miseries and afflictions. It is a stream of cool water; it is a wave of soothing breeze; it is the sweet fragrant scent of a flower garden for those tired and thirsty on the journey through the world.

"The end of bhavarog [the cycle of birth and death] starts with the sprouting of love in the heart. The awakened Shakti, or power, can be called "Love-Shakti," and latent Shakti can be called "Hate-Shakti." In the Shiva Sutra it is called apashu Shakti [non-animal force] and pashu Shakti [animal force]. In love, the animal force is destroyed and in hate, animal force persists. Love-Shakti is the cause of depletion of the impression of the animal nature, while hate causes its accumulation. The observation of the activities of Love-Shakti is sadhan itself. In love a sadhak laughs and cries, he dances when filled with love, and sometimes he is absorbed in love and meditation. When love grows he rises above his body because love is energy and hate is inertia.

"What is hate? It is air filled with the odor of filth accumulated in the mind. Hate is caused by attachments in the world, and it is due to aversion. It is like a corpse that no one wants to face, yet everyone embraces it. If hate is a sign of aversion then somewhere feelings of attachment must exist. Aversion cannot exist without attachment on the opposite pole. Thus hate consists of attachment and aversion. The greater the hate in the mind, the more the world will appear full of faults. The fault-finding tendency grows stronger with hate. Faults are imagined where there are none. Straight things appear twisted.

"What more is there to say? Hate is like a great ocean filled with filth. Hate is like an owl that cannot see in the day and flies in the darkness of night. Hate squeezes out all the joy from life and adds poison to it. Hate sows seeds in the mind that cannot be weeded for many lifetimes. It robs one of joy and happiness and also makes others miserable. The one who sinks in hate forgets the Self, and his original color is stained.

"Only the sadhak who enjoys watching blissful activities of the

Shakti after its awakening can be a real lover. When awakened Shakti starts to dig and throw up impressions, all the animal instincts and vasanas [mental tendencies] are tossed from the mind. The natural loving nature of the sadhak comes to light. This is the gift of the awakened Shakti."

Question: "It often appears that sadhaks have more attachment, aversions, hate, jealousy, and so forth, than average people. How and when will love manifest? When will they become true lovers?"

Answer: "When active Shakti brings out vices and vasanas at a fast pace, that affects the mind of the aspirant. It should not be allowed to affect one's mind, but generally it is harder for the aspirant to be successful at that. Consequently this wave, after affecting the mind of the aspirant, influences his behavior as well. This slows down the progress of the sadhak. But these defects are transient. The process of purification of the mind continues, but due to lack of caution, distractions take place that cause delay. One thing is certain though: Once Shakti is awakened, it does not leave until the chitta is totally purified, no matter how much delay takes place."

Question: "True, hate is the dark side of life. But if someone turns around and uses hate and anger to get rid of faults and vices, does not that make hate a virtue?"

Answer: "Vice will always remain a vice, but its use may be good. For example, someone is in the habit of taking opium and goes around keeping packets of it in his pocket. Now he begins to make good use of it by giving it to people as a medicine. Still, his old habit can arise at any time and he may start using the opium himself. The same situation exists with vices. After making good use of it in getting rid of vices hate itself must be thrown out. Otherwise it can start acting up again in the world."

Question: "Should one dispense with love after finding God?"

Answer: "You do not have to get rid of love. It dissolves by itself. This is the difference between good and bad vasanas [tendencies]. Bad tendencies never leave, even after numerous exploits. Good tendencies, on the contrary, leave after achieving their goal. When God is found, then the sense of individuality, along with feelings of love, will merge in God. A devotee is freed from the cycle of birth and death, and the feeling is also gone."

21. Destiny and Doership

When an aspirant starts his spiritual practice he does not know where to begin because he does not know what his first problem is. Not only new aspirants, but also senior aspirants cannot determine the basics of sadhana, or spiritual practice. They continue to grope around in the dark. A disciple asked this question to Maharajshri: When a person turns toward sadhana after seeing the miseries and futility of the world, what is his first and foremost problem?

"The first problem is prarabdha [destiny based on past karma]. Whatever may be his principles and spiritual path he has to deal with his destiny. Usually sadhaks do not pay attention to prarabdha and remain indifferent to it. Consequently prarabdha keeps them entangled and comes in the way of spiritual progress. Even when the world is worthless it seems useful. Even when it lacks joy the hope of attaining happiness burns on and keeps the individual going round and round in pursuit of tantalizing attractions and sensuous pleasures. Prarabdha is a power that, while remaining invisible, brings happiness and unhappiness. This creates favorable and unfavorable waves in the world and the mind. It stays with the individual every step of the way. Then how can it be ignored? As one begins sadhana it comes up and stands before you. It stands in the way like a great mountain.

"A sadhak focuses on efforts to turn his mind inward. Upon failing to do so he tries to find weaknesses in his sadhana. But this is the mischief of prarabdha. It keeps on pushing the mind outwards. Along with sadhana, one must pay attention to reducing prarabdha, then only will the mind turn inward. But a sadhak makes the mistake of ignoring prarabdha and emphasizing sadhana. Spirituality is a very deep subject. Often things that we think are insignificant become great obstacles.

"Prarabdha is like a bridge between the world and the individual. It pulls the individual back to the world. The individual remains restless but cannot leave the world. The mind keeps on running toward the world in spite of huge efforts to focus internally. The mind is of a harmonious nature, hence it is eager to find happiness. It is always hopeful that, somewhere, happiness will be available. Neither is happiness found, nor does the restlessness cease. This drama takes place in the background of prarabdha."

Question: "There must be some way to get rid of prarabdha."

Answer: "Yes. That way is to practice Karma Yoga with a sense of service and fulfillment of duty. Karma Yoga is the beginning of all types of sadhana. Karma Yoga is the door to spirituality. It is a logical technique to end prarabdha after experiencing the results of past karma. Without this, neither yama [internal disciplines] nor niyama [social and external codes of conduct] can be mastered, nor is pratyahar [withdrawal of the mind from the world] possible, nor does the mind become worthy of dharana [single-minded concentration] and dhyana [meditation]. However the practice of Karma Yoga is not that easy. In fact, this is the hardest part of the spiritual journey. It is not easy to leave the world and accept spirituality. The aspirant wants to leave the world but prarabdha does not allow him to do so. It pulls the aspirant into the world through vasanas [mental tendencies] and vritis [modifications of the mind]. Karma Yoga is like a war between the world and spirituality. The aspirant wins the war only when he knows the techniques of war, when he is full of patience and enthusiasm and has mastered the art of getting up after each fall."

Question: "Doesn't Karma Yoga simply mean withdrawing from action while performing sadhan? What is the difficulty in that? The real difficulty is doing sadhan. On the other hand, if you keep working in the world, the mind remains occupied [with worldly matters]."

Answer: "This is not a full explanation of Karma Yoga. Prior to starting Karma Yoga, the decision must be made whether karma will be performed for building new destiny or for depleting destiny. The karma of worldly people is for creating new destiny, and the karma of spiritual people is for depletion of already-formed destiny. Those who do karma for new destiny are worldly people. Spiritual people are encouraged to

purify the chitta [psyche] and perform worldly actions that cause depletion of destiny. Karma [actions] performed for creation of new prarabdha [destiny] cannot be Karma Yoga. Work done with attachment and
the desire for results, and work done with anger, greed, or for the sake of
pleasure are the causes of new destiny. They cannot be Karma Yoga.
Those who want to go toward the world perform action such that they
create destiny, and those who want to turn away from the world work
without attachment to reduce destiny. The action may be the same, but
one will create new destiny with that action, while another will reduce
prarabdha, or destiny, with the same action."

Question: "How is it possible to take any action without attachment, desire, expectation and ego? Why should one do anything then?"

Answer: "For reducing prarabdha. I said that karma forms prarabdha and karma also releases one from the bondage of prarabdha. Karma
with attachment means bowing down to the world, and pure Karma
Yoga is rebellion against the world. The first makes you sink in the unfathomable ocean of birth and death, and the second helps you swim
and go across the ocean. One is aimless wandering, while the other is a
guiding light. One is receding, while the other is progressive. The action
is the same but the results are different. Those who want to walk the
path of prarabdha annihilation will take interest in pure Karma Yoga.
Pure Karma Yoga is a straight path that will take you directly to the door
of spirituality."

Question: "Then what is the difficulty?"

Answer: "Our ego, fickle-mindedness, and desires for worldly happiness lure the mind repeatedly. While the aspirant is pursuing pure
Karma Yoga, even before he notices, attachment creeps in quietly. Even
before the aspirant can become careful attachment finishes its job. In
fact, it is already present in the mind. The aspirant tries to suppress it,
but like a ball which, when thumped down, bounces back with equal
force, attachment, when suppressed, bounces back with the same force.

"Another difficulty is the selfish world. People do not understand
his pure sentiments, but the aspirant has to deal with the world. Sadhan
is like going through a jungle on fire where nothing is visible due to

smoke, and there are difficulties at every step. If the aspirant tries to swim across the river of the world then violent creatures starts pulling his legs from below. In and out, everywhere, the fierce dance of desires and perversion is going on. Just imagine how difficult it would be to practice pure Karma Yoga under such circumstances."

Question: "Then what can the sadhak do?"

Answer: "The journey of Karma Yoga is very long. The path is full of difficulties. There are high peaks on one side and a thick jungle on the other. The ground is filled with rocks and thorns. It is slippery and full of obstacles. You must pass through a thick forest, cross many rivers, and face wild animals. You will have to spend dark nights in the forest alone. Thieves and robbers may rob you. You may have to go hungry and thirsty and bear wounds on your body. All this will require a lot of patience. For completing this journey, firm resolve and endurance are a must. Control over one's self, fearlessness and a steady mind are also essential for this."

At this I said, "Maharajshri, because of the way you have described the path of Karma Yoga, I am reminded of an incident from my life. I used to live in Nangal, and I used to go frequently to Himachal Pradesh to tour or to be in solitude. One day I went just to tour. There were no fixed tracks in the mountains. A man from a village accompanied me. When he was about to leave me he showed me a tree at the top of a mountain and asked me to go there. He said that there was a path on the other side of the mountain. If I went on that path for about two miles, I would reach the village I wanted to go to. I walked up to the tree and there I saw not only one, but three or four paths. Now which way should I go? I was confused. There was no one to ask. I waited for ten or fifteen minutes thinking someone would show up. No one came. Finally I started to walk on one of the paths. I kept on walking. I stopped and found myself in a thick forest.

"There was no way to go forward and there was no point in going back. It was a desolate, still jungle. I turned my head in one direction and started to walk. Ferocious noises made me quiver. While crossing a mountain spring I slipped and fell and was drenched. All my clothes were soaked. I did not encounter any wild animals, but I was fearful all the same. After I wandered for another one-and-a-half hours the jungle came to an end. I saw some human footprints covered by bushes. I started following the footprints. Finally I met a young man with a herd of goats. I asked him about the village but he did not understand my language. I asked by making hand gestures while saying the name of the village. He put up his hand in one direction. Here I learned what it meant to be lost. During my tours of Himachal Pradesh I had similar experiences many times. The journey of Karma Yoga must be somewhat like this. Difficulties arise at every step. Temptations, slipperiness and confusion are at every turn."

Maharajshri said, "Even more difficult and very long. This is only on the physical level, but on the journey of Karma Yoga difficulties and slippage occur on the mental as well as the physical plane, inside and outside. The jiva [individual soul] falls and gets lost, internally first, and then externally."

Question: "Does this mean that one must practice Karma Yoga and annihilate prarabdha first, and then do sadhan? How long will a person be involved in Karma Yoga?"

Answer: "No. Practicing Karma Yoga does not mean that one must not do sadhana at the same time. Karma Yoga and sadhana go hand-in-hand. They are complementary and support each other. Karma Yoga pushes the mind inward from outside, and sadhana pulls the mind inward from inside. The purpose of both is to turn the mind inward.

"The aspirant must do sadhana with Karma Yoga in mind. It makes no difference what you do, but there is a difference in your feelings about what you do. Your actions will take a form that is consistent with your feelings. First of all, the person whose heart is pure will not be able to take any bad action, and even if something bad happens his intentions are pure. To work with a sense of selfless service is one form of Karma Yoga, and to work with a sense of duty is another form. To do all the work for God, to offer all the fruits of your work to God, and to believe that all work is God's work, are different forms and levels of Karma Yoga. To work without aspiration and to work without attachment is a higher stage of Karma Yoga. To work as a medium of God with God as the real doer is another form of Karma Yoga. Each aspirant follows the type of Karma Yoga that suits his or her level and feelings."

Question: "Other than this, is there any other obstacle?"

Answer: "The next problem is the ego of doership. This ego is baseless and false, yet it plays a major role in the formation of prarabdha. The sense of doership is the powerful governor of all worldly affairs. The feeling of doership does not really exist, yet it is super powerful. It has no energy, yet it governs all the senses. It is that so-called element through which the sense of individuality manifests. It is like a person whose only accumulated capital is his ego. Just as Shakti contains Kriya-Shakti [the ability to act], false ego contains a false sense of doership. It is like an apparition of the court of Indra in the wilderness, which is based on mere imagination.

"How can there be a relationship between prarabdha and doership when both of these are imaginary and untrue? Still, both are experiential and their relationship is unshakable. It is like the rainbow that is only a reflection, yet its colors are visible. It looks like an arch in the sky, but none can catch it even if they fly thousands of miles. Similarly, prarabdha does not exist, yet one has to go through it. Doership is only a feeling, yet it makes the whole world go around. Here we must believe and act upon the fact that, as long as both can be experienced, they exist, and they are related to each other.

"Doership flourishes and grows larger due to likes, dislikes and attachment. With this growth of likes and dislikes the belief that the world is a reality is strengthened. Yearning to achieve desired things and to discard unwanted things is reinforced. Then the individual soul does all his work with attachment. His sense of self [I-ness] falls from pure consciousness to the level of the psyche. At that stage, while he is at the psychic level, he begins to believe that pure consciousness [chaitanya] is his Shakti [divine power] and his own quality, and then the sense of doership is born in him. All the activities done by his senses are in reality due to Shakti, but because of false ego he thinks he is the doer. As long as he had the experience that all was done by Shakti [and not by him], there was neither any ego, nor any prarabdha. As soon as the ego of 'I am the doer' enters the workings that are really those of Shakti, egoism starts to bubble up and memories of everything are engraved in the form of samskaras [accumulated impressions]. All this is imaginary, but still a jiva cannot rise above the accumulated impressions of its memories for many lifetimes.

"Prarabdha and doership are like robbers whose unity and mutual support are unforeseen. Together they rob the individual of his peace of mind and happiness. They are merciless, and rejoice in seeing the sufferings of the jiva. Ages may pass, but once in the grip of these two it is difficult to escape. They suck the blood, but do not allow jiva, the separated soul, to unite with God. Both of them continually influence the mind, and then make him run around and dance the way they please. Intellect also is not spared, and it thinks as both of them wish. Kabir has said, 'No one remains safe between the two grinding stones.' Possibly he was thinking of these two — prarabdha and doership — as the two grinding stones. The world is being crushed and the robbers enjoy watching."

Question: "What are the means of getting rid of this sense of doership?"

Answer: "We can look for treatments for the disease by examining its causes. The main reason for this sense of doership is the mistake made by the jiva [the individual soul] in believing that the Shakti belongs to him. Consequently the ego of the individual assumes the role of the doer. No matter how much knowledge is acquired, how many discourses are heard, how much sadhana is done, or prayer, japa and rituals are performed — the sense of doership does not diminish unless and until Shakti is experienced personally and directly.

"This is where the subject of Shakti awakening begins. Only this feeling known by personal experience [of awakened shakti] can diminish the ego of doership and give rise to a sense of surrender. Bhakti [devotion] and yoga start from here. The foremost objective of bhakti and yoga is only to get rid of prarabdha and its cause, the sense of doership.

"True surrender is the surrender that arises after the awakening of Shakti. Bhakti is defined in the *Narada Bhakti Sutra* as that ultimate love and devotion that arises toward the divine God energy [Shakti]. Bhakti is the ultimate love for the Shakti awakened within the aspirant that talks to him, listens to his prayers, and gives him guidance directly. Thus yoga and bhakti both begin with the awakening of Shakti. Just as the sense of doership is directly tied into the formation of prarabdha, destiny, similarly together they are directly related in depletion of prarabdha. First they are together in the growth of prarabdha, and then they are together during its annihilation. They are always together, in life and death.

"In the beginning the individual soul walks, as it were, holding the hand of his ego of doership. An individual soul cannot walk without any support because he does not have any energy. Prior to giving up his dependence upon doership he must find a bigger and better support. He gets this support in the form of the awakened Shakti. This support does not remain in the form of support forever, but at first it purifies the chitta [psyche] and then merges the purified chitta into Shakti. Subsequently it enables the aspirant to walk without any support. The awakened Shakti, on the one hand, transforms the doer into an observer and makes the doer surrender. On the other hand it weakens samskaras by turning them into kriyas [spontaneous activities of Shakti] and halts the formation of new prarabdha. It also imparts greater endurance to the sense of an observer and opens the path to diminish pre-existing prarabdha. It depends upon the aspirant then as to how far he utilizes tolerance and surrender [as tools for spiritual progress]."

Question: "In my opinion, aspirants are not able to utilize these qualities appropriately."

Answer: "Hence they do not get the desired results from sadhana. The aspirant starts to become proud about sadhana, whereas sadhana is done for lessening the ego. He grows attached to his sadhana and related experiences. The Shakti that grants the experiences and performs kriyas does not possess ego, nor does it have attachment. This is known as false pride.

"After awakening of the Shakti the aspirant becomes a witness and experiences kriyas. He does not have to make any efforts. He does not imagine any scene, and yet still he sees many sights. He may be totally ignorant of music, but he sings melodious, classical tunes. In the absence of any sound or light he sees light and hears divine sounds. Seeing all this he is struck with wonder, and he is certain that even without doing anything much can happen. He also begins to question whether he can really do anything or he only carries the false pride of doership. On the one hand, the practice of Karma Yoga weakens the base of prarabdha and, on the other hand, the weight of past impressions [samskaras] on the chitta [psyche] becomes lighter due to the effects of kriyas. Additionally, the ego of doership is hit hard by the experiences of autonomously-occurring kriyas. This is how the aspirant's inner journey commences."

Question: "Yes, but you have never explained what the technique is for awakening?"

Answer: "You people are already aware of Shaktipat. This is a scientific technique endorsed by scriptures. It is true that this technique sometimes vanishes and sometimes reappears. All techniques go through this. All principles, techniques and religious sects go through this. Nothing is spared from nature's law of change. Fifty years ago people were totally unaware of Shaktipat. Swami Narayan Tirth Dev Maharaj brought it to light for common people. Even today there are many people who do not believe in it. That is their problem. We have seen the results of this technique, and scriptures and the words of saints give testimony to it.

"However Shaktipat is not the only means of awakening. In my opinion Shaktipat is necessary even when the awakening of Shakti takes place by some other means. It makes the Shakti's awakening secure. By practicing spiritual techniques for a long period of time the awakening of Shakti is possible. We have seen cases where Shakti was even awakened without any spiritual practice. It was possibly the result of sadhana done in a past birth. It is also possible that awakening might have taken place in the past birth. Awakening from birth is acknowledged as a possibility in the path of yoga."

Question: "Is there any other problem?"

Answer: "There are many more problems, such as how to end the separate individual identity and experience yourself as part of the cosmic consciousness, and how to destroy avidya [false or negative knowledge about the Absolute Self] and get rid of ego identity. However these are the two most important difficulties in front of the aspirant. If an aspirant somehow solves these two problems then it is certain that the aspirant has made great progress on the spiritual path. It is very difficult to pass through these two stages. The subsequent path becomes much easier than expected.

"Destiny [prarabdha] and the sense of doership are the only two causes of fickle-mindedness, a restless intellect, attachment to the world, and the experience of joy and miseries. These two entangle the individual soul in the muddle of vasanas in such a way that he cannot escape even if he tries millions of times. The being restlessly suffers like an injured bird, moans like a woman at separation from her beloved husband, and wanders like a lost traveler. Prarabdha and doership continue to increase his suffering, intensify his moaning and add to his wandering. These two robbers have no mercy in their heart. The individual soul goes on consuming these two like sweet poison and wastes his life. Efforts to be free from these robbers is sadhana, this is spirituality.

"The sooner a jiva [individual soul] can free himself from the miserable imprisonment of prarabdha and doership the better for him. Prarabdha has an infinite stockpile of samskaras for luring, deceiving, entangling and tormenting the jiva. Doership also has many tricks, pretenses and techniques for keeping a jiva in its clutches. Both have the same objective: to torment the jiva and bring him back to the world after death, to torment him again and then bring him back again, and so on. Thus their amusement goes on. My purpose in telling you all this is to make you aware of the horrific nature and the powerful hold of prarabdha and doership.

"In the beginning, Karma Yoga involves the sense of doership, even when Karma Yoga is done for attaining freedom from prarabdha. Ego helps in these efforts, on the one hand, and, internally, it makes the efforts hollow. In the beginning one must take each step very carefully.

Slowly, over time, Karma Yoga becomes the aspirant's nature.

"Sadhana starts with Karma Yoga. The need for Karma Yoga diminishes as samskaras are depleted, inner experiences increase, and love and surrender toward God grow. An aspirant does not have to give up Karma Yoga. Eventually, at the right time, it drops away by itself. The quality of the practice of Karma Yoga is totally transformed, or should be transformed, after Shakti is awakened. Karma Yoga then becomes natural.

"Sadhana begins with anvopaaya [self-effort; effort at an individual level]. The jiva [individual soul or being] is atomic, or very small. His efforts are equal almost to zero but his ego is very big. He can start only from where his mental state is. Hence in the Indian tradition, spiritual practices for each individual are decided on the basis of his or her capability. Someone may like to do japa [repetition of God's name], and others may like reading and reciting scriptures. This decision is based on worthiness, state of mind, faith, preparedness and availability of time.

"At this point I refer to the awakening of Shakti because most people are prepared up to this stage and not beyond. Very often aspirants begin to do sadhana of a very high state, ignoring their own worthiness, and force themselves to renounce and retire from the world. They can neither stay in that state, nor can they fulfil their duties. It is best for an aspirant to take one step at a time and make progress in succession. Put each step on a firm ground, and when the foothold is strong and firm, then take the other step.

"After awakening the nature of sadhana changes. It becomes sadhan. The place of ego is taken by the kriya, spontaneous activities of Shakti. Hence the form of Karma Yoga also changes. It advances from anvopaaya [self-effort] to the level of shaktopaaya [effortless]. Whether to walk this path or not is in the hands of the aspirant. If the disciple does not cooperate then what can the Guru do? The disciple must be ready to give up everything to walk on this path. The lamp can give light only by burning itself."

22.   The Real Form of Miseries

A disciple once came to Maharajshri and opened his bag of miseries. His bag was filled with difficulties, calamities and complications. Maharajshri told him, "This is not only true for you. All the passengers in the boat of the world are in the middle of a storm and the boat is swaying. Someone is sad due to poverty, and others are worried about protecting their wealth. Some are troubled due to too much money and family quarrels caused by that, some are burning in the fire of jealousy, while others are afflicted with hate. Some have nothing to eat, and others are unable to eat because of bad health due to overeating. Some have a miserable married life, and others are exasperated with fights among brothers. Some do not have even a hut to hide from bad weather, and others have so much property that they are too busy taking care of legal issues related to it. Some are depressed that they do not get the desired sensual pleasures, and others are tirelessly trying to be free from them. Some want to do sadhana but cannot due to their restless mind, and others are sad because they are not satisfied with their progress. Some are concerned that their disciples are not doing sadhana, and others are miserable because they could not be Guru. Some are sad for an ashram, and others are sad due to the ashram. The point here is that no one in this world is happy. If you search in their hearts, you will find unhappiness in each of them. Yes, some people do put up a show of happiness.

"How can there be happiness? As long as one depends on the world for happiness he will only find unhappiness. The world is constantly changing and illusory. Whether a person is worldly or a renunciate, all are stuck somewhere. Everyone has his or her own dream about happiness. Some search for happiness in the scriptures, and others in temples. Some search for happiness in pleasures of the world, and others see happiness in giving up pleasures. As long as happiness is believed to be in some form, quality and circumstance, it will be fleeting. There may be illusory glimpse of happiness, sometimes."

Question: "The world is not the basis of happiness in sadhana, yet sadhaks experience unhappiness. Why?"

Answer: "The world goes beyond what is visible to the eyes. Your heart and psyche are also parts of this world. You cannot get out of the circumference of the world as long as the basis of your sadhana is your chitta [psyche]. As long as inner experiences are based on the chitta it is all Maya [illusion]. Rarely do sadhaks [spiritual aspirants] rise above the chitta and enter the realm of chaitanya [pure consciousness, or the conscious-self]. They mostly keep going up and down within the realm of Maya. The visible world keeps on influencing the chitta, and chitta affects the world."

Question: "Once Shakti is awakened, grants the status of a witness and turns one toward chaitanya, where is the association with the world?"

Answer: "It does not turn one toward chaitanya, rather it turns one toward activities of the conscious-self. Kriyas depend upon samskaras and they come to the surface in the form of kriyas on the ground of the chitta [psyche]. Samskaras are this world and the psyche is also this world. Therefore, for the witness, the psyche and kriyas are the world. Thus the world does not disappear instantly after the awakening of Shakti. The world disappears only after sadhan is done for a long time and with the grace of the Guru. That, too, happens only when the sadhak does not accumulate new samskaras and his mind is not influenced by spontaneously-occurring kriyas. The sadhak is established in the conscious-self only after all samskaras are uprooted. Kriyas are also based upon the dissolution of tattvas [elements]. That is when the world vanishes."

Question: "Does this mean that the spiritual journey is very long?"

Answer: "It is long, as well as arduous, unbearable, and filled with adversities. At every step of the way there is a possibility of slipping, getting lost. There are doubts and illusions. Generally aspirants remain satisfied in the preliminary stages. They neither rise above the physical level, nor are they able to experience even higher bliss."

Question: "Does this mean that the world is the cause of suffering?"

Answer: "No, the world is not the cause of suffering. It is only a base for the manifestation of joys and miseries. Human beings have made this world a cause of suffering. This world itself is the base for release from suffering. The responsibility lies with the aspirant, either to make this world a cause of suffering or a base for freedom from suffering. The real cause of suffering is illusion in the human mind, which has made room for itself there for life after life. Attachment and ego arise due to this illusion. The same illusion is the basis for the belief that the world causes suffering. Elimination of illusion is the goal of spirituality."

Question: "What is the role of Shakti in this?"

Answer: "Shakti is the power; she will only do the work that one urges her to do. If you want to untangle the knot of illusion, Shakti will do that. If you want to tighten the knot, she will do that also. If you want to build someone a home, she will do that. If you want to destroy, she will do that. If you want to be full of attachment and accumulate impressions, she will do that. If you want to awaken her to deplete impressions, she will do that. For Shakti, nothing is good or bad. The only task for her is to impart energy to the mind to make resolves and become functional through the medium of the senses. When Shakti becomes introverted, then mind stops making resolves and becomes only a witness. Then Shakti brings forth accumulated impressions and performs appropriate kriyas. The compassionate form of Shakti is visible when an aspirant, afraid of worldly suffering, takes refuge in Shakti. Then Shakti holds the aspirant's hand like a mother and takes him to her abode."

Question: "Then the spiritual journey becomes very easy. Simply hold the mother's hand and you arrive."

Answer: "No, the release from suffering is not that easy. Ego is the biggest obstacle. It does not allow you to surrender. Ego does not leave you alone even on the spiritual path. Ego wants to believe that its efforts are the only way. Holding the mother's hand is not an act of surrender, but of ego. Real surrender takes place when the mother takes hold of the child's hand and the child does not try to release it."

Question: "You have shown difficulties on the spiritual path so far. Please show some easy aspects also."

Answer: "Until the path becomes natural nothing is easy. Difficulties will come even after that, but they will not constrain progress and they will not interfere with inner bliss."

23. Discipline and Control Over the Mind

Today I remembered the old days, when Maharajshri had come to Nangal. We took him then to see Bhakra Dam. I do not remember who was with us, but I recollect there were three or four persons. To see the dam in those days one had to walk far. I do not know what the situation is today. We bought peanuts on the way. I tried to give Maharajshri some peanuts and he said, "I do not eat while walking." The rest of us walked and munched on peanuts. No one else paid attention, but a question was constantly on my mind. I hadn't the courage to ask Maharajshri, but this question spontaneously came to my mind at the time. Even after such a long time had passed, the question was still in my mind. Why does Maharajshri not eat while walking? How is this connected to spirituality?

I broached the subject the next morning. I reminded him of his visit to Nangal. Then I narrated the event of going to Bhakra Dam and mentioned the peanuts. I asked, "Is there any spiritual reason for not eating while walking, or is it just a custom? I do not see the connection between eating while walking and spirituality."

Maharajshri was silent for a few moments, as if he were trying to recollect something, and then he said, "On the surface there is no connection between this and spirituality. One can eat while sitting, one can lie down and eat, or eat while walking. One has to eat somehow or the other. But one thing should be remembered: Every step we take has a relationship to spirituality. Today we are in the strong grip of prarabdha [destiny], which is caused by past actions. Lack of discipline in our way of life has resulted in the collection of samskaras of fickle-mindedness, and our mind cannot be steady even for a moment. We are wandering in the world today due to an undisciplined life. Hence authors of scriptures have given rules for bringing discipline into life. Consequently we will accumulate samskaras of control, and our wanderings will reduce step-by-step.

"If you live a life of control for a long time then you will accumulate samskaras of discipline and samskaras of fickle-mindedness will diminish. Unripe seeds pressed in the ground will decay and be destroyed. With the passage of time a day will come when the mind will be completely influenced by samskaras of steadiness and control. Through fickle-mindedness and lack of control we stumble; by steadiness and control we ascend. Fickleness is the world and steadiness is spirituality. Fickle-mindedness makes you wander and steadiness gives you peace. If you consider not eating while walking in this context then it has a deep connection to spirituality. One small step is so significant for making life steady and peaceful. Perhaps you cannot see its effect immediately, but with the passage of time its effect is clearly visible, when enough samskaras of steadiness are accumulated. The rules for controlling the mind given by authors of the scriptures must be seen in this light. An aspirant may make his own rules in the light of his own mental state, in addition to the rules given in the scriptures.

"Now let us consider the subject from the perspective of yoga. When you offered me peanuts, for a moment I felt like accepting, but then I remembered the rule of not eating while walking and the feeling was controlled. Yoga is the restraint of the fluctuations of the mind. It is true that complete yoga is the control of all mental modifications, but that cannot be attained in one leap. You have to take one step at a time. If we wish, we can live a life of rules, watch mental modifications or fluctuations all day, and continue yoga sadhana all day. This way, one after another, mental modifications will be controlled, and we will keep marching forward in the direction of total control over mental activities.

"Sometimes an aspirant tries to control a particular mental modification but cannot halt its force. The mind does not listen to explanations nor to scolding. Then the aspirant must surrender to God. The unhappy aspirant yearns, 'Oh God, please protect me, protect me. In spite of your presence, the inner demon is creating havoc. The more I try to protect myself, the greater the harassment. You are sitting with eyes closed. O God, protect me, protect me.' The feelings in the devotee's heart become so intense that unwanted mental behaviors are washed away. Where knowledge and yoga do not work, devotion in the heart does.

"Some people make efforts in the beginning; when they are unsuccessful they call on God. Some have no ego of self-effort, and directly surrender. This state comes only when certain commandments are before you. Thus to practice control of the mental modifications rules must be followed. Otherwise life becomes unruly."

Question: "But in the path of Shaktipat there is no need for any such practices. Doesn't this sadhana depend upon surrender?"

Answer: "I have told you several times that surrender does not come through mere talk. The type of surrender needed in sadhana is rare. All hold on to ego in some form or the other. As long as ego exists you will have to take care of yourself."

Question: "I have one more doubt. We understand that you have risen above the boundaries of practices. Why do you need to make and follow rules?"

Answer: "Whether I need rules or not is irrelevant. You may think anything you like according to your feelings. But an aspirant must follow rules even after attaining everything, otherwise people will break all the rules and religious guidelines. They will free themselves from all rules."

24. Illusion in Kriyas

A couple came to visit Maharajshri and, during a conversation, said, "My wife's Guru Maharaj appears in her meditation and misbehaves with her."

Maharajshri asked how long it had been since she had met her Guru. The reply was that she hadn't met him since her wedding. Now he had left his mortal body, too.

Then Maharajshri said, "It is your illusion that you believe Guru Maharaj appears before her during meditation. Who knows what impressions of which lifetime are coming up in meditation? Some memories are dug up and come alive like a picture. Many different samskaras are mixed together and create a confusing picture inside. This is part of the Shakti's purification process. Therefore an aspirant need not be afraid. A time will come when the samskaras giving such experiences will lose their power, and this type of experience will end. If you are afraid of these experiences then there will be a delay in clearing the samskaras and the experiences will continue to occur. Hence, do not worry; watch the experiences as a witness."

The woman said, "My Guru Maharaj was extremely compassionate. He considered us to be his children. He was always active for our spiritual progress. Therefore it is impossible to imagine that he could behave this way. How come I am having such experiences?"

Maharajshri said, "Listen, daughter. It is beyond the capacity of an individual soul to understand the secret ways of the workings of Shakti. Only Shakti knows how many samskaras are mixed, how they manifest in the form of kriya, what their purpose is, and when the experiences will be transformed. When and how Shakti will display within is beyond the understanding of an individual soul. The jiva, individual soul, knows very little and Shakti knows everything. Shakti knows what a sadhak is filled with, and what vasanas or tendencies are deep-rooted. Shakti also knows who needs what type of strong kriyas. It is the duty of the sadhak not to interfere in Shakti's work."

The woman said, "I am only trying to understand, not interfere in the kriyas."

Answer: "To be afraid and wish not to experience these kriyas — isn't that interference? As far as knowing the reason is concerned, if the Shakti feels it is essential for you to understand, it will let you understand even without your asking. Both processes, explaining and understanding, are internal. External understanding is only an intellectual lecture. I can only tell you that there is nothing to worry about. Shakti will give you experiences according to requirements that are based on samskaras in the chitta. As soon as the samskaras are destroyed the experiences will also change. Your duty is to keep watching with surrender."

After they left Maharajshri said, "I have had many bizarre, misleading, strange experiences that shook my chitta. Often I would experience an illusion, but with the Guru's grace I was saved. An aspirant must maintain great caution. We do believe in ghosts, and I did have some such experiences, but our mind is the greatest ghost. The mind is expert in taking many different forms — threatening, scolding, and sometimes even wishing us well. The spoiled mind is a person's greatest enemy. All the tricks of the mind are taught by vasanas [tendencies]. A simple and innocent jiva is influenced and misled. When the mind returns to its natural state, then there is no other friend like the mind."

I said, "Maharajshri, I recall an event from my life. I had just entered my youth and was working in an office. My colleagues proposed going to a movie after work and everyone agreed happily. But I said my family would be worried because it would be 10:00 PM by the time we returned home. I tried calling my father at his office but he had left. Since they insisted, I went with them."

"When I reached home it was 10:00. I was afraid that I would be scolded. I extended my hand several times to knock on the door, but I did not dare to knock. I could hear the angry voice of my father, which completely discouraged me. I drew back. I stood at the street corner, thinking that there was no way to escape his anger. I was very afraid of my father but there was no alternative but to go home. The problem would worsen the longer I waited. I returned home. I extended my hand to knock on the door but found it open. I went in and saw that my father was smiling. He said, 'He has came back. Quickly serve him food.' Then he turned towards me and said, 'Give up this job. If you work so hard your health will suffer. There must be a reasonable time for returning home.' I became like a statue and began to reflect. Father was shouting with anger a few minutes ago, and now there was no trace of anger. I ate my dinner without any joy.

"Later, I asked mother whether father was upset with me. She said, 'No. He said we should make you leave the job since you had to work so late at the office. It would not be good for your health.' I told my father the real reason for returning late. He was pleased to hear the truth and said, 'It is good that you are aware of your mistake. That is sufficient.'

"Thus I had imagined a fierce form of my father in my mind, but his true state at that time was quite the opposite. There was an immediate reason for this, but there must have been some past impressions that played a role in my fear."

Maharajshri said, "Certainly samskaras play a primary role in the events that take place in our lives. Current happenings are present before us, while samskaras are invisible. They are like a river flowing under the Earth that can surface at any point. We only see the flow on the surface and do not see the river constantly flowing beneath."

25. Analysis of Selfishness

It was a full moon in autumn [Sharad purnima]. A very large pot of milk was kept in the front yard so that it would absorb the moonlight. With the moon shining down upon it, the hill above us seemed like an ornamented dancer, adorned with lunar light, performing a serene dance. A variety of flowers all around graced the landscape. The whole environment was filled with joy. For some time bhajans were sung. Maharajshri was sitting on a chair in the open. Devotees were sitting all around him. A spiritual discussion began.

Maharajshri said, "Literature and worldly usage have given a strange meaning to the word 'swartha' [selfishness], just as they have altered the meaning of the word 'purushartha' [self-effort]. The way in which purushartha means 'for the soul,' swartha means 'for the Self,' Now, the question arises: What is the Self? Often we consider our body as the Self.

"Swartha [selfishness] is the greedy attachment to accumulating means of comfort and happiness for the body, and for things related to the body. A selfish person only thinks about his selfish needs. A thief or someone who picks pockets will never think of the difficulties of the other person. He wants, somehow or the other, to snatch someone else's property. Generally, selfish people live like gentlemen in the world and employ tricks to consume other people's property. On the surface, all criticize selfishness while remaining fully immersed in it. From the point of view of spirituality and devotion, selfishness is a serious vice. The lowest state of greed is swartha [selfishness]. A selfish person will not hesitate to inflict a loss of a hundred rupees upon another for the sake of getting one rupee.

"Selfishness need not be related to money alone. It can be directed toward power, fame, sensual pleasures or protection of the body. It may involve the desire to be a well-known artist, actor or scholar. Jealousy, hate and disgust are sentiments helpful to selfishness. Once someone starts to sink into selfishness, then he continues to sink more and more. A selfish person is never content. Even if he has all the comforts in the world, he continues to want more and more. It is understandable that someone should want something for himself, but when the personal interests of someone else are chopped down, one sees the worst form of selfishness.

"A selfish person is jealous of those who have greater comfort and happiness. He despises those who have nothing. He flatters those who may be able to fulfill his selfish needs. He is afraid of those who may snatch his selfish accumulations. He is friendly to those who may help in achieving his selfish ends. In a nutshell, the mind of a selfish person is never at peace. He is always busy with some manipulation or the other. The world is full of selfish people, even though selfishness is full of miseries, worries and restlessness.

"Selfishness is like a river that may flood in any season. It is like a well that is never filled. It is a hunger that it is never satisfied. It is like a desert where owls continuously howl. It is like a thorny bush in the desert that hurts all those who pass by. It is like a pot with a hole at the bottom that cannot retain any water. It is like a whirlpool that has swallowed many boats in its belly. It is a tornado that not only lifts those who want to go with it, but also drags up those who may not want to. The whole world burns in the fire of selfishness."

Question: "The world does not respect selflessness. It is believed that no one can be selfless. Selfless service has become so difficult."

Answer: "Selfless service has been very difficult in all eras, but for an aspirant, the example is not the world but the inner Shakti, which is totally selfless. The difficulty is that the aspirant must work in the world while keeping the ideal in front of him. Just as two different points cannot meet, similarly selfishness and selfless service cannot survive in the same place. Either the chitta will have selfishness or selflessness. A selfless servant will not be influenced or shaken from his path no matter how many difficulties arise. Yes, it is different if someone has put on a false garb of being selfless. Then selflessness is a pretense."

Question: "When the flow of the current itself is full of selfishness, how then is selflessness possible?"

Answer: "It is difficult, but it is not impossible. Generosity and tolerance are absolutely essential for this. The path of sadhana is definitely very hard. A selfless servant will always be peaceful and joyful, irrespective of how many difficulties come his way. People may insult him, call him names, try to shake his selflessness, but he will always observe all these things like waves of the ocean and forgive everyone. This is the way to stay in the world and yet apart from the world. Many people use the metaphor of a lotus untouched by water, but the secret of this metaphor is known only to a selfless person."

Question: "Where did selfishness come from, when the nature of consciousness is selfless, and an individual soul is, in reality, this consciousness?"

Answer: "From misconception, from attachment, from samskaras. The true nature is selfless, but the original true nature and form has been forgotten and the individual soul has become selfish. The affliction of attachment and the cover of samskaras solidify this misconception. Then the nature of the individual soul appears to be selfish.

"Saints totally lack this selfishness. Kabir, Mirabai, Surdas, Tukaram, Jnaneshwar — who of these was selfish? They lived for the benefit of others, and for ultimate spiritual benefit. It may be said that a saint is that person who is not selfish at all.

"The basic nature of an unselfish person is spiritually oriented. Hence his selfish pursuit is to attain the true nature of the spirit. The world is in selfish pursuit of the body, while spiritual selfishness is for ultimate spiritual benefit. The word 'selfishness,' here, is the same, but there is such a difference in the implication. The progression of selfishness can be described as follows:

(1) Worldly Selfishness — directed towards physical purposes only.

(2) Selflessness — the effort to get rid of worldly selfishness.

(3) Spiritual Selfishness — the desire to merge with the Absolute Self. The ultimate spiritual goal is such selfishness.

"If worldly selfishness is the heat of desires then selflessness protects one from this heat, and spiritual selfishness is like a cooling shade. Travelers feel peace and joy as soon as they come under its shade. Selflessness and surrender are two sides of the same coin; the only difference is in the perspective. Purushartha, or self-effort, can also be placed in the same category, because it is nothing other than surrender and selflessness. All of them have only one goal: to establish in the Absolute Self. Hence the use of the prefixes swa [self] and para [real].

"The wealth of an aspirant is true selfishness. Only true selfishness can destroy all the inner enemies. True selfishness is the herb that can eradicate the disease of birth, life and death from its deepest roots. True selfishness is a garden full of different varieties of fragrant flowers. It is the flow of the holy river Ganges, which can wash all sins. And true selfishness is that level of sadhana from which one does not have to return to the world.

"But, in the end, I must remind you that only a rare person can attain true selfishness. Physical selfishness has become so powerful that a person's discretion is swept away by its force."

Question: "Does this mean that efforts in this direction are useless because one can rarely attain it?"

Answer: "No, it does not mean that. When I said that only a rare person attains selfishness, it was in reference to the fullest degree of real selfishness. As a man begins to walk in the direction of reaching that state his mind becomes peaceful and free from miseries. To establish one's self with the Absolute Self is not easy for everyone. However, one can be free from great miseries of life if he can attain an unselfish [in the worldly sense of the term] state of mind that is not easily perturbed."

26. Pure and Impure Selfishness

The next day, during the morning walk, I asked a question related to the same discussion. "What is the role of Shakti in worldly selfishness and spiritual selfishness?"

Maharajshri said, "Shakti not only destroys worldly selfishness, it also destroys its root cause. Samskaras come before it after awakening, and the cause of selfishness is samskaras. Samskaras take the form of vasanas, behavioral tendencies that create waves in the mind and give rise to a mind filled with desires and volition. Thus abolition of samskaras is the main problem in the way of elimination of selfishness. Some call it the abolition of tendencies and others call it purification of samskaras. As such, vasanas are the result of samskaras. Therefore the process of purification of samskaras includes abolition of vasanas.

"Now a different perspective will be presented: impure selfishness and pure selfishness. Impure selfishness is worldly, and the mind is filled with worldly desires, attachments, hate and jealousy. It is also filled with vengeance, anger and egoism. The mind does not hesitate a bit before causing harm to others. There is pride of wealth, youth and power. These are the qualities of impure selfishness. In pure selfishness, worldly desires, attachments, hate, jealousy, vengeance, and so forth, withdraw. They are replaced with the desire for self-realization, and give rise to qualities such as detachment toward the world, love of God, restlessness due to separation from God, tolerance, forgiveness, compassion, and so forth. Impure selfishness burns one all the time, whereas in self-realization, pure selfishness merges into the soul along with all the virtues.

"With the kriyas of Shakti and seva [selfless service], impure selfishness diminishes and pure samskaras increase, which gives rise to the good qualities mentioned above. Then Shakti, with the help of kriyas, consumes these good qualities and finally merges itself into the soul."

Question: "However, from a worldly and practical standpoint, this effect is rarely seen. Let us forget about worldly people; even most of the aspirants who claim to have spiritual experiences of a higher nature are in a state of mind that is contrary to this. Anger, ego, attachments, hatred, disgust, and so forth, fully occupy their mind. For such people, even the names of qualities like tolerance, forgiveness and generosity do not exist. They get upset at small matters. Events leave a marked impression on their psyche, as if a line were engraved in stone. This is hard to understand. On the one hand there is the joy of sadhana, and on the other hand there is such a state of mind.

Answer: "I have told you before that only a rare person can enter into the Lord's city of love. Many start on the inner journey, but only a few lucky ones reach their destination. Most of them fall to the ground before reaching it. What I talked about is the usual sequence of progress of Shakti. It is the duty and responsibility of the aspirant to allow selfishness to transform into kriyas of Shakti. It is also said that the psychic tendencies, impressions and selfishness do not leave you at once. They perish and are reborn again and again. They disappear and manifest again. This is the play of Maya [the grand illusion]. Even in the dry desert the harvest of faults is very rich. A sadhak may be absorbed in his sadhana, but this selfishness is busy weakening its roots from inside. In reality, this is the carelessness of an aspirant. The Gita says that a devotee is alert. Alertness is moving forward on the spiritual path and, simultaneously, remaining cautious about inner enemies.

"Parallel to the journey on the spiritual path, there is another journey that is known as the journey of prarabdha, or destiny. One foot of the sadhak is on the path of sadhan; the other foot is on the path of his prarabdha. As long as both feet fail to take synchronized steps one cannot go forward on the spiritual journey. Generally sadhaks take an interest in the journey of sadhan, but neglect the journey of prarabdha. One foot tries to move forward, but the other foot is tied to vasanas and the stone of selfishness and does not want to rise up. Consequently the psyche remains impure.

"The journey on the path of prarabdha is even harder than the journey on the path of spiritual practice, because in this the foot tries to alter the path over and over again. If the foot on prarabdha moves further away then the foot on the sadhana path slips. The journey of prarabdha has a greater effect on the journey of sadhan than the journey of sadhan has on the journey of prarabdha. On the journey of prarabdha you have to remove rocks in the way and you have to prevent new rocks from falling in your path. This work is not easy, but it is an absolute requirement to progress on the spiritual path. Often aspirants tend to overlook this very important task, or they cannot manage to do this in spite of millions of attempts.

"I have tried to explain again and again that walking on the spiritual path is not easy. Only a rare, brave person, who has wagered his head and body, can proceed on this path. Others fall flat upon meeting obstacles. How many catastrophes I had to face and tackle, and what kind of difficulties I had to endure, only I know. To describe them would be arrogance, so it is better not to talk about them."

Maharajshri went on talking and, as I listened attentively, an incident from my days prior to ashram life came to mind. I was reminded how difficult spiritual life can be. The incident involved getting lost in Himachal Pradesh.

"Five or six of us were walking on a road. Some were chatting about things of very little interest to me. I was walking behind them at a distance doing japa. My mind was totally focused on japa, and I became oblivious to everything around me. Other people were so engrossed in their conversation that they never looked back at me. At one point we were to leave the road and make a turn onto a mountainous footpath. Everyone turned and started on the footpath, but I was so absorbed in japa that I missed it. I kept on walking along the road. I came back to Earth after about an hour and realized that I had gone three or four miles too far. Darkness was descending. There was no time to return. I met a traveler on the way and gave him the name of the village I was traveling to. He said it was five or six miles by road. Since it was getting dark, it would not be a good idea to go through the forest, but if I had the courage to go over the mountain, the village was on the other side.

"I thought for a little while, checked my courage, and decided to go over the mountain. I was young; my body was strong and energetic. Still the climb was very steep, covered with trees and bushes. It was pitch dark, there was no path, and I was afraid of snakes and scorpions. The task was difficult but I started climbing. I usually wore pants, a shirt and shoes in those days. I was fixed on one obsession: climbing the mountain. Holding trees and jumping like a monkey from one branch to another, falling and getting up, I went on climbing. The jungle became so thick that not even a ray of moonlight could pierce through the trees and strike the ground. My efforts were being carried out in this pitch darkness.

After climbing for about half an hour I reached the peak and saw the moon. The other side was clearly visible in the moonlight. Lamps twinkled in some places. I could see farms full of grains glistening in the milky white moonlight. As I looked at this beautiful sight all my fatigue disappeared. After enjoying the view for a few minutes I started to climb down. That was even harder. Somehow I managed to reach the base of the hill. There I slipped in a field of grain. The farms were all muddy, and I looked like a ghost smeared with mud. Somehow I reached the village.

"Sadhan is also similar to climbing a mountain in the dark. The deep darkness of illusion, ego, desire, anger, greed, selfishness and wild animal instincts in the form of vasanas [deep-rooted psychic tendencies] make it difficult to see the path ahead. Sometimes we need to grab the branch of japa, and sometimes we need the help of scripture study, singing God's praise and prayer in order to climb the steep incline of sadhan. If one foot slips, you can slide thousands of feet into the valley. How difficult is the climb of sadhan. The awakening of Shakti does make it somewhat easier, but difficulties and hardships persist."

Maharajshri said, "You are right. Sadhan is a similar journey, filled with difficulties. Only a few people turn toward this. Of those, a few begin the climb and, of those, some succeed in climbing one peak. The biggest obstacle is prarabdha. A sadhak may start to climb but prarabdha pulls one down.

"I was staying in an ashram. The Dewas ashram did not exist then. People come to where there are ascetics. The priest in charge of the ashram did not like people coming to me. At night he told me to leave the ashram. I was very angry. You know that anger is a very big obstacle, nevertheless I convinced myself that this was a play of prarabdha and accepted the situation. If I had given over control to anger, I would have accumulated too many samskaras and the routine of sadhan would have been disturbed for a few days. Such occasions come in life at every step of the way. A sadhak gets carried away by them. He even forgets that he is a sadhak. His behavior as a sadhak must continue through all his social interactions — while eating, drinking, and while performing all his activities. Very often a sadhak cannot maintain this. Some believe anger to be an ornament of a sadhak, but what good is an ornament if it makes you ugly?

"If someone comes to clean your room and you sit in his way, how will he be able to clean where you are? You have to get up. To vacate the space to be cleaned is the same as surrender in spirituality. The psyche of the sadhak is covered with ego and selfishness. For some time ego must be steadied in the state of a witness and withdrawn from the mind. Then only will Shakti be able to clean. Not only that, Shakti will also provide your chitta the foundation for spiritual experiences. This is sadhan.

"When a sadhak descends from sadhan and acts in the world, he commits this mistake: His ego, selfishness and doership take on a strong form again, and their effect is clearly visible in his behavior and attitude. He again becomes responsible for the fruits of his action. Again samskaras are accumulated. All that was earned during the time of sadhan is gone. His special spiritual income is lost. It is as if the person has a dual personality — one of a sadhak and the other of a worldly person. He is angelic at the time of sadhan, and back in the world becomes a demon. At the time of sadhan he undoes knots, and after sadhan he tightens them.

"Due to this dual personality he cannot make progress in sadhan and spirituality. He complains about the lack of progress in sadhan, and he also looks for limitations in his sadhan. As long as every moment of life, every action, every thought and feeling rising within is not spiritual, to look for progress is like daydreaming."

27. The Ephemeral World

In those days Maharajshri used to go up the hill on his morning walk. The hill was very different then. There were no paths, no trees and no electricity. Dewas was the only city in India that had been ruled by two kings. The city had been divided into two sections, namely, Badi Pati [Old Dewas] and Choti Pati [New Dewas]. The hill was equally divided between the two sections. The temple of the Mother Goddess of Old Dewas was in New Dewas and the temple for the Mother Goddess of New Dewas was in Old Dewas. A pathway with steps to climb the hill was in Old Dewas, and a there was a walkway to New Dewas. However these divisions did not exist after the recent abolition of the princely states in India when Dewas became a district. The city was now like one big village with a population of 12-14,000 people.

We had reached the top of the hill. Maharajshri was facing the city of Dewas. He said, "This world is so mutable. At one time there were two kingdoms and now there is one district. Newer boundaries are formed and broken. There are no borders in the world; they are all imaginary. The borders change with changes in imagination. New countries come into existence and disappear. New organizations are created and come to an end. New principles, traditions and languages are created, and with the passage of time they exist only in the pages of history. A line is drawn; a country's formation is announced. It is considered holy and people are ready to die for it in the name of patriotism. One principle is formed, some rules are made, an organization is made, a new religion is named, and people grow attached to it and are ready to die for it. Then a time comes when that country, that language and that culture all come to an end. The wheel of time keeps moving and new countries, languages, religions, traditions, systems of thought, art forms and cultures rise and fall. People create divisions in their country, language and religion. They even segregate scriptures and great personalities. The wheel of time continues to move, and neither are the people alive any longer, nor are their faiths and beliefs. Everything changes. Perhaps, therefore, the world is said to be a play. New actors come, show their skills, and then go backstage. The only thing that remains is the thundering sound of applause. That, too, is momentary, and eventually is lost in the skies.

"When small kingdoms existed here the royal families were in power. Their language was the official language. Their culture was the culture of the society. Their food habits, way of dressing, and so forth, influenced their citizens. They had authority; they were special. Today they stand in the same line as a common citizen. There was an age of Hitler. The whole world shivered at the sound of his name. If he lifted his finger toward a country, it would surrender. A day followed when it was hard even to find his corpse. People, countries, languages and artists keep on changing. The world goes on. There was a time when the sun never set on the British empire.

"It is said that once upon a time the entire Earth was one single land mass. Slowly it broke up into Asia, Africa, America and other continents. Many islands emerged from the ocean beds. It is also said that where the Himalayas are standing high today, there once was the deepest ocean in the world. Sometimes ice from the North Pole melts away, and at other times ice from the South Pole. Once upon a time the Ganges River used to meet the ocean near Panipat [a city in North India]. Rajasthan [a western state in India with many deserts] was a sea. The world is changeable. If some great change takes place suddenly then people take notice, but change is going on at every moment, all the time.

"Change is an intrinsic quality of nature. Just like the world, changes take place in the body, too. First of all, we see many different colors, shapes, sizes and languages among humans. Some are accustomed to living in icy, cold weather and cannot stand heat. Some live in hot places and cannot stand cold. Even within the human body itself changes go on. A child comes into existence from who knows where, and does not attain youth in a moment. The process moves slowly. The process of daily change goes unnoticed. The young man does not become old in one day. Yes, death can come anytime, just as someone completes his performance and leaves the stage at once. Death itself is a major change; it is like a curtain falling on the ever-changing life. Besides, the body also sometimes feels more energetic and sometimes weak; sometimes it is healthy and sometimes sick; sometimes hungry, sleepy, lazy and refreshed. Thus the body also does not remain the same.

"The chitta [psyche], just like the body and the world, is also a part of nature. The body is a miniature form of the world. The chitta spreads out and manifests in the form of the physical body. The only difference is that the body and the world are physical and visible, whereas the chitta, being subtle, cannot be seen. As far as change is concerned, it takes place in the chitta also. The state of the chitta changes constantly. Sometimes the influence of tamo guna [inertial tendencies] becomes overwhelming and the onslaught of deficiency, laziness, sluggishness, indulgence, anger, sleep, and so forth, increases. Sometimes it is under the influence of rajo guna [quality of activity] and it runs around in the world. Sometimes it is ruled by sattva guna [harmonious tendencies] and it does good deeds, prays and meditates. Then the chitta manifests good qualities such as calmness, compassion, tolerance, generosity, sobriety, and so forth. Just as the world and body keep changing, so does the predominance of the gunas [the three qualities mentioned above]. They are never in balance. If a perfect balance of the gunas occurs then the body, the world and the chitta will cease to exist.

"Vasanas [psychic tendencies] and samskaras [accumulated impressions] play a vital role in the changes within the state of the chitta. Shakti always vibrates on the basis of the chitta, but strengthening these vibrations and changing their direction is the work of vasanas. These vibrations of Shakti ultimately manifest in the form of modifications of the mind. There are innumerable variations, forms and levels of mental modifications. Desire, anger, greed, jealousy, hatred, and so forth, are different types of modifications. These modifications take place when true knowledge has arisen, when there are false assumptions, or when baseless illusions fill up the mind. When a specific feeling arises in the mind, then others subside. The mind is considered fickle when it rapidly jumps from one subject to another and displays different feelings. Fickle-mindedness is defined as an effort to focus attention on the mutable. The body and the world are manifested forms of the vibrations of Shakti. The greater the focus on these, the greater the inconstancy of the chitta.

"When anger arises in the chitta, the signs and symptoms of anger generally show in the face. Some people suppress anger inside, nevertheless there is a change in the chitta. This is true for other feelings, mental modifications and mental events. Events within the chitta [psyche] affect the world, and the sense organs act in the world according to the effects on the body. Sometimes the chitta affects the world, and sometimes the world influences the chitta by bringing the mental tendencies to the surface. This body is the link between the world and the chitta.

"The world, the body and the chitta are like waves. A wave rises, takes form, and then disappears. The body takes form in the world. It goes through childhood, youth and old age and then disappears. In the chitta, feelings, thoughts and resolves arise and then disappear. Spirituality is the name of that force which detaches you from these effects, changes and waves. An individual soul caught in a wave goes up and down with the tide and takes a form in accordance with the wave. When one wave subsides a new one takes its place and the being becomes involved in that. The world is the result of the vibration of Shakti and the imbalance in the three gunas, but the main problem for a being is not the world, but the vibration and imbalance in the chitta. The jiva has grabbed the world because of that. For the same reason one is entangled in the waves of the world and has fallen from his real state.

"The Ramayana has an episode related to Kak Bhushundi. [Kak Bhushundi is an immortal being living in the form of a crow since the beginning of all manifestation.] He was detached from the world and watched the activities and changes in the world as a divine sport of God. He was not affected by Maya, the grand illusion, or in other words, was not influenced by these changes. Kak Bhushundi is an ideal to follow in spirituality. There were others before him who were also ideals, but for a common person he is the greatest ideal. It is not easy to attain this goal. We have established oneness with the waves of the world. Kak Bhushundi did not attain his detached state in just one lifetime. He fell many times and got up every time. For many births he remained firm on the path of spirituality. And eventually, with the grace of God, he attained this state.

"Shakti does the same thing after awakening. For a short time it makes the individual soul like Kak Bhushundi. It makes him stand on the side and watch the play of Shakti. This state does not last forever, as is the case with Kak Bhushundi, and is only an example. The sadhak goes beyond Maya for a short period of time and watches the play of Shakti on the stage of his chitta [psyche], independent of himself. He understands what he has to do and where he has to go in the future. The samskaras that were the cause of his happiness and misery so far now become the basis for the workings of Shakti. The chitta, which was colored by vasanas until then, now appears before the individual soul, the observer, in the form of the activities of the Shakti. If a sadhak thinks about it he recognizes this as a great attainment. It is a powerful ray of hope for a being wandering in the dark. It is a support for the unsupported. It is a guide post for a lost soul. This is a rope by which the individual can reach the Self.

"It is the duty of the individual to take this from the level of practice to the level of natural behavior. If the aspirant is honest and committed then Shakti will definitely help to the fullest extent. The state of an observer that is attained during meditation should be brought to physical and worldly levels. This is not just a matter of the aspirant's efforts. The role of Shakti is very important, and the effort and surrender of the aspirant are also important. It is the responsibility of the aspirant to maintain a balance between effort and surrender.

"When Shakti turns accumulated impressions [samskaras] into kriyas before they become mental tendencies [vasanas], at that time the basis of kriyas is samskaras and not vasanas. Kriyas may be in accordance with the vasanas or samskaras. Samskaras do not have an opportunity to transform into action through the mind and senses. This is what is called "burning samskaras in the fire of yoga." Here samskaras lose the potential of sprouting in the future. Burned samskaras cannot develop, even while performing actions. Thus the process of purification of the chitta continues further. Eventually a state of mind develops in which, just like

Kak Bhushundi, an aspirant becomes a witness and observes the changes in the body and mind like a movie, separate from the Self.

"Generally an aspirant is unable to maintain such awareness even during sadhana. His ego, attachment and selfishness do not let him settle into a state of surrender. He feels a sense of ego and attachment towards his kriyas. Consequently the samskaras, instead of becoming like burnt seeds, begin to sprout and the sequence of progress is stalled."

28. Mutual Likes and Dislikes

There was discord between two residents of the ashram. They would criticize each other whenever they conversed with anyone. Their own minds were burning in a fire of dislike, and they were spoiling the minds of others. They rarely talked to each other, and whenever they did it was curt and cold. This was poisoning the ashram environment.

When Maharajshri heard about it he called them and said, "I have given you initiation for spiritual benefit. I wished you both well at the time of your initiation. Your animosity toward each other is a path to unhappiness. This will increase the impressions of dislike, hatred and enmity, and that will contaminate your minds. Your behavior is contrary to my will. How can you hope to benefit by behaving contrary to your Guru's wish?

"Lord Shiva resides within both of you, but you are busy hiding him in the cover of likes and dislikes, jealousy and hatred, and so forth. The nature of Shiva is love and detachment, whereas you are drawing far away from the nature of Shiva by going towards the world. The basis of your spiritual practice is mutual love, whereas you are getting deeper in the mud of mutual hatred. Know your path. Understand your duty. If you develop love for each other, your Shakti will increase; otherwise it will be depleted in your conflict.

"Love is the essence of the world. Love is God's commandment. Love is a human obligation. Love is a ship that takes one across the ocean of life and death. Love is a medicine that brings peace to a mind burning in likes and dislikes. Love is a wave of cooling breeze that brings fragrance to life. Love is a high peak of life from which one sees the value and worthlessness of the world. Love is an instrument that offers the sweet and immortal nectar of God's name to a person to drink when he is burning in the fire of the world. It is an invaluable and holy gem. Leaving such an invaluable and beneficial jewel aside, why do you fight with each other with the intent of drinking the pot of poison?

"First of all your minds should be pure toward each other. There are faults on both sides. Develop a habit of looking at your own faults instead of looking at other's faults. Then only will you be able to nurture love for each other. Then your heart will become magnanimous and generous. Love will expand in your heart. You will not only love each other, but you will also love birds and animals, fish and serpents. Your heart will be filled with love for the mountains, deserts, rivers and oceans. Lord Shiva will come alive for you in every living being, in nature and in every particle.

"On the other hand, if the process of falling deeper into the darkness of likes and dislikes, jealousy and hate continues, darkness will continue to increase. In the dark you do not even know whose throat you may cut. It is the job of darkness to make you fight with strangers, as well as with your own people. Darkness takes away your clarity about friends and foes. You will want to kill whoever approaches you. In the dark you can see neither yourself, nor your path, nor your destination. The individual continues to sink deeper into the darkness, and believes peace and happiness are hiding somewhere in the dark. If someone tries to lead him to the light, he thinks he is being tricked and harmed.

"The darkness of hate and disgust cannot be sustained in a heart in which the light of love is present. Those who are filled with the darkness of hate cannot see even a single ray of the light of love. Although love is our true nature, we have covered ourselves in hate. These covers have only hidden love, but love cannot be estranged. How long will you remain unaware of your nature? How long will you remain under this pile of unnatural garbage? How long will you burn in the fire of illusion? Get hold of the torch of love and move forward. How long do you want to be lost from your path?

"As long as your mind is filled with hate you will be unable to enjoy the bliss of love. You will not be able to see even a glimpse of love. So, either enhance the light of love in such a way that the darkness of hate is ended, or drive away the darkness of hate in such a way that the love hidden within manifests spontaneously. The light of love indicates that the darkness of hate is gone. The darkness of hate means that the light of love does not exist. Love is spirituality and hate is worldliness. If you talk about spirituality but continue to descend the ladder into the darkness of hate, then spirituality cannot shine.

"Love is a natural feeling of the heart. It does not have anything to do with time and space. The person who loves today will also love tomorrow. The one who is a lover in India will be a lover in America. It is the same story with hate. Feelings of hate are not limited by boundaries of time and space. If you love or hate each other while living in the ashram, the same feelings will persist outside the ashram. If you go to sleep with certain feelings, you will wake up with the same feelings. As long as the state of the chitta remains unchanged, feelings do not change. Feelings that depend upon the state of the chitta change with a change in the state of the chitta. The love that depends upon the state of the chitta is not love. True love is an intrinsic quality of the soul."

One of the ashram residents said to Maharajshri, "We accept our mistake. We will devote our best efforts to purifying our minds. So far the fire of revenge was aflame in our hearts. Your advice has given us some peace. With your blessings, our hearts will be filled with love in place of enmity. One question arises in the mind: Is there any connection between the practice of love and Shaktipat? The practice of love increases the feelings of love in the heart. Is that correct?"

Answer: "You are repeating the same mistake. Shakti, by its activities, removes filth and layers. Consequently the natural qualities of love, generosity and detachment manifest. Until that happens, practices done with a conscious effort are required to help the processes of Shakti."

Both residents changed tremendously after that day. Most people were very happy to see their behavior toward each other. Some jealous people were unhappy. With this change, their spiritual practice was also enhanced significantly.

29.   Mango Juice and the Juice of Joy

Behind the temple there were two mango trees. Both of them have now been removed for the expansion of the ashram. Maharajshri was sitting under one of them on a chair. Some devotees were sitting on a mat on the ground. Ripe mangos were hanging on the tree. It was a pleasant evening. Maharajshri was looking at the mangos and thinking, and suddenly said, "The sweet juice of the mangos is still hanging on the tree while people are busy drinking the bitter juice of worldly pleasure. Worldly pleasure can never give them satisfaction. Goddess Shakti is always inviting her children, 'Come! Drink the nectar of my love and be content.' But people, like restless children, keep running after the toys of sensuous pleasures. They remain far from the natural juice of love, sweet like the mango juice. Gurus, saints and scriptures stand like trees, bending with the weight of knowledge, inviting everyone to come and drink the juice of God's name, but people are busy drinking something else.

"Have you ever looked into your psyche and seen how the mango orchard has turned into a jungle full of useless growth, weeds and uneven soil? The jungle-like environment inside not only stunts the growth of the mango trees, but it strangles the new shoots, flowers and fruits. Why waste life wandering in this deep jungle?"

Question: "Man is busy tending the garden outside. He has neither the time, nor the desire, to look at the garden within. His mango orchard inside is barren and dry, bugs devour it, and branches break in high winds. Useless thorny bushes have covered the mango trees."

Answer: "This is the irony of human behavior. Instead of carrying a well of sweet mango juice within, one is lost in the external world and pours poison inside. He has lost inner bliss, and chases desires, anger and ego like a blind man. These beautiful mangos hanging on the branches of the tree are symbols of the natural inner juice. The man of today is bent on reducing his sweetness by picking unripe mangos, and then ripening them with chemicals.

"Have you ever considered what a mango gives you in return for being cut by a knife? Sweetness. This tolerance and generosity is the sadhana of the mango. This is its benevolence. The mango is an example of the true saint. It spreads joy in the world by losing the self. Selfish people cannot comprehend this. For them this is stupidity because they experience sweetness in selfishness. However, over time, this sweetness proves to be poison. The mango does not put a knife in the stomach of the person cutting it; instead the mango fills his stomach with sweetness. No resistance, no revenge, only sweetness. This is his saintliness.

When a mango tree starts to shrivel it is in need of water. The leaves turn yellow, the branches dry out, but when watered again it comes alive. The leaves get firm again. The branches become strong and straight again. Your life, similarly, needs the water of love [for God]. The aridity of likes and dislikes, hate and selfishness has ruined your face. You need the water of love to make your life green and lush, and to fill it with sweetness. Love may appear painful on the surface but it will fill your heart with joy.

"Worldly love is no love. It is a misnomer for infatuation and lust. True love is the love of the soul. It is the giver of inner bliss. It causes release from worldly anguish. It is sweet like mango juice. Mango juice reminds one of the same inner bliss. The sweetness of mango juice fills each and every cell. The juice of love also saturates every part of the body, the heart, and all the senses. When the nectar of love spreads throughout the mind and the body it cannot be hidden even if one wants to hide it. Like the fragrance of flowers, it rides on a horse of air and spreads in all four directions. Love changes one's perceptions. The world appears beautiful where all the beloved people reside. Love drives away all the narrow selfish feelings such as ego, likes and dislikes, anger, and all negativity.

"The lover loves the whole world and the whole world is his beloved. His connection is spiritual and not physical. He sees the Atma, the highest personal principle of life, the Self, in all beings because the atma-tattva [the Ultimate Reality] is manifest within. He knows the secret of love. He knows that hate depletes the soul, whereas love awakens and illumines the soul. The Ultimate Reality remains a stranger as long as there is hatred, dislike or jealousy even toward a single person. If there is dislike and aversion toward something, favoritism, too, must be hidden somewhere. This shows that the person is still within the sphere of likes and dislikes.

"Egoism is the enemy of love. The ego in the mind prevents the expression of love. The layer of ego, even though it is unnatural, is a cover all the same and it covers natural love. Ego is merely an illusion, it is treachery, and it is false. How can the soul that has fallen in the deep trench of ego know the hidden essence of love?

"The mango is a living symbol of love and joy. It offers itself not only to humans, but also to birds. Such self-sacrifice is possible only by a lover of God, just as king Shibi offered a part of his body to save a pigeon. How can the soul, dying for selfishness, be familiar with the joy of love? But you are spiritual aspirants. You meditate everyday; you have the grace of a Guru; you talk about divine experiences; you have no excuse for being without love. If you try to find excuses then you fall from the level of an aspirant. Think about it and decide once and for all. If you want to be worldly then do whatever comes to mind. If you want to be an aspirant then be ready to give up everything like a lover.

"You suck the juice from a mango and throw the seed away. You do not accept and develop the qualities of the mango. You start shouting at the slightest difficulty. People break leaves from the mango tree. They strike it with axes. It bears the cold, heat and rain and does not even complain. People keep eating its fruit; it goes on giving juice to all. Its seed is discarded. It sprouts and is ready to serve again. Such a selfless life must be that of an aspirant. Then only will he be able to spread sweetness, love and joy. Then only will he be able to find joy within."

30. Swami Muktananda

The families of a few disciples lived in Mumbai [Bombay]. They were always inviting Maharajshri to come. Finally their request was accepted. They arranged for Maharajshri's stay near the Mahalaxmi temple. I want to draw the attention of readers to an important event that took place during this trip. Mahatma Swami Nityananda was very well-known in those days. He was originally from South India, but he had followers from many different states. He spent most of his time in the Avadhuta state [a state wherein one is free from worldly feeling and obligation]. Arrangements were made for Maharajshri to seek his company

Swami Nityananda had a disciple named Muktananda, who eventually did noteworthy work in the field of Shaktipat. He traveled through America, Europe, Australia and many other countries showing the path of Shaktipat to the masses and earning international fame. In those days he lived in a cottage near the ashram of Swami Nityananda. It is now a huge ashram, almost like a palace. This was in 1962.

Among the disciples of Maharajshri there was a doctor who was a trustee for Swami Nityananda's ashram, and also knew Swami Muktananda. When Swami Muktananda heard that Maharajshri was coming to meet Swami Nityananda, he asked the doctor to bring Maharajshri to his cottage for a visit, even if it was for a brief moment. It was decided that Swami Muktananda would stand on the street across from his cottage and wave, and the doctor would stop his car. At that time Swami Muktananda would ask Maharajshri to visit his cottage.

The next day, at the scheduled time, the car arrived at Ganeshpuri near Swami Nityananda's ashram, and Swami Muktananda was waiting on the street according to the plan. He saw the car coming from a distance and waved. The doctor was driving. He stopped near Swami Muktananda. Swami Muktananda bowed to Maharajshri. The doctor said, "This is Swami Muktananda. He is a disciple of Swami Nityananda and lives in the cottage nearby. He requests that you please visit his cottage." Maharajshri paused briefly, then got out of the car and walked to the cottage.

Swami Muktananda had already made preparations to offer puja [to worship Maharajshri]. He had laid a woolen seat at an appropriate place. Maharajshri was respectfully seated on the woolen seat. Swami Muktananda did Maharajshri's puja. After completing the puja Swami Muktananda immediately fell into the lap of Maharajshri. His eyes were half closed. Maharajshri's eyes were closed and his hand was on the head of Swami Muktananda. This divine scene lasted for about fifteen minutes. The whole room was saturated with Shakti, as if waves of Shakti were silently circulating throughout the room. Only Maharajshri and Swami Muktananda knew their inner states, but all those present in the room felt an extraordinary intoxication. Swami Muktananda opened his eyes after about a quarter of an hour. Maharajshri's hand also moved away from his head. He sat up. Both were silent, looking at each other. Neither did Maharajshri say anything, nor did Swami Muktananda utter a word. A silent discourse. Maharajshri left.

No one could see the process that took place on the subtle level, but the goal that cannot be accomplished with thousands of lectures and long-term spiritual practice and propitiation was accomplished in no time, without a single word spoken or heard. That state for which ascetics remain engrossed in austerities in the jungles and still fail to attain was experienced by Swamiji Muktananda while lying in the lap of Maharajshri. After the experience Swami Muktananda's face was shining with divine lustre and Maharajshri's face had unfathomable solemnity.

Only a saint can know the greatness of other saints. How can a worldly soul, lost in the thick forest of pleasures, be capable of understanding mysteries on a subtle level? What a saint does, when he does it, and to whom, is known only to the saint. Scriptures have described saints with precision. These detached mahatmas are free from the bondage of the world and they do not expect anything from anyone. The play of their life is only for the benefit of the world. They also have karmic

debts to others from past births. Only the fortunate can benefit from
the grace of a saint.

Maharajshri returned after meeting Swami Nityananda. On our
way back, these were his words in the car: "This Muktananda took a lot
— much more than I had expected."

The next day Swami Muktananda came to where Maharajshri was
staying to see him. He was asked how he came to know about Maharajshri and Shaktipat. This is what he said, of his own accord:

"I was a wandering monk in those days. I came to a village in
Maharashtra (I do not remember the name of the village now.) and
stayed at the house of a village chief for the night. I was put up in their
guest house. Just above the place where I was seated there was a cup-
board in the wall. I was sitting in the dark doing japa, and again and
again one book there grabbed my attention. I was trying hard to concentrate on doing my japa, but again and again I was distracted by this same
book. I turned on the flashlight and took the book. It was a book by
Swami Yogananda [Maharajshri's Shaktipat Guru] named *Mahayoga Vijnana*.
I read a few pages by the light of a flashlight. That night I experienced
all the kriyas I read about in the book. Thus I knew about this branch of
knowledge. I had already heard the name of Maharajshri. I also knew
that he was the worthy successor of Swami Yogananda. Thus I had a
pre-existing desire to meet him, and God fulfilled my wish."

Maharajshri and Swami Muktananda met three times after that.
Once in 1966, when Maharajshri came to Mumbai, he went to see Swami
Muktananda at Ganeshpuri. By then the cottage with the two rooms
had taken the form of a large ashram. Later, when Swami Muktananda
invited Maharajshri, he went there for an overnight stay. The third meeting took place in 1968, in Delhi, when Maharajshri's health was not
good. Swami Muktananda had come to Delhi and, upon hearing about
Maharajshri's ailing health, came to see him. These three meetings are
not the subject of this book. If God grants me time and preserves my
health then it will be more appropriate to write about these meetings in
the third part of *Churning of the Heart*. This book only describes the period up until 1965.

31. Mirdad

Maharajshri often used to discuss a book entitled *The Book of Mirdad*. A Christian Arab living in Lebanon wrote this book, originally in English. Eventually, it was translated into Arabic and many other languages of the world. Now the Radhaswami group in Punjab has published its Hindi and Punjabi translations. I do not remember how Maharajshri came across this book, but he was definitely moved by it.

The author of the book is Mikhail Naimy, who was born in 1889 and died in 1988. He studied in Lebanon, Russia and America. He wrote many books, but *The Book of Mirdad* is considered his best.

According to many mythological accounts, in ancient times a group of people survived the dissolution of the world by boarding a ship, as God had instructed them. The whole earth was submerged under water. For many days the ship swayed on the waves of the ocean. After the ocean became calm and the water level receded the ship came ashore. The population began to grow again. This story is related in almost all the religious traditions, with minor variations. Christians, Muslims and Jews call the captain of the ship Noah, and the Hindus call him Manu. Mirdad was one of the eight persons who were with Noah. The collection of his teachings is *The Book of Mirdad*.

When Noah was very old and saw that his end was near, he called his son, Shem. He said, "There is no certainty about life and, in any case, I have grown old. Be happy with your family. A time will come when everyone will be so involved in worldly affairs that no one will remember the creator. You should build a monastery on the top of this mountain and call it 'Noah's Ark.' Spread the divine gospel. Only nine of us were on the ship, therefore there must only be nine residents in the monastery. When one resident of the monastery dies, a new member will arrive automatically." Noah's Ark was established. Noah spent the rest of his life there.

Time passed and the population grew. Village after village sprouted up around Noah's Ark. People served the monastery very well due to their faith. The monastery became wealthy. Gradually the world began to influence the monastery. All kinds of facilities were added to it. Luxuries and amenities were in abundance. Ego, anger and greed crept in.

Once a resident of the monastery died and a new person came to take his place. He had torn clothes, matted hair, bare feet and a foul odor. The chief of the monastery refused to accept him. As a result of his repeated demands he was finally admitted as a servant. No one else came to live at the ashram. Eventually this man was accepted as a resident. After eight years he revealed his secret. He announced that he was Mirdad, one of the nine on Noah's ark. As a result he was given the seat of the Guru among all the residents of the monastery. The head of the ashram became envious. Mirdad gave away all the wealth of the monastery. He told the head of the ashram that his soul would wander in the ruins of the monastery for 150 years due to his greed and attachment. "Then from a certain direction a hungry, thirsty, ragged, naked man will come to you. You will be freed when you give him this book. Then you will turn to stone. How long you remain a stone cannot be said now with any certainty."

Later a man came, climbing the mountain by way of the specified path. His food, clothing and walking stick had been stolen from him. The chief's spirit gave the man the book and then turned to stone. This is *The Book of Mirdad*. Maharajshri advised us not to get involved in the history and events described in the book, but to digest the essence of its wisdom.

Maharajshri said, "The teaching of Mirdad, that the ark is no longer an ark, is so pertinent. So much gold, silver, luxury and gross objects, as the means of pleasure, have been heaped on its deck that it is ready to sink. The ocean is ready to swallow it into its belly. The ark, which was a monastery of renunciation, detachment, generosity and tolerance during the times of Noah, had become a home for selfishness, ego, anger and revenge. How can it be called an ark [a monastery]? Is such a ship capable of ferrying anyone across? Then Mirdad tells his companions,

'You might have loaded the ship with gold and silver, expanded the circle of followers and expanded its kingdom, but now the ship is about to sink. This great monument will soon become a ruin. It will exist only in history books. Only rumors will survive. The soul of the ship has died. It has lost all its high values of renunciation, love and spirituality.'

"Mirdad also says, 'The one who creates can also destroy, and it takes him but a moment. The one who lifts you up can also throw you down; in fact he raises some only to throw them down. He can give birth to many like himself, within himself, and merge them back at his own will. His creation is unique. Your ego is an extension of your consciousness. Your world expands according to your ego. If you are established in the single, undivided consciousness then you will see oneness in the whole world. If multiplicity exists in your consciousness then you will see multiplicity outside as well. You will experience the world as the same as your ego. This life is supported by ego. It is an extension of ego, and this life itself is ego. If your ego gives up the feeling of separateness then you yourself are the cosmic consciousness.'

"How close these words are to the thoughts written in the Upanishads. It feels as if these are the words of some ancient sage, but these are the words of an Arabic philosopher that echoed thousands of years ago. It seems that the same thought-process was prevalent throughout the entire world.

"Mirdad says, 'A man listens to the mind very quickly. How fast he is misdirected by the senses! Although he knows that the mind is deceitful and the senses are fooled by pleasures, he still trusts them easily. Is this not his foolishness? Where is his sense of discernment A man knows very well that whatever is visible in the world is a playful spectacle, yet he runs after things in the hope of achieving happiness. Why? He becomes tired of running, falls down, and fails to find happiness. Yet he continues to believe.'

"Mirdad continues, 'Whatever expands in the world one day is destroyed another day. Whatever is done is one day undone. Whatever exists is annihilated.' But the Shakti, which is the cause behind all creation and destruction, all growth and decline, neither expands nor diminishes. These are the characteristics of worldly things and scenery. Shakti is always the same, everlasting and beyond all changes.

"How philosophical are Mirdad's words! These can only be the words of a person who is fully illuminated within; who has directly seen the essence of cosmic consciousness and is fully familiar with the real nature of the visible world; who is not only a scholar, but has also experienced the truth personally.

"Mirdad says further, 'Spirituality is not a house or a flower garden. It is not a object or an element, it is not a chair or a table, and it cannot be sold or bought. It is a special state of the psyche. It can be attained anywhere. You do not need to go anywhere; you do not need any instrument. You do not have to run after anything. It can be attained very easily on this earth, under this sky, breathing the same air.'

"In fact, spirituality is very simple but the world and the mind together have made it very complex. The mind must simply turn away from the world. When Bulleshah [a Sufi saint from Punjab] asked the same thing of his Guru, he said, 'What is the difficulty in attaining God! The mind must simply be detached from the world and attached to God.' But the individual soul has become so weak that this simple task is very hard. What could be a more pitiable state for a human than this?"

The next day I took up the discussion again and asked, "Have you met Mirdad in the same way that you have met Agasha?"

Maharajshri said, "Mirdad was one of Noah's companions. Agasha was a pure soul. But it seems as though Mirdad never died. To contact him one does not need to channel. He can manifest whenever he wishes. He can be touched and he can be seen working like a common person. He lived during the times of Noah and, even centuries after Noah had passed away, he lived in Noah's monastery, namely Noah's Ark, with the head of the monastery, Shamadam. He was seen eating, walking and working like a common resident of the monastery. Anyone could meet him when they wanted. This means that Mirdad is not only a spirit, but a spirit that existed in a mortal form with the power to become invisible, just as he existed during the centuries that passed between Noah and Shamadam. There is no mention of his death anywhere. Hence, possibly, he lives in an invisible form somewhere. It is possible that he is visible to some aspirants, and some may sense his presence. No one has introduced himself as Mirdad to me so far.

"Agasha is in a different state. He lived in Egypt 7,000 years ago. He is busy helping souls through some medium or the other even today. He does not have a body. For contacting people he requires the assistance of someone with a body. He can also connect with highly evolved souls directly without a medium. My contact with him was without any medium. This contact was always on a subtle level. Agasha's direct contact is possible only for those who can reach those subtle levels.

"The Lord's Maya is strange. On the one hand he has thrown out the net of Maya and made arrangements for tormenting the individual soul; on the other hand he has given many spiritual practices and made holy beings who are immortal and entrusted with helping people. Another such example is Hanuman. He remains invisible despite having a physical body, and whenever necessary he manifests. There are possibly more temples of Hanuman then of Lord Rama in India. It seems that Mirdad is a similar, immortal, holy spirit, still having a physical body, remaining invisible, and active in helping spiritual aspirants and devotees.

"Now, whether I have met Mirdad or not, no one has asked me this question before, nor have I told anyone anything. Experiences of sadhan must be kept secret, otherwise the ego will strengthen and people will generate unnecessary judgements. Throughout the world invisible beings are moving around. In some places they make a permanent residence, but they frequent some regions more often than others. Their stay is also longer in these places. Malwa in Madhya Pradesh is one such region. Many invisible, holy beings reside and visit Malwa. When some people sense their presence, they consider them to be ghosts because they do not understand the difference between ghosts and holy spirits.

"Their work of helping people takes place in the morning, generally, when most spiritual aspirants are doing their sadhana. Some holy spirits stay in one place in meditation and spread spiritual vibrations. Others travel to bless aspirants, then move on. If someone is sleeping at that time, they miss the benefit of receiving blessings. Some holy spirits grant the experience of their presence and arouse knowledge in the heart of the aspirant. Some remain invisible but can be heard, whereas others manifest physically and talk to the devotee directly.

"I have had all kinds of experiences in meditation — from feeling the presence of holy beings to seeing them personally. Some of them introduced themselves and others did not. I do not know why, mostly they talk in Hindi. Perhaps they know all the languages of the world and talk to aspirants in their own language. Perhaps Mirdad came to me but did not introduce himself. Holy beings in costumes of different countries have manifested before me. The line of thinking of Mirdad significantly influences me. Judging from the manner of speaking, I did once feel that a being visiting me was Mirdad, but I cannot say anything with certainty."

Question: "Did any of them introduce themselves to you?"

Answer: "Yes, the great sage Galav [a disciple of Sage Vishwamitra] introduced himself to me, and so did Ashwatthama. My introduction to Aswatthama also involved his wound. I request that you not tell this to anyone while I am alive."

Question: "Is it possible that an aspirant may harbor a specific desire and that, over time, this feeling might take a form before the aspirant that could be interpreted as an invisible great being?"

Answer: "Yes, it is possible. But that is not the case with me. I am not talking about the vision of heavenly beings. If one does sadhana with a desire for contact with them, it is possible that this desire might bear fruition. However, meetings with invisible great beings can take place at any time, even when someone is not worshipping or meditating. Often, when I am talking to people, some invisible great soul will suddenly manifest and start talking to me. At that time I become silent for a little while and listen. People think I am trying to remember something, but I am engrossed in listening to the invisible great person."

Question: "In what form does Agasha meet you?"

Answer: "Agasha manifests in the form of a shadow and speaks to me in English. I do not know which language was spoken in Egypt 7,000 years ago, but now he talks only in English.

Question: "And what about Mirdad?"

Answer: "I already told you that I am not sure about seeing Mirdad."

Question: "Did you get any spiritual benefit from these encounters?"

Answer: "Definitely. Some clarify my doubts verbally, while others become the cause of some inexplicable experience within. The great sage Galav made me sit with him in meditation and nothing could be experienced except subtle vibrations of Shakti. My ego also dissolved in it."

Question: "Then how did this 'I' come back?"

Answer: "This is only a formality. One must accept the help of certain words for communication."

Question: "Did you feel the vibrations of Shakti at that very moment?"

Answer: "I am experiencing them even now. The world seems like a sport. Even in your talking I experience the activity of Shakti."

Question: "Does the Guru-Shakti [the power of the Guru] not do anything, so that you felt the need for the grace of these invisible masters?

Answer: "It is the grace of Guru-Shakti that manifests through the medium of these great invisible masters. Without the grace of the Guru these great masters would not manifest."

Question: "Do all aspirants receive the grace of invisible masters?"

Answer: "No. The level of sadhana of all aspirants does not reach these heights. When an aspirant is climbing the heights of spirituality, sadhan gets harder and harder. Invisible ascended masters see them struggling, then they descend a little and help out. Generally an aspirant is unable to rise to the level where he can come under the gaze of these ascended masters."

Question: "Is it necessary for all aspirants to see these invisible, great, holy souls? I have heard that upon attaining very high states, when unexpected siddhis [supernatural powers] arise, at that time the heavenly beings try to make aspirants fall down with the help of many different enticements."

Answer: "This is where the help of perfect, invisible holy spirits and ascended masters is essential. The inner fight between the heavenly beings and the holy spirits takes place at an extremely subtle level. However it is not necessary that all aspirants have such an opportunity."

While listening to all this I felt that I was still wandering in a wasteland, still searching along the path. Grains of the sand of worldly gross desires were hurting my eyes, the thirst for pleasure was drying my throat, and my body was aching with fatigue. A faint ray of hope was visible in the grace of the Guru, and yet it was not clear to me due to imperfections in my spiritual vision. Only Gurudev can help.

32. The Influence of Mirdad

The effect of Mirdad's thinking was clearly visible on Maharajshri when he used to compare the human body to a boat. It is a boat in which the human being must cross the vast, infinite and deep ocean of life and death. It is a boat that can face any calamity. It is a boat whose rudder is held by the Lord himself. But what can you say to the individual soul? He has snatched the rudder from the hands of God and seized control. He has become the captain of the boat, but has left it to the pounding, high waves of the ocean. He has even lost control of the boat. Now the boat is rocking helplessly in the fathomless sea. The waves take it wherever they want. It is always overcast with the danger of storm, rain and the wild creatures in the ocean.

In the fierce cyclone of ambitions, impurities and deep-rooted tendencies his boat rocks violently. Yet the boatman lies unconscious. Even if he wants to do something he cannot, because the oar has slipped from his hand and fallen into the sea. His companion, the mind, has deceived him and flown away in a tempest of desires. His senses, which once worked like obedient servants, have also abandoned him. A lonely and helpless soul, a boatman without an oar: What a wretched state he has brought upon himself and the boat!

The philosophical style of Mirdad would be visible when Maharajshri would say, "People of the world are engrossed in raising mountains of samskaras within themselves. The intoxication of suffering is so heavy that it seems as if people are happy only in anguish. Suffering is the only way of life for them. They have no idea where they want to go or where they are going. They have chosen a path that has no destination. They are going round and round in the same place as if in a maze. Their life has become that of a bullock

that is tied to a mortar stone. Nobody has time to search within himself.
So many weeds have grown within, so many thorny bushes have grown,
so many poisonous vines have spread and dense darkness has descended.
Who cares?"

Here, too, Mirdad appears to talk through Maharajshri, "Do not
let the water of pleasure and desire fill your boat or it will sink. Then
you will be unable to go on your journey. The water that has seeped into
your boat must be thrown back into the ocean. Your boat will be lighter.
However, do not waste your whole life throwing water from your boat.
Your goal is not to throw the water out of the boat. Your goal is the
journey, and this is only the preparation for the journey. Do not waste
time in washing and painting the boat. Do not pay attention to the
beauty of the boat, but on it usefulness. Do the appropriate work for
maintaining the boat because it is a vehicle for the journey. But do not
become overly involved in servicing it."

Every individual is either influenced by a specific personality or by
a number of them. Similarly, Maharajshri's personality was clearly influenced by Adi Shankaracharya, the great Tantra Master Abhinava Gupta,
the masters of our lineage, and other devotee saints. In the same way, his
thinking and discourses clearly reflected the influence of Mirdad. There
is no means to find out which other ascended masters came in contact
with him, and what he received from them. He also had an independent
line of thinking. He used to contemplate and study ideas from everywhere with an open mind and intellect, and accept ideas from one and
all without any prejudice. If an idea appealed to him he would accept it;
if not he would leave it. He would put it to test at the touchstone of his
experiences in meditation. If it did not pass the test completely he would
not accept it. Maharajshri did not have any difficulty in accepting the
thoughts of Mirdad. They had such clarity, simplicity, logical appeal and
in-depth philosophy in them that Maharajshri had no reservations in
accepting his style of thinking.

33. The Experience of Two Bodies

It was a hot summer afternoon. I was sitting on a bench on the verandah of the building near the cave. My eyes were open. My mind was filled with unusual peace. It felt as if the entire world had distanced itself from me. Suddenly I saw my own body before my eyes, separated from me, strolling in the garden in front of me. For a moment I was stunned. Then again I saw my body start to walk. Sometimes it climbed the stairs and at times it came down, At times it would pluck a flower from the chandani trees in the front and sometimes it would leap and jump like a monkey. The scene stayed before me for a while and then disappeared.

I thought, "What was that? I have two bodies! The body had the same face, the same height, weight and form, the same clothes. How is this possible? What kind of illusion is this? Which is my real body, this or that? Was I sitting on the bench or strolling in the garden! Am I going mad?" I remained lost in this mystery for quite sometime.

After Maharajshri went to bed at night I went to the cave to meditate. For some time physical kriyas occurred. Thoughts about the experience of the day came simultaneously. Suddenly the physical kriyas stopped. The torrent of thoughts also stopped. My mind became dazed and tranquil. I went into a kind of meditative state, and in that state saw my dead body lying on the floor. I was standing next to it watching it. Relatives and friends were hugging the dead body and crying. The house was gripped with mourning. I stood there laughing. I also felt like crying at the foolishness of the mourners. How foolish they are! Those who believe that their body belongs to them do not know that, one day, the condition of their body will be the same.

What an experience Goddess Kriya-Shakti gave! I was alive and dead at the same time! I was the seer as well as the seen. How did one body become two? I was the one for whom people were crying, as well the one who watched them cry. What an amazing experience of life and death together! I drowned deep in thought again. One wave of thought would subside in the mind and another would rise. Now I was lying on a bed in a half-awake state. I experienced my body starting to separate and become two. Slowly a second body came out of the first and stood apart in the air. My body lay there like a corpse. I looked at it for a little while, then started to fly. I crossed the sky, flew over rivers, forests and towns, and reached a land of lush greenery full of flowers and fragrance. After traveling over that land I returned and found my body still lying lifeless. I re-entered my body. The body was filled with life again. My trance was broken.

Within a few hours I had three experiences of my body becoming two. These experiences made me think deeply. I was unable to under-stand what Kriya-Shakti was trying to explain to me. What samskaras were being cleared? What sheath was being removed? I am only one. My whole life I have been only one. How then can I experience myself as two? What is the secret? Is my dual personality manifesting? All kinds of questions and doubts began to erupt. I passed the entire night in thought.

During the morning walk I expressed my problem to Maharajshri. I described the three experiences and asked him what they meant. Maharajshri said, "Attachment to the body is not cleared without such experi-ences. No matter how much reflection and contemplation you do, no matter how much self-study, japa and worhip you do, yoga and pranayaama you do, your attachment to the body will not be destroyed. Repeated experiences like these bring the understanding that life is separate from the body and may leave the being at any time. Then the process of de-tachment from the body begins. A single experience like this is not enough. I will explain the subject systematically.

"Your first experience is called Swaroopa Darshan, seeing one's own form separate from one's self. You see your body separate from yourself just as you see your form in a mirror. There aren't two bodies, but it seems as if there are. This experience does not depend on the subtle body; the physical body is simply seen as a reflection. A second body arising out of one body is experienced when the subtle body is separated from the physical body. Nothing like this takes place in Swaroopa Darshan. Swaroopa Darshan is not an experience, but a feeling of an experience. This feeling does not even begin to destroy bodily attachment, but it is a first step in that direction. It initiates the awareness of two bodies from only one body. The activity of your second body is definitely similar to that of your original body, based upon the same samskaras, but your ego did not leave the body. The ego identity was still present in the physical body only.

"In the second experience, you saw your corpse. The end of your physical body was right there, present in front of you. When death is visible, one is afraid because of one's attachment to the body. The destruction of attachment to the body can begin. Your attachment to the body has not yet ended because your ego identity still exists in the body. In that experience, the death that you see is not of your body but of the image of the body. It is as if someone were to act like he was dying, and then saw a picture of his own act of being dead. This is a very gross example, whereas your experience took place at the subtle level. Here, also, the subtle body did not separate from the physical body. It is also only a feeling, in which the subtle ego identity remains in the physical body. It is based on accumulated impressions. Thus it is much more significant and has greater effect. Seeing friends and relatives cry strengthens the sense of the futility of the world. This is part of the journey of detachment from the body.

"Your third experience is clearer because in that you observe your body after separating from it. Your physical body becomes your body's reflection. Your ego identity, the witness, escapes from the physical body along with your subtle body and the body lies like a corpse. This is not a feeling; it is an experience. Prana [life force] still remains in the physical body, but all its activities are at a standstill. Both bodies remain tied through a thin thread of consciousness, which keeps the physical body alive, but its activities take place in the subtle body only. This is the experience of death while being alive. Here the subtle body separates from the experiences of the physical body. This is the beginning of the destruction of attachment to the body. The destruction is not complete until impressions of this experience remain in the psyche. While such experiences are taking place attachment to the body appears to have ended, but as soon as the experience is over attachment resurfaces. Therefore such experiences must occur repeatedly.

"There is one more thing: Right now these experiences are not under the control of your resolve. They are a play of Shakti, depending upon your accumulated impressions. They may occur often based on certain factors. A stage may come where they come under the control of your resolve, then the subtle body could leave the physical body and remain separate as long as you wish and re-enter when you please. Then the attachment to the body really begins to be destroyed. Now the kriya controls you; then the kriya will be in your control. But to reach this stage the ego identity must rise above the psyche [chitta] and settle in pure consciousness. The science of entering another body is related to this. If you attain mastery in this science then you may enter any dead body with your subtle body. The body then will be less important to you and your attachment to it will end.

"We often experience in our dreams that we are one of the characters in the dream, and we see the reflection of our individual self along with the entire dream, like a spectator. One of our forms is a part of the dream; another form is the spectator watching the dream. However the form that is a part of the dream does not have the sense of an observer or any ego, and hence this experience does not destroy attachment to the body.

"The physical body is enwrapped by a subtle body. The subtle senses of the subtle body manifest and become gross. Sometimes they take the form of a human, and sometimes of an animal or bird. At death the subtle senses merge back into the subtle body. Some aspirants experience this while they are alive. Subtle senses, along with the mind and ego, separate from the physical body and merge into the subtle body. The aspirant realizes that the physical body is lifeless. The subtle body is the true personality of the individual soul. The subtle body is tied to the physical body by a cord of consciousness. Through the medium of this subtle cord, the subtle senses manifest as physical senses. Through the same cord of consciousness, resolves, mental tendencies, emotions and ill will reach the physical senses. Death means the breaking of this cord that connects the subtle and physical bodies. When the subtle body moves out and goes away while the subtle cord remains connected, it gives the experience of the separateness of the subtle and gross bodies."

This analysis clarified the following:

(1) The separation of the subtle body from the gross physical body is an experience.

(2) This experience can occur frequently on the basis of accumulated impressions.

(3) It is also possible that this experience may never repeat.

(4) The goal of this experience is to remove the sense of attachment to the body.

(5) It may be regarded as a siddhi [supernatural power] that arises in sadhan.

Question: "There doesn't seem to be any mention of this science in *Yoga Darshan*."

Answer: "It is mentioned in the form of an aphorism in *Yoga Darshan*. A chitta [psyche] may be formed that is free from mind-stuff and does not have any accumulated impressions. If this technique is used with the help of the subtle body for some special purpose then it is not the nirmaana-chitta [the created psyche] but it is a siddha-chitta [the pure psyche]. This is what Adi Shankaracharya did. When Bharati, the wife of Mandan Mishra, initiated a debate pertaining to the science of sex, he did not have any knowledge of that field and so he asked for a period of one month to prepare his answer. A king of the area had just died. Shankaracharya established his own body in a meditative state in a cave. He left his physical body and entered the dead body of the king with his subtle body. The king came to life. While maintaining the chastity of his own body, Shankaracharya attained knowledge of the science of sex through the king's gross physical body. His subtle body was present in the gross physical body of the king. Hence the impressions of that knowledge could accumulate in it and the memory of that knowledge was also retained This was not the nirmaana-chitta, it was a siddha-chitta. However, if the ego identity remains in the physical body and a new chitta that is free from ego is created then it is a nirmaana-chitta. This is how it is referred to in *Yoga Darshan*. Since *Yoga Darshan* is a scripture written in the form of aphorisms, most things are conveyed through hints."

Question: "Without this experience, are there no other means of getting rid of attachment to the body?'

Answer: "No. That is not the case. It is not necessary to have the experience of a subtle body giving up the physical body. But it is necessary that, somehow, the separation of the subtle body and physical body be experienced. Only after this experience will the aspirant believe himself to be separate from the physical body. Knowledge of the scriptures can make one think — the aspirant can fly high in the sky of imagination — but it cannot give direct experiential knowledge. Only after this experience does the aspirant's detachment mature. Bear in mind that this experience is only about the distinction of the gross and subtle levels in the nature, not about the difference between inertness and consciousness. Nonetheless, the aspirant must go through this experience first."

Question: "If, in the tradition of Shaktipat, an aspirant experiences consciousness from the very beginning then what is the need for the experience of gross and subtle levels of creation?"

Answer: "The experience of consciousness that you are talking about in the tradition of Shaktipat is not the experience of Shakti, but that of the activities of Shakti, through the medium of the chitta and senses, based on samskaras [accumulated impressions]. This does not lift the aspirant above the body, nor does he begin to experience a feeling of separation of the body from the self. Layers must be removed from the chitta in order to experience separateness of the subtle body from the physical body. This is the first thing Shakti does after awakening. This is the primary stage of any aspirant, no matter what his experiences are and how intense they are. Up until that point he has believed himself to be a part of the physical world only. Full knowledge of the distinction between the physical and subtle bodies is acquired only after the layers covering the chitta are removed."

Question: "Does that mean that the study of scriptures, the recital of verses from the scriptures, worship and spiritual practice, japa and pranayaama, and so forth, are all useless?"

Answer: "No, they are not useless. But they are not the ultimate answer to everything. They represent efforts of the aspirant toward awakening. The experience of the physical and subtle levels does not depend on these efforts. It depends on the experience of the workings of the Shakti. All these efforts are done to initiate the activities of the Shakti."

Question: "Is attachment to the body destroyed once the distinction of the physical and subtle bodies is experienced?"

Answer: "No. Attachment to the body does not go away with one such experience. One must have that experience repeatedly. Each time samskaras will diminish a little. Eventually total detachment will arise, and attachment to the body will go away completely."

Question: "This indicates that the spiritual journey is very long. Aspirants very quickly begin to celebrate, believing that they are fulfilled. But the reality is that the layers over their chitta are not yet removed and the attachment to their body is intact. There is no question that there remain many steep climbs and other milestones along the way."

Answer: "Each aspirant can decide this independently, by looking within. The experience of separation of the gross and subtle bodies takes place at a very subtle level, whereas, mostly, aspirants are still involved in the external characteristics of materialism, such as desires, anger, ego and selfishness. This is why it is conveyed repeatedly that spirituality is not a subject only of words. The layers of Maya dissolve one after another. It is going to take time. This is a journey of many lifetimes, and that, too, if it goes on continually."

34. Swami Narayan Tirth Dev Maharaj

In those days, during my spare time, I was trying to write a book, *Narayan Upadeshamrit* [a biographical sketch, in Hindi, of Swami Narayan Tirth Dev Maharaj]. It was quite a job to collect the required material. The Guru brother of Maharajshri, Swami Pranavananda, was staying in the Dewas ashram during that time. He had lived with Narayan Tirth Dev Maharaj for a few days in his ashram. I learned some things from him, but Swami Pranavananda left after a short stay and I was unable to collect enough material for the book. Only thirty to forty pages were possible. In the meantime I found a book written by Narayan Tirth Dev Maharaj in Bengali. Maharajshri knew some Bengali so he would translate for me. I could write the book based on that. The thoughts presented by Maharajshri regarding Narayan Tirth Dev Maharaj included what follows:

(1) Shri Narayan Tirth Dev Swamiji was a great being of such high caliber that his Gurudev [Swami Gangadhar Tirth Maharaj] put all his faith in him, which proved to be very fruitful. His Gurudev was a renunciate, an ascetic, who loved solitude, and yet he wished for the spiritual elevation of the populace. He was in search of a person who would live a simple ascetic life and work for the spiritual elevation of the people. In Swamiji he found such a personality. Shri Swamiji never sought money. He never gave initiation for the sake of money. Like ancient seers he ran the ashram on donations and lived in extreme poverty. Many kings and landlords came for initiation but he turned them down. He thought twice before trusting a rich person. On the other hand, his Shakti flowed like the River Ganges; all of India is swimming in it even today. Among his disciples there were great teachers such as Shankar Purushottam Tirth Maharaj, Shri Yoganandji Maharaj and Shri Ashwini Kumar Bhattacharya. They expanded his work. Spirituality grows in a life of poverty, renunciation and asceticism like a lotus grows in mud. A true example of this

was Swamiji Maharaj.

(2) The second example offered by Swamiji was of lasting patience. His Guruji instructed him to return home and fulfill his family duties. He further told him that his Shakti would remain dormant during that time. "When your duties are completed then the Shakti will become active again."

He went back home, took a job, and fulfilled all his family responsibilities while continuing his sadhana. For almost twenty years he carried on his japa, waiting for Shakti to be activated. He recited the Gita, sang God's praise, and so forth. He hungered for spirituality while performing his householder duties. This is an example everyone must contemplate and imitate. His patience, enthusiasm and perseverance for spirituality were so high that no difficulties or duties could interfere. In all kinds of circumstances he kept on marching on the spiritual path. After nineteen and a half years, the day came for which he had been waiting. The activity of Shakti manifested. And when it manifested, it was such that Swamiji started to shine like a brilliant star in the sky of spirituality.

(3) What was his ashram? Two huts of straw and an idol of mother Kali under a banyan tree. There was no room for sadhana, no room for satsang [spiritual discourse], no room for people to come and stay, and no bathroom. Those living in the ashram and those who visited led a very simple life. They bathed in the lake, and meals and sadhana took place under the trees. There was no unnecessary conversation and no waste of time. Strict discipline was followed, but the atmosphere was full of divine love. There was no room for likes, dislikes, anger or gossiping. Every nook and corner of the ashram was overflowing with experiences of Shakti. The meditation room was wherever you sat; the temple of God was wherever you went. You could feel the presence of Swamiji Maharaj wherever you went. It felt as if devotion and Shakti were dancing everywhere in the ashram.

(4) East Bengal [now Bangladesh] was a very strange country. In the rainy season all the rivers and streams would swell and become one. Water flowing from Assam would come down and spread throughout the land. A major part of the country would be under water. In the

middle of farms, soil would be piled to build hills on which houses could be constructed. One would need a boat to go from one house to another. Swamiji Maharaj used to go out for alms in such difficult conditions. For fire he would go to the forest and fetch wood, then do sadhan. How ascetic the life was, and how spiritual the aspirations were! When Bramhachari Atma Prakash [Swami Shankar Purushottam Tirth Maharaj] went to live there, he began going out for alms. Bramhachariji stayed in the service of Guru Maharaj for eight years. By then other people had also arrived. How a spiritual person can live in poverty was demonstrated by the way in which the ashram was run by Swamiji Maharaj. He was more interested in giving initiation to those who had little. Thus there was negligible funding from the disciples.

(5) It was a rule in the ashram that if any visitor got food from the market it must be shared with everyone. If it was not for all then it could not be for one's self either. Time was not to be wasted, and all the time was spent in reading and spiritual activities. If, at any time, anyone misbehaved or said something inappropriate then it was tolerated. No one could waste any gifts of nature. It was one's duty to live in such a way as to present an example of spirituality, and to present a brilliant example of a life of endurance, generosity and asceticism. Those who arrived from outside burned with the fire of desires, tendencies, and likes and dislike; they were in dire need of affection, love and peace. If people came to the ashram and had to face the same worldly behavior then their coming to the ashram would be a waste.

(6) Swamiji Maharaj was the founding teacher of Shaktipat. This school of knowledge and practice had existed in the past, but it was like a river flowing underground. Swamiji Maharaj began the great task of unearthing it, just as one might excavate hidden treasure from the earth and offer it to the people. It was the responsibility of his holiness to bring it to the world in its pure form. He emphasized that one should not include the fulfillment of desires in spirituality. By involving desires in sadhana, it becomes impure. He explained this to the disciples repeatedly. He also demonstrated, through his own behavior, how to live without desires. He taught how to endure difficulties and sufferings caused

by destiny [prarabdha]. Had he wished, he could have accumulated many things for his comfort and luxury. There was no shortage of rich people desiring initiation from him. But he never paid attention. He always based his decision whether or not to give initiation on the state of mind of the person.

(7) Swamiji used to rise at three o' clock in the morning. Residents of, and visitors to, the ashram were also awakened. Exceptions were made to this daily discipline only when someone was sick. Drinking tea in the morning was not a norm. Therefore, after performing the morning ablutions, the only thing to do was sadhan.

(8) Swamiji Maharaj had met his Guru Maharaj only once when he received diksha. Yet he constantly remembered his Guru's instructions. He followed his instructions throughout his life. After returning home he remembered Guru Maharaj daily before doing his prayers, puja, and so forth. Only after that did he undertake worldly affairs. Even while he was busy with worldly duties he remembered Gurudev and experienced his presence near him at all times. When he became a Guru he used to always feel that he was doing this work as a service to his Guru. Even though the Guru was physically distant, the Guru was always with him mentally.

(9) The account of Swamiji Maharaj would be incomplete without mention of the service of Atma Prakashji. It would be difficult to find such devoted service rendered to any Guru, incessantly for eight years. He was so intoxicated in serving his Guru that he could not think of anything else. He would go out for alms by swimming across the waters, bring wood for fuel, sweep the ashram, and still be ready for all the work of the ashram. He would rise at three in the morning for sadhan and then get busy with the ashram duties. He was like a Bramhachari in the times of the ancient rishis [sages] and believed that the Guru was his God. Guru-seva, the service of the Guru, was his worship. In comparison to his, the services of other disciples seemed meager.

Later on, when he was established as Swami Shankar Purushottam Maharaj, he still worked with feelings of Guru-seva in his mind, just as before. For him doing Guru-seva while living in the ashram, and sitting on the Guru's chair, were two different forms of Guru-seva. If one nurtures the ego of being a Guru himself, it leads to his downfall.

(10) We have moved away from the path shown by Narayan Tirth Dev Maharaj. Ashrams have added all kinds of comforts. The attitude of seva has vanished. The lack of commitment to sadhan has grown. No one follows the Guru's instructions. Initiations are given in order to increase the number of disciples. Discrimination of worthy and unworthy is getting lost. Generally, greed and ego are on the high pinnacle. Sadhan is done with an aim to fulfill desires.

When a religious tradition or philosophical school first begins, its form is different. Slowly impurities start to enter and separate groups are formed. When secret knowledge is revealed to a great being it is pure. With wider exposure the number of its followers grows but its purity declines. All paths have had the same fate, and recent ones have suffered the same. As a path proliferates, its original goal is lost and the distance from its original form increases. With the rise of a new path of knowledge its decline begins.

Question: "If you have had encounters with so many invisible ascended masters then you must definitely be seeing Narayan Tirthji also."

Answer: "Yes, I do see him. All this is the fruit of his grace. He definitely manifests before me, and I see him in all other masters, too. I also see in their hearts the feelings of faith and surrender to Gurudev. He has been the source of my inspiration at each and every step.

"Coming back to what I was saying, every path of knowledge goes through the process of manifestation and disappearance. The path of Shaktipat is no exception. The path that rises will fall one day. Someday only the external shell of Shaktipat will remain and its soul will be gone. Slowly people will forget the concept of Shaktipat."

Question: "Then what will happen to the resolve of Swami Gangadhar Tirth Maharaj, the Gurudev of Swami Narayan Tirth Dev Maharaj? He revealed the path of Shaktipat because it is very hard to perform spiritual practice in the Kaliyuga [the Dark Age]."

Answer: "No resolve can remain effective forever. The Lord's resolve to create the cosmos also ends with pralaya [the Grand Dissolution]. Every resolve rises and then dissolves. Those who are serious about sadhan have support. It cannot last forever. Many great beings have come and tried to bring people onto a good path, but only a few have been able to follow. The world continues to tread on in its old ways."

Question: "Please tell me why Narayan Tirthji never went back to meet his Guru?"

Answer: "Those days were very different from today. Railways, buses and roads were not developed. Most people journeyed on horse-carts, bullock-carts, or on foot. The distance between Madaripur in East Bengal and Jagannathpuri was not short. Due to poverty, Narayan Tirthji was not able to bear a large expense. If he went on foot, it would take a long time. The main duty for him was to do as Gurudev had instructed him. Fulfilling his duties with the sense of Guru-seva was more important than meeting him.

"Once a gentleman went to Jagannathpuri and, upon his return, gave the news of Gurudev's merging with the Divine, but Gurudev never departed from Swamiji's heart. He possibly passed his responsibilities to Narayan Tirthji Maharaj and ended the play of his mortal form."

Now I wanted to stay in solitude somewhere and complete the book. In those days a mahatma named Vilinatma used to come to visit Maharajshri. I went with him to a farmhouse in Lasalgaon, in Nasik district. I stayed there for fifteen days, completed the book and came back.

35. The Subject of Succession

One day, during the morning walk, Maharajshri said, "Now I am seventy-five years old and my health is likely to deteriorate slowly. I would like to spend the remaining time in quiet, retired from all activities. Therefore I suggest that you accept the succession of this lineage and take care of ashram responsibilities."

I was not ready for such a thing. The idea was placed before me so suddenly. After being silent for a little while I said, "Maharajshri, I am a person who likes solitude. It is your Shakti that makes me do all this work for the ashram; without that my skill in worldly affairs is nothing. Before coming to Dewas I lived in solitude. Besides, I have hardly been able to become a disciple. How can I be a Guru? This is why I have not yet been able to follow your instruction to give initiation. Thirdly, I am younger than everyone. Many other worthy people were here before me. From among them, whomever in your opinion is deserving, please, announce him as your successor."

After listening to me that day Maharajshri did not say anything more. But two or three days later he opened the subject, asking, "So what have you been thinking about the subject of being my successor?"

I pleaded, "I presented my thoughts to you the other day." Maharajshri became silent again.

Now I began to think of ways to avoid the problem of succession. If he was still considering the idea he would ask the question again in a few days. After thinking for some time I proposed the name of a certain Bramhachariji and presented a strong case in his favor. Maharajshri relented.

A letter was sent to that Bramhachariji inviting him to come. When a proposal of succession was placed before him he accepted it after some hesitation. I breathed a deep sigh of relief. I could not even imagine such a thing for me. There was no comparison between Maharajshri and me.

Where was his perfect personality, scholarship, high level of sadhana and worldly wisdom, and where was I?

In the evening, after a few visitors had come to the ashram, Maharajshri announced Bramhachariji as his successor. "I have appointed this person as my successor and he has accepted happily. I will depart for Rishikesh in a few days. In my absence the ashram will be the responsibility of Bramhachariji. I hope that you will all give him full support and cooperation."

I began to explain the functioning of the ashram to the Bramhachariji the same day. In my absence Maharajshri also explained a few things to him. I suggested to Maharajshri that, since a successor had been appointed, we send out a written announcement. He responded by saying, "What is the hurry?"

We went to Rishikesh with a few residents of Dewas, and Bramhachariji started to take care of the ashram. He gave discourses and watched over the administration of the ashram. But suddenly, something happened and he became uncomfortable. Perhaps someone said something unpleasant. Perhaps there was an argument with someone or someone threatened him. He was disturbed. Residents of the ashram tried to pacify him, but he did not listen and left. When we received the information by letter, Maharajshri said, "See? You asked me to send out a written announcement. But I knew that he would not last."

36. The Stay in Rishikesh

Towards the end of 1962, Maharajshri went to Rishikesh. Several people from Dewas were with him. Maharajshri preferred to go there in the winter. In the first place, very few tourists went there during winter, and many saints living there traveled during that season, so the environment was peaceful. The cottage of a saint became available for Maharajshri right on the banks of the Ganges, near Triveni Ghat. We all stayed in the cottage. Maharajshri used to take a bath in the Ganges every day. First he would take 8-10 dips in the river, then rub his body, then again dip in the river, then rub his body again. He enjoyed bathing in the Ganges in all seasons. He would visit Garuda Chatti at least once during these trips to Rishikesh. Now there is a road on the other side of the Ganges, but in those days, beyond Rishikesh, there were only footpaths. The first stop used to be Garuda Chatti. Now Garuda Chatti exists only in name. Only a small tea stall, an empty ruin of Kali Kamali Dharmashala, and a deserted temple of Garuda remain, about four miles after crossing the Laxman Jhula. The beauty of the Himalayas can be seen there.

I still remember the scene of Maharajshri seated in the courtyard of the Garuda Temple, surrounded by devotees. The discussion was spiritual. Maharajshri said, "A human being is in such an illusion. He believes that the world is the cause of happiness and misery. The world is before him, as well as within. He sleeps and wakes up in the world. He does not know anything besides the world, neither is he interested in knowing more. Every moment is spent in illusion, and every step is taken within the same illusion. He forgets that the world is inert and cannot be active without being mixed with life force, the power of consciousness. The lifelessness of the body is realized at death. At that time the life force [Prana-Shakti] has ceased working through the medium of the body and has left the body. Every act of an individual is also lifeless. He may be served food, but he cannot eat a bite until the life force puts the hand in motion to take the food and place it in the mouth.

"The fruit of karma of an individual is also lifeless, because life force is required to turn karma into prarabdha [destiny]. To experience the fruits of karma the body alone is not enough; it needs to combine with life force. The individual soul is so unintelligent that he has forgotten the power of the life force and considers the world, karma and the fruits of karma as everything. The shining of the sun, the floating of clouds, the rain, the growing trees, the karma of an individual soul, resolves, feelings — everything is the activity of the power of consciousness. How misdirected the individual soul is! Can a jail arrest someone and lock someone up on its own? Can a jiva [the individual soul] take even a breath in the absence of the active life force? Can dinner be ready just by getting all the ingredients together? Can one go anywhere without the motion of the body? The experience of that life force is spirituality. The removal of the illusion is spirituality. Manifestation of the truth is spirituality.

"The world is unnecessarily blamed for being the cause of bondage. How can the lifeless world be the cause of bondage or liberation? If you must believe then believe that the world is the cause of liberation as well as bondage. In reality, it is not the world but attachment to the world that is the cause of bondage, and detachment from the world is the cause of liberation. This attachment is the main problem for the individual soul. When it arises it becomes the cause of bondage, and when it withdraws it gives liberation. The world is only an apparent screen on which attachment rises and sets. The real basis is the chitta [psyche], on which the play of attachment goes on and on. This drama keeps the being so engrossed that he has lost all his senses and is submerged in the world.

"The divine power is everywhere. It is in each and every cell of the body, and in each and every particle. It is the doer, the giver and the cause of every undulation in the chitta [psyche] of the individual soul. When the chitta of the jiva abandons its refuge in the divine power and becomes egoistic, then the omnipresence of God disappears. The chitta of the individual soul, his body and the world become inanimate, and when this quality of inertia expands further it persists for life after life. A living being takes birth in dense oblivion, it lives a life in stupor, and dies in ignorance. This dense oblivion also is nothing other than a state of the chitta [psyche], and it does not end for a long time."

High mountain peaks lush with greenery were towering all around. In the center the sweet sound of the flowing Ganges was pleasing to the ears. Somewhere streams were flowing and somewhere birds were chirping. Maharajshri went on talking in this peaceful place, so abundant with natural beauty, and all the devotees were listening as if enchanted by his words. A few persons from the village in the mountains also came and sat in the back. Whether they were able to understand anything or not they alone could tell, but they were sitting comfortably and quietly.

"Like two ends of a line, at one end of the world there is bondage and on the other there is liberation. Bondage and liberation coexist in the chitta [psyche]. But liberation is suppressed in one corner and bondage is dancing freely. The kingdom of bondage is huge; his army is strong and always ready to face the enemy. Great warriors, such as desire, lust, anger and selfishness, are his generals. Just as King Indra [king of the heavenly beings] had to flee due to fear of demons, so moksha [liberation] hides its head. Moksha [liberation] is always alone, without any army and without any companion. It possesses limitless strength but all that strength is bottled up. The entire kingdom belongs to him, but he owns nothing. Moksha [liberation] is like Shiva. Although he gives everything to the world, Shiva himself applies ashes to his body and lives in a cemetery, or goes to the Kailash Mountain peak and remains in samadhi. He gives blessings and strength even to the demons and he himself falls into difficulty.

"Moksha [liberation] means freedom from the duality of happiness and misery in the world. The world is filled with duality. With the affluence of the world the dichotomy of happiness and misery increases. Even if affluence does not continue for as long as the world itself, duality remains. The affluence, comforts and luxuries of the world perpetuate duality, and as long as there is prarabdha the world is not going to leave you alone. It is like a black blanket that will not leave you even if you wish to give it up. In reality, the individual soul has grabbed the world and is crying out. What stupidity, what ignorance! The individual soul puts his hand in the fire and then shouts, 'Help! I am burning!'

"The world is an enigma. When was it created? How was it made? Why was it made? Nobody knows. It is even hard to say whether God has answers. God only knows. It is said that God knows, but common people are troubled by it. It is said that the world only appears to be real. It may be so, but it has been influencing our chitta [psyche] and our chitta goes on collecting the effects. The science of spirituality says the cause of this is attachment. This attachment transforms ego into pride. Attachment creates prarabdha [destiny] and causes experiences of happiness and miseries. Therefore the individual soul must give up attachment.

"Attachment makes one imagine a different world within than the world made by God, a world of my family, my money, my body, my karma and its fruits. This 'Me, mine and yours' is nothing but attachment, whereas, in reality, nothing is yours. All this is given to the individual soul for experiencing and fulfilling one's duties. As soon as the feeling of 'mine' appears happiness and miseries arise. Then why in the world succumb to 'me and mine'? Why not experience everything as God's? This is where the journey of spirituality begins. Whatever prarabdha presents — happiness or misery — both are taken as the grace of God. If there is fame or disgrace one endures them equally. Thus each and every moment of life is spent in the service of God. This is the basis of spirituality."

Question: "We came from Dewas and are listening to your nectar-like words in the beautiful surroundings of the Himalaya. Is this also prarabdha?"

Answer: "Yes, this is prarabdha, and the difficulties along the journey were also prarabdha. Prarabdha presents different circumstances, and your reaction to them is your karma."

Question: "To endure prarabdha with peaceful acceptance is sadhan?"

Answer: "Yes, tolerance, or peaceful acceptance, is definitely sadhan.

But prarabdha is mainly for depleting existing samskaras and preventing the accumulation of new samskaras. Earnestness, generosity and forgiveness play a major role in this. But if this is the limit of the aspirant's sadhana then it is not easy to hold fast to this mood, and when it is disturbed the sadhan of depleting prarabdha is lost. Therefore cultivating a feeling of God's omnipresence is essential. A mood is only a mood; it changes continually. To hold fast to this mood it is essential to keep doing puja, reciting scriptures, mantras, japa, and so forth. Once the experience of God's energy occurs within, then that experience becomes a support for the mood [of detachment] that opens the pathway to the experience of God's presence everywhere in the world.

"The world is a beautiful garden full of flowers, vines and trees. It is attractive, and the basis of its beauty and fragrance is God's omnipresence. But the truth is hidden behind the beauty and fragrance of the garden. The garden will perish one day. The blooming flowers will wilt one day. Trees and vines spread, but they will dry one day. This garden is temporary, but the omnipresent Shakti of God is eternal and real. As long as the mind of a person clings to the world, it goes on blooming and wilting, spreading and drying along with the world. This is the experience of happiness and unhappiness. Therefore attention must be focused on the omnipresence of God, and experiences in the world must be lived with detachment."

Evening was approaching so it was best to return. The villagers from the mountain also were ready to get up and go. The sun was going behind the mountains and the shadows of the trees were very long. Everyone had a cup of tea at the tea stall and started to go towards Rishikesh. Maharajshri continued with the spiritual discussion along the way.

"Garuda is considered to be the vehicle of Lord Vishnu. He flies in the sky at a very high speed. Nothing can interfere with his high speed. Second, Garuda is the enemy of poisonous snakes. He eats them. In the old days there were two main problems for travelers. One was fatigue and the other was fear of poisonous snakes in the jungle. At the first stop a temple of Garuda was constructed. Travelers prayed to Garuda for a speedy completion of their yatra [pilgrimage]. They would pray,

'Let us not grow tired, just as you do not get tired while flying. Let us fly as you do. Oh, Lord, please protect us from poisonous snakes along the way. We are on a pilgrimage for a glimpse of Lord Vishnu, thus we surrender to you.'

"Now we will try to understand this allegory from a spiritual point of view. The journey of the Uttara Khanda [the northern sector] is an external symbol of the inner spiritual journey. The inner journey is very long, hard and arduous. Repeatedly the aspirant is disappointed and says, 'I cannot continue.' The poisonous snakes of worldly pleasure move about him and at times even bite. The poison of the bites creates huge obstacles. Garuda is a symbol of Prana-Shakti [life force]. Prana-Shakti moves our vital air around. It performs internal and external functions with spontaneity. Shakti is the only destroyer of worldly desires. Lord Vishnu maintains the world and helps devotees through the medium of Shakti. To move forward to reach Lord Vishnu, devotees must surrender to the inner Shakti in the form of Garuda. This is the secret of Garuda puja.

"In the path of devotion, Garuda is the Kundalini. Lord Vishnu sends his vehicle, Garuda, meaning Shakti, to bring his devotees. In other words, with the awakening of Shakti a vehicle is made available to the devotee. You all know that the spiritual journey, after awakening, becomes easy like a railway journey. That is why it is called Shaktopaaya [solution through Shakti]. Anvopaaya is like walking on foot. Garuda is a vehicle that not only helps in completing the journey speedily, but also removes obstacles. Lord Vishnu does not really need a vehicle for himself because he is omnipresent from the beginning. His vehicle is useful to his devotees in his name. The power of Vishnu is called Garuda in some places, and Mahamaya in others."

By now we had arrived at Laxman Jhula. We had crossed the Ganges while looking into its depths. Horse carriages were available for hire. Now even taxis are available. Now there is also a bridge between Rishikesh and Laxman Jhula. In those days such facilities did not exist.

37. A Description of the Ganges River

It was evening; the sun was ready to set. Maharajshri was sitting on the sandy bank of the Ganges and watching the river continuously. Suddenly he said, "Like the Ganges, the inner Ganga [river] is also very deep and fast. Who knows what samskaras are stuck in the depth of our chitta and how old they are? Ganga dives forcefully to great depths and brings up samskaras from the bottom to the surface of its flowing waters. In reality, this inner Ganga is much deeper. Many of its kriyas [spontaneous activities] take place so invisibly and secretly that even the aspirant himself is not aware of them. The way in which the Ganges makes a loud noise when its waters strike large rocks — similarly, when samskaras are brought out and many obstacles come forth, multifarious kriyas manifest and the inner Ganga marches on and on. When the Ganges strikes the rocks, the rocks continue to exist, but the inner Ganga takes a sigh of relief only after removing inner obstacles.

"There is a mythological story in the scriptures that says when Ganga was brought to Earth by Bhagiratha, it first descended into the locks of Lord Shankar's hair. Its flow started from there. The visible world is knotted and spread out like the locks of Lord Shankar's hair. The whole creation, animate and inanimate nature, has spread like the matted locks of Lord Shiva's hair. The whole creation, including the mind, intellect, sushumna and the six chakras, are part of the expanse of the matted locks of Shiva's hair. The Earth is the grossest form of his locks, and it is the element pertaining to the Mooladhar chakra. The Ganga descends into the Mooladhar chakra. This is the awakening of the Shakti. First, the Ganges wanders in the locks of Shiva's hair. Kundalini has to move in circles to open the kundals [twirls], and only after that does it start to rise in the sushumna. Removing one obstacle after another, passing through waves of various moods and plays, the inner Ganga proceeds to merge with her beloved, the soul. Sometimes her flow separates into many streams, and at other times it merges back into one. During floods she breaks through her banks, then again returns within her main boundaries and starts the journey again to meet her beloved. As the beloved ocean approaches near, her noise and force subside and her kriyas becomes very serene. The work of destroying deep samskaras is over. Still the eagerness and joy of meeting her beloved keeps on growing. After she merges with the ocean the individual's separate identity vanishes."

Question: "Yesterday you made Shakti the high flying Garuda, and today you made it the Ganges and took it to the depths of patal— the nether world. Which of the two similes are appropriate? I am in a dilemma."

Answer: "The same subject can be analyzed from many angles, styles and attitudes. As you go deeper into the chitta [psyche], you will start rising into the sky within the chitta. The great saint Kabir says, 'I dove into the ocean, but came out in the sky.' In the same way, the higher Garuda flies the deeper the aspirant will dive. As the flow of Ganga touches greater depths, the higher in the sky of the heart the aspirant will dwell. All these ups and downs are the imagination of the mind. The aspirant attains a state beyond dimension only after rising above the land of imagination."

It grew dark so everyone came into the cottage. I was busy preparing dinner but my ears were attending Maharajshri. Maharajshri continued further on the subject of the Ganges. "The Ganges river has attained the status of the main pillar of Indian spiritual culture. Sanyasis [renunciates] desire to be swept away by the waters of the Ganges after death. Remains of householders after cremation are immersed in the flow of the Ganges. These are external symbols of one's desire to flow in the inner Ganga. On the banks of the Ganges there are thousands of ashrams and cottages of mahatmas. My Shaktipat initiation and sanyas diksha [initiation into the monastic order] took place on the banks of the Ganges. I also wish to take my last breath on the banks of the Ganges, and that my body be immersed in its flow. I do not wish that a shrine be built over my body because eventually it will be turned into a source of income.

"Yes, so I was talking about the Ganges. Focusing on the Ganges, devotees have given rise to many different feelings. These sentiments have proven beneficial to devotees and other people. People look at the Ganges not as a river, but as a mother. Thus devotees have had many divine experiences in the beauty of the Ganges. God has given me a beautiful ashram in Dewas; the lure of the Ganges forces me to come back again and again."

38. Vrindavan: A Form of Sadhan

After a few days a Bramhachariji who used to visit Maharajshri frequently, had great faith in Maharajshri, and knew Maharajshri's nature and needs, came to Rishikesh. I also loved him dearly and he served Maharajshri with enormous fervor. After a few days I thought, "Why not take a trip to Uttarkashi? Bramhachariji will take care of Maharajshri. Thus Bramhachariji would have an opportunity to serve Maharajshri fully." After receiving permission from Maharajshri I went to Uttarkashi. Those who were visiting from Dewas had all returned.

In the Shankar Math, in Uttarkashi, Swami Pranavananda [cf. chapter 34] was visiting during those days. He was very pleased to see me. A certain Bramhachariji was also there. After we were introduced I came to know that he had behaved very badly toward Maharajshri when he visited Uttarkashi during the 1940s. I became very angry when I saw him, but I swallowed the anger and never talked to him again.

Swami Narayan Tirth Maharaj came there after a few days. Swamiji was very generous-hearted, sociable and easy going — a joyful and simple mahatma. He was very benevolent toward me. In 1965 he was to grant me sanyas diksha. I stayed in Uttarkashi for three months. During this period I did not receive any news about Maharajshri. I returned to Rishikesh, and then, with Maharajshri, to Dewas. On the way we stopped for a few days in Delhi and Vrindavan.

Maharajshri said that Chaitanya Mahaprabhu disseminated knowledge to the people about the lila [divine sport] of Lord Krishna in Vrindavan. He saw every location in a state of divine ecstasy, and every place where he experienced a specific lila of the Lord, that place was associated with that particular lila. Chaitanya Mahaprabhu used to sing and dance in divine ecstasy. He was the pillar of Krishna Bhakti [devotion toward Lord Krishna] in Bengal.

Question: "Did Vrindavan not exist before that?"

Answer: "Vrindavan did exist, and it was honored as a pilgrimage site, too. But its recent expansion and various locations of Krishna lila were only enunciated after Chaitanya Mahaprabhu's time. After Chaitanya Mahaprabhu the number of Bengali devotees in Vrindavan grew tremendously."

Question: "Today there are many devotees of Lord Krishna, but at one time there was a kind of flood of Krishna devotees. On the one hand there were devotees such as Chaitanya Mahaprabhu, Jayadeva, Tukaram and Jnaneshwar, and on the other Surdas, Meera and Narsi Mehta gained fame. The whole country was drenched in the devotion of Lord Krishna."

Answer: "Yes, but as you know, we believe that different paths and spiritual practices are different levels and sequences of the same spiritual practice. One devotee may have more of certain sentiments, while another may have a preference for a certain form of God. Some feel that love for God is primary, and others feel that surrender and service to God are primary. Some may see God in the form of Vishnu, Shiva or certain Goddesses, and others may believe in Nanak, Mohammed or Jesus. God does not have any form, and all forms are his. Although there is no relationship with God, yet all relations are with him. There are no feelings for him, yet all feelings are for attaining him. Thus there is variation in the level of devotees and the nature of devotees. Some emphasize prayers, puja, and japa, while others prioritize meditation, knowledge, yoga and karma. Spiritual practices of some involve efforts, and others are on the path of natural and spontaneous spirituality. Depending on the preferred form of God, spiritual practices, histories, locations, disciplines, scriptures and principles develop.

"The world is nothing but the waves of Shakti. Just as waves arise in worldly sentiments, waves of devotion, too, arise in various forms. At one time the waves of devotion for Rama and Krishna arose in India and the whole country was colored with it. Historians of Hindi literature call it The Age of Devotion. Prior to that India was ravaged by wars and killings. Warriors displayed their bravery everywhere. This was also a wave. That period is called The Period of Bravery. In both these waves worldly and spiritual people were swept up. True spirituality is to remain aloof from these waves and watch them, but prior to such detachment a person will, for some time, be swept up in the waves. Those who swim through these currents and arrive at the shore are the true brave warriors."

Question: "What is sadhan then?"

Answer: "To cross the river of sadhan is sadhan itself. Everyone talks about the river of life and death because that is the river related to the world. But after that the aspirant must cross the river of sadhan. To cross this river is as difficult as crossing the river of birth and death. Just as one is attached to the world, so one gets attached to sadhan."

Question: "This means that attachment follows an aspirant for a long time."

Answer: "Yes, until one totally frees one's self from bondage."

Question: "Is Vrindavan the devotees' state of freedom from bondage?"

Answer: "It is so from a spiritual perspective. Feelings of devotion for Krishna can develop on the basis of Vrindavan, and his childhood lila can attract the minds of devotees. Those who are crazy after Krishna become crazy after Vrindavan, also. When one rises above all feelings, then the mind and the whole world become Vrindavan. Their ideal is Lord Krishna, the giver of the wisdom of the Gita. They want to live life according to the teachings of the Gita, and their focal point becomes the Gita. Furthermore, their body becomes a Kurukshetra. On further progress, the chitta [psyche] becomes a battlefield. Thus the aspirant moves forward."

Question: "However, there have been many proponents of bhakti in this world, such as Ramanuja, Vallabhacharya and Nimbakacharya, who established many different principles and sects."

Answer: "A devotee does not get involved in such arguments. He believes in devotion based on his sentiments. Whatever he is, he will come forth through God's grace. It is not good to be attached to certain principles related to devotion before knowing anything. The purpose of devotion is to attain the grace of God and not to formulate principles."

Question: "Then what about the awakening of Shakti?"

Answer: "It is impossible to be a devotee without it. The awakening of Shakti strengthens and awakens devotion. Devotion is attained only after awakening."

39. The Subject of Succession Resurfaces

Maharajshri had an inner desire that he give up his mortal body on the banks of the Ganges. He would express this desire occasionally. The thought would come to him because the Ganges River was not near Dewas. This shortcoming of the ashram would come to his notice from time to time, and he would be tormented by memories of the Ganges. This topic came up while traveling to Rishikesh, too. We checked a few places in Rishikesh and Haridwar. An agreement to purchase a building in Rishikesh was almost finalized, but it did not go through for some reason. Maharajshri used to say that he did not want an ashram in Rishikesh, only a room where he could take his last breath.

The discussion of this matter started up again after returning to Dewas. His devotees and disciples also took this discussion seriously, thinking that since he was mentioning it frequently that day must not be too distant. Maharajshri's health was perfect and nothing of this sort was apparent, yet Maharajshri's comments raised doubts. People began to accumulate funds to purchase a place on the banks of the Ganges. For me, there was another reason for entertaining doubt. He talked often about succession. This issue came up on our return to Dewas. Maharajshri raised the question again during the morning walk. "Bramhachariji has gone away. Now what is your thought? Someone or the other must carry out this responsibility."

I pleaded, " My shoulders are not strong enough to carry this weight. In a way my journey has barely begun. So much garbage is still accumulated in my mind. How can I sit on the chair of the Guru and give discourses? This seems very awkward for me. Besides, my mental state is not worthy of running an ashram. I still remember the mountain ranges and rivers of Himachal Pradesh. The gushing sound of the Sutlej River still echoes in my ears. How will I be able to run an ashram?"

Maharajshri replied, "An aspirant has to perform certain tasks that he does not wish to, either due to sentiments or a sense of duty. This is the life of an aspirant. Regard this as one such task. Is it not enough that I am asking this of you? Do you think there is a difference between a Guru's wish and a command? Don't you owe anything to the lineage through which you have had spiritual benefit? Think all this over with a calm mind."

Maharajshri said all this, and I was in a dilemma. On the one hand there was Maharajshri's wish, along with my duty toward the lineage, and on the other hand my mind was just not ready to accept this responsibility. Why should a free, flying bird prepare for imprisonment in a cage? Besides, I did not think I was worthy of this. In the last four or five years I had gained some experience of the ashram. How enormous was this entanglement! It seemed so much bigger than the life of a householder. I thought that after accepting responsibility for the ashram I might have to live a double life. One would be internal, my real self, filled with weaknesses and impurities. The second would be external, a mere pretense, a facade, misleading people, and that would be deceitful. Thinking about the different personas — the internal and the external — I shivered and involuntarily uttered, 'No. No.'

I made a mental resolve, but how could I explain that to Maharajshri. Suddenly I thought of a gentleman who had taken initiation about twenty years prior to me. He had just retired and wanted to live a spiritual life. My heart began to shine with a ray of hope as soon as I remembered him. The next day I proposed his name to Maharajshri. Maharajshri heard me quietly and said, "This means that you are not ready then?"

I pleaded, "If you can forgive me it will be a great favor."

Maharajshri thought for a moment and said, "Whatever you wish."

I shared my thoughts with a few other people. I also met with the gentleman and informed him of what Maharajshri was thinking. After receiving his acceptance I told Maharajshri. Now I was very happy that the large problem was solved. The ashram is a cause of likes and dislikes and conflicts. This problem is even greater when the ashram is inherited through a lineage. One may receive a ready-made ashram with a group of disciples and other facilities, but many complexities are attached to it.

I put aside my worries and busied myself in the service of Guru Maharaj and ashram work. A certain Bramhachariji came to live in the ashram on a permanent basis. He took many responsibilities from my shoulders so I had an opportunity to attend many discourses. I also had more time to serve Maharajshri personally.

Maharajshri began one discourse by saying, "Spirituality and the world can never meet. They are like the East and West; like two banks of a river that can never meet. The mind will have only one sentiment, either spiritual or worldly. Either there will be the desire for pleasures, or the desire for liberation."

Question: "This is difficult for me to comprehend because spirituality develops while living in this world. Has God made a different world for sadhan, bhajan, japa, study of scriptures, and so forth? Devotees live in the world, yet they consider it untouchable."

Answer: "The issue is not about living in this world. As long as the body is alive it will live in this world. The discussion is about whether one keeps the mind in the world, or keeps the world in the mind. The body does not accumulate samskaras, the chitta does. It does not matter where the body lives. Wherever the mind lives, it will accumulate impressions of that place. When I said that spirituality and the world couldn't coexist, I was talking not with reference to the body, but to the mind. I have said this to you many times, but it seems that the idea is not clear in your mind. If you are sitting in a temple or in the company of holy men, and if your mind is somewhere else, then your body is in the temple but you are not in the temple. And if you are at a place that is not appropriate from a spiritual standpoint, but your mind is floating in pure sentiments, then you are not in that place even though you are physically there. The act may appear impure, but it is pure.

"Only one from each pair — pure-impure, dharma-adharma, worldly-spiritual, tempting-beneficial — can exist in the mind at any given moment. Either the world will exist, or spirituality will exist. If you try to keep both then both will disappear. The person who remains in a dilemma attains neither the world, nor spirituality. Either there will be supremacy of angels or of devils in the mind. Either the mind will be oriented towards spiritual welfare, or towards worldly happiness. The path that goes to the world will take you to the world, and the path that goes to spirituality will take you to spirituality. There is no single path to attain both. Therefore saints say that friendship between a yogi and a bhogi [person engrossed in pleasures] is not possible. How can Lord Rama manifest in the mind in which worldly desires dominate? How can worldly desires flourish in the mind in which Lord Rama shines? If desires flourish then Lord Rama has not yet illumined."

Question: "Yes, but you advise us to do pure karma [action]. Karma can be performed with the senses. How does the mind enter the picture?"

Answer: "Yes, advice is given to do pure and pious karma. Once you understand the definition of pure karma your misunderstanding will be removed. The impurity of your mind speaks through this question, not you. The desireless state cannot be attained instantaneously. It develops in stages. When the mind remains indifferent towards worldly pleasures, and they start to give unhappiness, the appetite for spirituality flares up. Then the person has taken his first step on the spiritual path, although his samskaras and vasanas still persist. This is the start of moving away from the world. This condition gives a person the right to walk on the spiritual path and be initiated.

"When the chitta [psyche] attains this state, renunciation starts. Although this state is far from total renunciation, still first steps are taken in the direction of renunciation. In this state an aspirant needs the help of a real Guru. This is the first stop on a spiritual journey. From here Garuda takes off on the flight to see Lord Vishnu. This is the foundation stone of the mansion of spirituality. This is where distaste for the world begins.

"The subject of shreya [spiritual welfare] and preya [worldly pleasures or comforts] is very subtle. Even an intelligent person, at times, is misled in this decision. The shackles of the mind are such that it is hard to describe even through simile. Many times the mind presents undeserving activities with such convincing explanations that the individual soul is deceived. The intelligent person is one who can correctly decipher shreya from preya. Hence, at this time, a Guru is needed. When a Guru sees such a condition in a disciple, he knows that it is his duty to help.

"The path of preya is the path leading to the world. And the path to shreya is the path to spirituality. When directions are opposite they are unlikely to meet. One goes down and the other goes up. One goes after the world and the other turns away from the world. One is light and the other is darkness. One is extrovert and the other is introvert. One is always hanging on hope and the other is self-fulfilled. A person must choose one of the two paths. The one who runs after the world and talks about spirituality deceives the world and himself. A wise person always takes the path of shreya [spiritual welfare]. Ancient Indian sages were never interested in the physical sciences. It was totally clear to them that it would not bring peace and happiness to the world. It cannot solve problems of the world, either. On the contrary, with the progress of the physical sciences the world has become more restless. There is more animosity, distrust and suspicion. Along with comforts and luxuries, instruments of mass destruction are developing at a fast pace. Excessive use of natural resources has caused an imbalance of natural forces. Man has become the prisoner of scientific comforts. Physical sciences are oriented toward preya [worldly comforts]."

Question: "Isn't physical science related to the growth in population? With the growth in population, human needs also grow. One must make use of science. This opens up the path for progress."

Answer: Population growth is also indicative of preya. The life of people inclined toward shreya is moderate and self-controlled. They do not create this problem. First, an aptitude toward preya was developed, then began the progression of modern science. Consequently craving for pleasures grew and the desire to live in comfort and luxury heightened. Many diseases, worries and problems grew along with them. Man was not so restless, unhappy and unsafe in the absence of all this progress, as he is today.

"This is about the materialistic attitude of people. Religious practices done with the purpose of fulfilling worldly desires are no less a hindrance to spiritual progress. For solving problems of life people run after deities. Not only that, they desire heavenly pleasures. They do not experience a reduction of attachment. In fact, it grows further. They desire pleasures of the world that do not even exist in the world. What a flight of imagination!

"The person who desires heavenly pleasures is in the clutches of attachment and has not taken a single step toward detachment or spirituality. The bondage remains the same as before, even if you attain heaven. Even then anger, greed and pride are the same. The sense of individuality remains the same. The chitta is still engulfed in Maya as before. As good deeds are exhausted they will be pushed out of heaven as if they never belonged there. The desire for heaven is like a king begging in front of his palace. A king becoming a beggar. What a paradox! What a downfall of mankind!

"Only that person deserves spirituality who has no desires of the world, is detached and hungry for spirituality. The Guru who will initiate the disciple must decide whether the person is ready for initiation into bhakti or not, otherwise the disciple is likely to become entangled in desires and hopes. There is a greater need for caution in giving Shaktipat initiation than in giving initiation into other, effort-based spiritual practices."

40. Many Forms of God

The next day someone suggested that, with so many types of spiritual practices and so many forms and images of God, an average person gets confused.

Maharajshri replied, "God has many forms based on various principles. The form of God that is appropriate to a specific spiritual practice is formulated according to the need. For example, in saguna bhakti [devotion to God with qualities] a god is needed that the devotee can be dependent on. A god who speaks and acts like the devotee, listens to his prayers, is compassionate and forgiving. A god who can destroy evil and guide his devotee. Hence their god is in human form, like Rama, Krishna, Shankar and Bhagavati. Even while retaining his impersonal nature he incarnates in the midst of Maya.

"Yogis contemplate God within. They meditate on the formless — that is, there is no idol; only the feeling exists. A yogi performs all his actions knowing that God is the doer, and that he, himself, must be the non-doer. If he accumulates any impressions he still knows that the god within has no impressions. He reaps the fruits of his actions, but since, ultimately, it is God reaping the fruits, there is nothing to reap. And so a person following the path of yoga is established in individuality but his god is the Supreme Being. There are no signs of individuality in God and this is what makes him exceptional. For the practice of yoga, he requires no other god than this. He does not get into arguments over the qualities of God, such as eternal, pure, totally aware, etc.

"And as for the seeker of knowledge, the foundation on which his chitta is based is different from that of a yogi or devotee. Bramha is impersonal, formless, beyond vibrations and one and only. Bramha is eternal, pure, boundless truth, consciousness and bliss in nature. Bramha is beyond the reach of the mind, and the senses cannot even reach there. Due to the power of his discrimination, the emptiness and the transient-nature of the world has become apparent to the seeker of knowledge. The sorrowful nature of the world also is apparent to him. That is why he is in search of the eternal element, which is God, the one who is ever blissful in nature. He also knows that the mind, the senses and his intellect cannot reach there. That is why he always makes efforts to lift himself above all these.

"The point here is that the image of God is dependent upon the state of mind of the aspirant — his sentiments, faith and spiritual path. Someone asked Swami Vivekananda how large God is. His answer was, 'He is as big as the devotee.'

"For some people God is a mountain, a tree or a river. With the development of the psyche, the image of God also develops. At first a temple is God's abode. Slowly one progresses to believe in his omnipresence. At first the way to attain God is a special mantra. But this belief keeps on changing with the development of the chitta. Hence a true sadhak does not try to change anyone else's belief. Otherwise the natural faith of that person might be destroyed, when he could not accept any higher faith due to the limitations of his state of mind. Then the person would not be at home anywhere. On the contrary, an aspirant tries to further support and strengthen the faith of the person. And when he develops his faith he will automatically change.

"The perspective of a sadhak is totally different from that of the world. He seeks spiritual welfare for the world and for himself. He does not hesitate if he has to stop and wait for a while for the good of others to manifest. He does not assault anyone's sentiments. He does not hurt anyone's ego. This is true for the imagined God as well. He does not play with anybody's faith. He does not repudiate their belief. He helps."

Question: "You did not say anything about the God of sadhaks of Shakti."

Answer: "In the imagination of sadhaks of Shakti the conscious form of God is of prime importance. In other words, the nature of their God is chaitanya [consciousness]. They do not have to imagine this because the activities of consciousness are visibly present within. The power of consciousness is detached from the senses, but its activities are experienced through the mind and the senses. This path of Shakti-sadhan is the path to reach Shakti, by holding onto the rope of the kriyas of Shakti. Joy is experienced as soon as Shakti becomes active, but in the beginning one may need to imagine Shakti as eternal, omnipresent and singular. The oneness of Shiva and Shakti is a subject to be understood only after the destruction of ignorance.

"The God of Shakti-sadhaks imparts energy for activating the senses, and also manifests in the form of the world around the sadhak. Nothing is possible in the world without this divine power. The vibrations of Shakti are active in every form, every feeling and every resolve. In spite of that it does not do anything.

"Debates about God are meaningless. Principles have been established according to the experiences of the spiritual masters. On the basis of those principles many different views have developed and followers of these traditions have begun to dispute. God must be wondering, 'What kind of a living being have I created? On the basis of imagination they are ready to cut each other's throats. Without any experience they are swinging sticks in the dark.' A wise and thoughtful sadhak does not get involved in any argument. He understands that these differences are due to different perspectives and experiences. Otherwise, nobody can bind God in any definition, description or explanation.

"For example, if you go to a temple in North India, the costumes of Lord Krishna and Radha will be in a North Indian style. If you go to Maharashtra, it will be Maharashtrian. At a place where I stayed, the head of the household was devoted to rituals. He felt like smoking a hukka [an Indian pipe for smoking tobacco]. He prepared a small hukka and kept it in front of the idol of God. After that he prepared his own hukka and started to smoke. When I asked him why, he said, 'If I smoke a hukka why should not my God?'

"A journalist went to Afghanistan. He learned of a temple of Lord Rama. He became curious and went to see the temple. He saw that the priest brought food for God on a plate covered with a piece of cloth. He kept on watching. When the priest lifted the cloth the journalist was struck with wonder. There were meat dishes. After the offering was finished the journalist enquired about the meat offerings to God. The priest replied, 'Lord Rama was a kshatriya [a member of the warrior caste]. He used to hunt so he must eat meat as well. What is so surprising about that?'

"The main reason for this is that everyone in Afghanistan is a non-vegetarian, hence their God is also a non-vegetarian.

"It is human nature to try to imagine things that are beyond one's reach. A human writes articles and gets involved in arguments about subjects that are beyond his intellect. He knows that his mind and senses cannot reach God, yet he makes temples and places of pilgrimage to try to reach him.

"Human beings have an attachment for the body on the one hand, and, on the other, they try to attain God. The essence of this is:

(1) God cannot be defined. He cannot be limited either by thoughts, sentiments, forms, shapes or words.

(2) Humans are helpless due to their nature, and continually try to understand and explain God.

(3) Although God is unmanifest, formless and beyond qualities, an aspirant needs some basis upon which to worship God. Consequently he tries to find support in an idol, fire, water, sun, thought, emotion, books, and so forth.

(4) Everyone should follow their faith based on their state of mind. When their state of mind changes, their idea of God will also change."

41. Spirituality in Daily Life

Now Maharajshri addressed some practical issues, a subject most useful for spiritual aspirants. He began, "A human being is a social animal. Neither can he avoid interacting with people, nor can he accomplish much without doing so. This situation continues from childhood until the end. If he gets too involved in this interaction, however, it causes problems. A spiritual aspirant does not want to be anyone's enemy, nor should he become too attached to anybody. Neither attachment, nor hatred. This is the only way to remain in the world while being untouched by it, and people fail to understand this. As a result a human being increases his involvement with people until it turns into attachment.

"Not only does infatuation grow by excessive interaction, meetings and dialogue, it also leads to overstepping ones boundaries. Sometimes this may also result in arguments and mutual discord. It also stops any mutual dialogue. People then say, 'What happened to them? They had a lot of love for each other.' In reality, the cause of this is infatuation, an increase in their mutual expectations, and the inability to stay within boundaries. I am not asking you not to love anyone. I am asking you to love the whole world, but keep in mind limits and boundaries.

"Just like people, excessive association with places and things is the cause of infatuation. It destroys faith, limits and feelings. People have limitless faith and emotions for the Ganges. People come from far away, spending time and money, to bathe in the waters of the Ganges. But those who live in Rishikesh and Haridwar on the banks of the Ganges seem to be more attached to their families and businesses. Rarely do they care to bathe in the holy waters of the Ganges. On the contrary, they wash their clothes in the Ganges. The dirty water of the cities is dumped into the Ganges. This happens due to excessive contact with the Ganges.

"Like aversions, attachment also pollutes the mind and increases attachment further. There is always a chance that attachment may turn into aversion, anger and disgust. Attachment and aversion are both obstacles in spiritual progress. Spirituality starts with the elimination of attachment and hate. There is no shortage of people who raised their children with delusory attachment, who expected many things, but when these children grew up they turned away from their parents. The lives of such people were filled with hopelessness and despair because they harbored expectations for others. Too much familiarity increases expectations. Expectation is the mother of despair. The story of Jad Bharat [a great saint from India] is famous. He started to rear a fawn. He became attached to the deer and, eventually, had to be reborn as a deer.

"If work and social conduct are performed with a sense of duty then they are not a cause of attachment and bondage. However, do not do anything with reciprocal expectations. If you help someone in difficulty, do not expect to get help during your hard times.

Self-examination: "The second thing to do is to observe your own self. This is only possible for that person who is weary of worldly pleasures, who has started seeing the miseries they entail, and who wants to gain spiritual benefit because he knows that the flow of the world is incessant, that feelings of joy and sorrow will never end. Under such circumstances, when will you examine your own self, and when will the hunger for spiritual welfare awaken? The mind is fickle, yet the sorrows associated with worldly pleasures are easy to perceive. As such, self-examination is a constant process, but even if slight attention was directed towards it in the beginning life could be transformed significantly. The more you look inward, the greater will be the guidance and clarification of doubts you will receive from within. This inner satisfaction is real and natural. There will be no need for you to wander around asking questions. The first and foremost requirement for self-examination is solitude. There should be no work, and no obstacle of any kind, only undisturbed contemplation. Maybe at night before going to bed or waking up just before dawn, even if it is for a brief interval, look within and reflect upon the following questions with closed eyes and a peaceful mind.

(I) A man himself does not know who he is. His thoughts, feelings and resolve change constantly. The form and state of the body that he thinks is his also keeps changing. It is definite that in our constantly changing state there is an element that always stays the same. That element is not influenced by these changes. What is that element? What is its form? What are its qualities and nature? This is a subject of inquiry.

(2) The second question is, Where have I come from? Just as he cannot find an answer to the first question, in the same way this question also remains unanswered in front of man. In the path of yoga, types of states are described in which past samskaras manifest before him. Samskaras exist in the form of a chain reaction. If a person gets hold of the chain of samskaras and goes into the past he can know his past lives. This process is not so simple. For this a special development of the psyche is required. Until this state is achieved, man must think about this constantly. This process is also limited to the subtle body, which is not eternal. It does not focus on the atma-tattva [the ultimate reality]. So the question is, Where did the atma-tattva come from? What is that level, state and entity of which the individual soul is a part? It is not necessary to know about past births to attain the Self, but it is certainly one of the stages in sadhana.

(3) What is mine in the world? This question helps to develop detachment toward the world. Money, luxury, house, family, fame, and so forth, are certainly not mine, because they may exist today and not tomorrow. Whatever is mine should remain with me forever, but I will leave these or they will leave me. The mind, intellect, resolves, modifications, feelings and the world are not mine because they keep on changing. They arise and they dissolve. The ideas that I believe are mine also keep changing with time. Then what is mine in this world? Only the ego. But is ego mine? Ego is only an illusion. It is only an imagination. Scriptures say that only God is yours. He never leaves you alone, nor does he change. But where is my God? If God is mine then it is my duty to bring him before me. It is not enough to just say, 'God is mine, God is mine.' As long as he does not manifest and I do not see him, I am like an atheist.

(4) There is no means of finding out where we are to go. By grasp-

ing the chain of samskaras it is possible to know about past lives, but for the future neither samskaras exist, nor a chain. It depends on the state of mind at the time of death. Good karmas will result in a birth in a higher species and bad karmas will result in a lower species. But the cycle of rebirths does not end with that. This wheel of rising and falling will continue to turn. There must be some way to stop this merry-go-round of entering and leaving different life forms. Why not perform karmas [actions] that are neither good nor bad?

(5) Why did I fall from my atma, the highest personal principle of life? Due to what factors was I born into this present-day pitiable condition? I understand that the world is unreal, but I still keep running after the world. I know that the pleasures of the world are full of sorrows, but I am dying with cravings for them. If this is not a misconception then what is it? Is this misconception the cause of my pitiable condition? It is definitely a misconception that I am attached to this world with an expectation of worldly happiness. It is definitely a misconception that is making me dance around. So how can this misconception be destroyed?

(6) Due to this misconception I developed a sense of doership, which made me accumulate impressions. Now I am restless, like a bird entangled in the net of prarabdha. I want to escape from the net but I cannot. The grip is tightening. I do not see any way to escape. Prarabdha is so strong and powerful that it does not leave me alone before bearing fruits. With the accumulation of new samskaras, the wheel of samskaras keeps turning. Why not go through prarabdha without being happy or unhappy so that new samskaras are not accumulated. Can I do this? How much endurance and how much patience will I need for that? I will have to destroy my mind to succeed.

(7) The followers of Shaktipat sadhana must also examine how much the sense of surrender is present in the mind. With Shaktipat the sense of an observer may develop, but surrender is different from that. Not to interfere with spontaneous kriyas, to have equanimity in joy and misery, and to fulfill duties without concern for results are parts of surrender. One must ask, 'Am I able to do that? Does not my ego increase repeatedly and lead me astray from the path of surrender?'

(8) An aspirant must not think about his own virtues, and must never praise himself. This can give rise to ego, and ego is the worst vice. This may mean that those virtues have not yet become natural because nature [temperament] does not have any ego. If one has ego about virtues then it is certain that those virtues are not part of his nature. In the first place, you must not look at your own virtues, and second, never examine the virtues and vices of others. One cannot learn from other's virtues, while vices can influence the mind very easily. Do I also have these vices? Am I learning from other's virtues?

(9) One must look at one's own vices. A common man does not know about his own vices. Even if he comes to know about his vices, he tries to justify them. Consequently faults remain within and keep growing. So long as he is not disgusted with his own vices, the path to control the mind will not open. Only after becoming disgusted will he try to find ways to free himself from those defects. Is there a feeling of disgust towards these faults? Do I try in any way to get released from them?

(10) Are my lifestyle and food habits sattvic [harmonious]? Do I behave humbly? Are my words and actions the same? Do I react strongly to small things? Did I betray someone's trust in me? Do I keep my appointments? Do I go to bed early and get up early in the morning? Do I study some scriptures everyday? Do I sit in sadhan regularly? Do I waste time? Do I take interest in gossip or listen to gossip about others?

"Some questions have been suggested here that would help a sadhak in self-examination. A sadhak must assign some convenient time for this. He must scold himself for his mistakes. He must repent and make a resolution not to repeat the same mistake again. This must be contemplative throughout the day, while doing every activity. This way a sadhak can ride on his mind all day. The meaning of sadhan is to change the direction of the flow of life. If life does not change then it shows there is some deficiency or defect."

42. Kama-Kala:
The Art of Procreation

The subject of kama-kala [the art of procreation] is a very mysterious one. People have given a wrong meaning to these words because of their convoluted thinking. One day Maharajshri was speaking on this subject.

"The secret of kama-kala is known to God only. He created the universes in conjunction with Shakti, and thus Shakti became known as the mother of universe. But neither God nor Shakti has any sense organs, hence there was no question of sensual pleasure or desire involved in the creation of this child: the universe. This act of procreation was at a pure spiritual level, but the extroverted jiva [individual soul] brought it down to the level of sensuality. Kama [procreation or union] was reduced to nothing but the union of two bodies, and it became an instrument for the gratification of the sense of touch. Kama took the form of desire. What a downfall of Kama!

"All the arts are included in kama-kala because an artist gives birth to artistic creations. The greatest artist is God, who created a unique, exceptional and most beautiful world without any marble or hammer, without any colors and canvas, without any instrument. This is the artistry of God's creation.

"The essence of Kala [art] is an effect, which, by virtue of uniting more than one thing, gives birth to a new form. The universe was created by God through the vibrations of Shakti. This displays the artistry of Shakti, this is kama-kala, the art of procreation, this is the creative aspect of God. But this act of procreation is free from expectations and desires, there is no trace of attraction and attachment. There is not even an ounce of pride involved in the physical development of their child. An individual soul cannot even imagine this sport of creation. So long as he fails to rise above his senses, he will be absolutely incapable of understanding this fact. As soon as we talk about kama, procreation, he starts to visualize sensual gratification. How can he comprehend that creation can take place without the senses?

"However, the ecstasy, happiness and work of God are all beyond the senses. Still the creation of the universe is taking place. This is the artistry of God's creation.

"God does not need a person separate from him for the sport of creation. He manifests, within himself, the Shakti that is already latent within him. He acts like two while being one within. He gives birth to the universe through the procreative sport within. These actions, sports and effects are merely the lila [divine sport] of the Lord. On the contrary, the procreative desire of a living being is hunger for physical gratification. There are attachment for, and expectations of, the children. For God all this is a divine sport, but for an individual soul all this appears to be reality. He needs another person who is separate from him to unite with in sexual excitement, but this cannot be. For a moment he forgets his existence, his personality, but very soon he realizes his separateness. This is the kama-kala of an individual soul.

"When a living being has children, they have aspects of both parents. Often the love of a mother is compared to Bhagawati, the mother of the universe. This comparison is totally incomplete. In this world the child is separate from the mother, and the mother has attachment to the child. However the world is not separate from its mother. Just as her beloved is not separate from her, her child — the world — also is not separate from her. It is impossible for a worldly person to understand this difference, but such is the lila of the Lord. This is why God's lila is called Mahamaya [the Grand Illusion]. It has covered the psyche of the individual soul with Maya, and reduced the pure form of kama down to a level of sensual pleasure. Both parties wish to get lost in the other's body. This is the kama-kala of an individual soul.

"A man and woman become separate after procreative sexual play, but God is always united with Shakti — before, during and after the sport. He is the basis of Shakti. Shakti cannot be imagined without God. When the foundation of union is the physical senses, a separation is bound to take place. But God and his Shakti are beyond senses. How can they separate? An individual soul unites as well as separates, and is restless when separated. This is the kama-kala of the individual soul.

"The impressions of the procreative sport of the Lord are not accumulated. There are no senses. There is no chitta. How and where can impressions be accumulated? But the individual soul has senses, a chitta, desires and attachments in the chitta. Memories and impressions of the pleasure experienced through the senses are imprinted on the chitta. Thus prarabdha is generated and, accordingly, the individual soul has to wander through lower or higher life forms to fulfil his sensual desires. In this way the procreative play of the individual soul is the cause of his cycle of birth and death. This is the kama-kala of an individual soul.

"The essence of this is that God's kama-kala is beyond Maya. It is invisible, and takes place at a level subtler than subtle. Kama-kala of an individual soul is within Maya, and takes place at the most gross and visible level. God remains free after the sport of procreation, whereas a living being falls into bondage.

"For spiritual growth one must understand and experience the procreative sport of the Lord. It is like a river that must be crossed to go to the other side. It is like an insurmountable pass that must be crossed to climb the high mountains of spirituality. The job for the individual soul is very difficult. He must not only change the basis and the form of his procreative play, but he will have to understand and know the form and secret of God's procreative sport. For this he will have to change his life completely. He will have to rise above the body, the mind and the chitta, and establish a relationship with the cosmic consciousness."

43. The Circle of Aura

I was going for a morning walk with Maharajshri. There was not a single building near the railway station in those days. It used to be a deserted road. Once in a while a railway traveler or a horse carriage would appear. There were very few trees on either side of the road. As it was fall, the leaves, too, had fallen, and hence the birds had migrated elsewhere. Even the shadows of the trees had given up their company. What could be done? The world is such. The world leaves you alone as soon as clouds of adversity start to form over your head. But so what? We were only going for a walk. We were interested in our spiritual discussion, and Maharajshri was telling a story from his life.

"I was travelling to Gujarat with a Swamiji [an ascetic]. He had taken sanyas [the vow of renunciation] one or two years earlier. Swamiji got upset with me for something and said, "I will never see your ugly face ever again." He left after saying that. I was very sad. Am I really so bad that people would not want to see my face again? I remained dispirited for three or four days. I did not feel like eating anything. I regained my normal self after five or six days. I pacified my mind thinking this must be a play of prarabdha.

"Subsequently, I went south and reached the ashram of Shri Ramana Maharshi after wandering here and there. Ramana Maharshi was alive then. The atmosphere of his ashram was very peaceful and pleasant. There was peace all around. Maharshiji was very diligent about his morning walk. When he returned from his walk people stood on both sides of the road to see him. I did not have a particular question, I only wanted to have the privilege of his company.

"Afterwards I went to see a nearby temple. I had a very strange experience there. While walking around the temple my mind became absolutely quiet at a particular spot. During the second round my mind again reached the same state at the same spot. My mind would become totally thoughtless and free from any emotions. I noticed that my mind would get filled with a peculiar kind of ecstasy as it was being pulled deeper and deeper within. I looked around and saw that a gentleman was meditating. Perhaps he was in samadhi. The atmosphere was peaceful due to the effect of his state."

Question: "Was everyone's mind overwhelmed with peacefulness when they came to this spot, just like yours?"

Answer: "No. Not everyone. When someone is established in such a high inner state, then a sphere of influence develops by virtue of that state, in which the spiritual vibrations of the meditating person spread out. Only that person can have such an experience whose mind is capable of receiving these subtle vibrations. Everyone is affected to some degree, whether they like it or not.

"You must have read in the Ramayana that, when Garuda became deluded, Lord Shiva sent him to Kak Bhushundi to dispel it. From a distance, when he saw the peak of the mountain under which Kak Bhushundi had his ashram, Garuda's mindset was transformed and his delusion was cleared. Garuda's mind was pure. Only a wave of delusion had come up. Therefore, as soon as he entered the circle of the aura of Kak Bhushundi he could receive its power and be healed."

Question: "You could feel the tranquillity of the mind only at one point while circling the temple, whereas Garuda's mind was affected just by seeing the peak of the mountain."

Answer: "Everyone's circle of influence has its own range and everyone has his own capacity for grasping that power. The deeper a sadhak goes within himself, the greater is his circle of influence. The spiritual vibrations spread more widely. One person's circle may be smaller and another's may be bigger. Our scriptures present Kak Bhushundi as the highest spiritual personality, therefore his circle of influence is great. Garuda's delusion was removed just by seeing the peak from a distance."

Question: "Do only sattvic [harmonious or pious] people have a circle of influence? What about tamasic [inertial] and rajasic [with disturbing qualities] people?"

Answer: ""Everyone has an aura. A sattvic person spreads sattvic qualities within a certain area and people dominated by tamasic and rajasic qualities spread those. Only rare people are dominated by sattvic qualities. The whole world is busy spreading the effects of tamas and rajas everywhere. One can distribute only what they have. An unhappy mind will distribute unhappiness, a fickle mind fickleness, a joyous mind joy, and an indulgent mind spreads indulgence. Just as a fickle mind cannot grasp the effects of sattvic qualities, so a sattvic mind rejects the effects of rajasic and tamasic qualities."

Question: "Does this mean that one must have a predisposition for a quality to grasp its effect?"

Answer: "First of all, most people try to avoid contact with a sattvic aura. The whole world is miserable, but how many people could actually reach the ashram of Kak Bhushundi? If a holy person lives near a town, how many people from the town come in contact with that holy man? The majority continue to struggle with their own miseries. The population of Dewas must be twelve to fourteen thousand. From that number, perhaps fifty come to the ashram regularly. If someone comes only occasionally, he cannot receive the effects of the peace of the ashram. His mindset is not appropriate. If the mind is receptive, then only will it be able to receive. The psyche will grasp the effect only of that quality which is predominant in itself. The miserable world does not want to find happiness. It avoids the place where happiness may be found."

44. Consecration of an Idol: Shaktipat

A new temple of Bhagawati was built in Indore. A big celebration was held at the time. Maharajshri was invited to preside. After seeing the idol Maharajshri said, "The idol has received Shaktipat. Now this place is alive." Shaktipat of an idol! It sounded strange. Finally I had to ask, "Maharajshri, devotees consider the idol to be a representation of a goddess. Shaktipat on God? I cannot understand this."

Maharajshri said, "Understand this now: The idol is first a piece of stone. Then the artist gives it a beautiful form with his art. The piece of stone does not become worthy of worship just because it has been shaped into an idol until prana pratishtha [the ritual of invoking life; consecration] is performed. This means that the idol is not revered, but the prana [life-force] is revered. The idol is worthy of worship only after the life-force, or prana, is invoked in it. If prana is not poured into the idol then it is not venerable. This means that the idol is only a medium, a symbol, a vehicle. Some saints have criticized idol worship because people consider the symbol to be God. The medium itself is worshipped. As a result of this the basis of worshipping the life-force through the medium of the idol has been totally shaken. No one can criticize if the symbol is considered as a symbol and, through the medium of the symbol, God is worshipped. The Upanishads mention symbolic worship, but there is no mention of idol worship.

"These days consecration has become a mere show. Recitation of mantras from the Vedas, the bathing of the idol with water and grains, a fire ceremony, the worship of the nine planets, and so forth, are performed, and the attention of the brahmin is on the donation he will receive rather than on invoking prana. Organizers of the temple are more concerned with their reputation than with prana. Consequently consecration becomes secondary. In other eras the learned, ascetics and seers who were detached and had renounced the world, who had no expectations, were invited to perform the consecration. They had experience of the kriyas of prana and had control over prana as well. Earning money was secondary for them; invoking prana into the idol was the primary goal. They were capable of extending their own prana-Shakti into the idol.

"However the nature of rituals has undergone a change. The purpose used to be to invoke prana in the idol. Now, instead, it has been restricted to a ritual only. Even the form of the rituals has changed significantly. Now it includes showmanship, greed and the desire for fame. Often idols in the temple lack prana, the life-force, in spite of the ritual of consecration. Devotees only see the statue and not the prana. Many saints have criticized this form of idol worship.

"Meera, Surdas and Tukaram loved the idols of their deities to the point of being obsessed by them because they were able to experience prana, the sound of prana, and other kriyas in the idol. The best idol is the human body that is filled by God with his own prana. The human body is the best and highest creation of the divine art of God. In every cell and every limb of the human body prana-Shakti is active and shining."

Question: "What is the need for Shaktipat when God himself has put prana into humans?"

Answer: "Shaktipat is not done for bringing prana into human beings because it is already there. It is done to change the direction of the flow of prana inwards, away from the world and toward the atma [soul]."

Question: "But in an idol, prana does not flow inwards or outwards. Then why Shaktipat?"

Answer: "Shaktipat is done to invoke prana in the statue. A statue is worthy of worship only after consecration."

Question: "But an idol made of stone is passive in the process of receiving prana or not receiving prana. How can it receive the effect?"

Answer: "Shaktipat on a stone is like writing something on it. It neither invites someone to write, nor does it prohibit writing on it."

Question: "Did you feel the effect of Shaktipat on the idol?"

Answer: "I did not say that the idol has received Shaktipat for no reason. The work that could not be accomplished by priests even after an extensive show of chanting Vedic hymns, bathing and rituals happened in just a moment. The atmosphere around the idol has been transformed."

Question: "What do you think about people who worship an idol without doing the ceremony of consecration?"

Answer: "If the devotion is strong, faith unshakable and worship continuous then, after a long time, an idol can come alive, but this happens very rarely. A devotee may worship, but he cannot maintain his devotion. Consequently his worship is also merely a show. The beginning of our lineage took place with Shaktipat on an idol. Swami Narayan Tirth Dev Maharaj was building a cottage on a cremation ground. He was intoxicated with sadhan. Kriya was going on spontaneously. One day, in a devotional upsurge, he started to wash the idol of Goddess Kali in the cottage. The statue became so luminous that no one could look directly at the light coming out of it. This was the first Shaktipat of the Guru of Shaktipat of this age. In those days I was a traveler, and I stayed for a short time among the ruins of a temple in the district of Muraina. It was a run down temple of Hanuman. It was deserted and quiet all around. Weeds had grown up around it. Sometimes shepherds used to come to rest there. The temple statue was totally ignored. There was neither water, nor anything else for worship. Shaktipat took place as soon as the idol came into my sight. The statue came alive. It started to shine with divine luster. I had an opportunity to go there one year later, and in the place of the ruin was a big temple. A few shops were there, also. A priest had been appointed to conduct prayers. A residence was built for him, and the flow of devotees was constant."

Question: "You called Swami Narayan Tirth Dev Maharaj the founder of Shaktipat, whereas this knowledge existed even before him."

Answer: "Yes, it did exist before him. But it was hidden. Until then this knowledge was flowing internally. Knowledge is never lost completely. At some time or the other an exceptional sadhak would follow this path. The general population was totally ignorant of it. This hidden Ganga was brought to light by Swami Narayan Tirth Dev Maharaj. It's auspicious beginning was through the Shaktipat on an idol. This is why he is called the founder."

45.   The Value of Time in Sadhan

I was accompanying Maharajshri on a morning walk toward the railway station. The morning train was two hours late. Here came the train, blowing smoke as it entered the platform, and over there people ran down the road to catch it. I started to think, "Why are people running to catch the train when the train is already two hours late? They should have been waiting at the platform."

Possibly Maharajshri was thinking the same thing. He said, "Such is the condition of we Indians when it comes to punctuality. We do not value time at all. People should have arrived at the station to wait for the train. While waiting, they could have made good use of their time by reading or doing japa, but they are running now. The train stops here only for two minutes. Most of the people will not be able to catch the train.

"This is the situation in life, also. No one does sadhan in the prime of life, when it is the proper time. They wait for the train to arrive [old age], and remain involved in worldly pleasures. When old age comes the train has been missed. The opportunity to do sadhan has been missed. The body becomes weak by then. The train has already left the platform. Desires in the mind are still young, but the body is old. How can one do sadhan then? In old age the mind is even more restless.

"There is no greater wealth than time. There is no greater sadhan than good use of time. There could be no worse luck than missing the train of time. No one is more intelligent than the person who under-stands the importance of the speed of time. No one is more brave than the person who runs against time. There is no greater stupidity than disrespecting time. There is no greater foolishness than waiting for the right time.

"An aspirant does not wait for a conducive time. His train of sadhan is at the platform in every situation. He knows how to make the best use of the given circumstances. He accepts every situation as God's grace, and lives the life of sadhan as far as possible. For him every circumstance is a test, and he passes every test.

"Sadhan is such a priceless and effective herb. If used properly, over time, it will cure the disease of life and death at its root. With the passage of time, an adverse time becomes the propitious time. Rest taken at the proper time releases tension, bringing renewed freshness. Only over time can a real friend or enemy be recognized. Once the serpent of time has passed by there is no point in striking at its trail. The haste of these people to catch the train is like striking the trail.

"The one who is not aware at the right time does not attain anything. As time passes the one who sees death approaching will always be cautious. The one who does not waste any time always gains. The one who takes advantage of a suitable time, and hides his limbs like a turtle when time is against him, is always saved from calamities. The one who spends every moment remembering God and sadhan burns all his accumulated sins. This is why time is said to be the greatest wealth of all.

"A wilted flower cannot bloom again. A leaf torn from the tree cannot be attached again. A dead person cannot come to life again. And time that has gone by cannot come back. Time has a flow like water. The flow of time never stops; it never pauses. It has been flowing forever and it will keep on flowing forever. Day and night are in the boundaries of time. Birth and death are in the boundaries of time. The activities of life are within the boundaries of time. The entire play of Maya is also bound by time. Time is Maya's strongest medium. All objects change their appearances, qualities and functions over time. At the place of a high mountain a deep ocean may roar. Lush farms may turn into deserts. The body declines and the state of mind changes."

Question: "Is it true that the flow of time stops during meditation?"

Answer: "The flow of time does not stop. Attention is diverted from time and one is not aware of time. If you turn your face you will not be able to see behind your back, but what may be seen there remains the same. When the attention of a yogi is focused on an object, it becomes totally one-pointed and merges with it. Then nothing else is in awareness, neither time, nor anything else. The world is destroyed for those who attain the ultimate spiritual goal, whereas it goes on as before for all others."

Question: "On the one hand you say that time is the greatest wealth, and on the other hand you are asking us to go beyond time. Which of these is the truth?"

Answer: "Both. Only by making the right use of time can you go beyond time. Time is the greatest wealth for a sadhak, but a siddha [a perfected master] gives up this wealth of time. Just as you have to make use of the mountain to climb the mountain, but once you are on the other side the mountain is left behind, similarly time is also left behind. A sadhak never ignores time because he wants to go beyond time. He uses each and every moment."

Question: "Is Shakti also within the boundaries of time?"

Answer: "No. Shakti is divine and beyond Maya. Maya and time are like parallel rivers. When one flows the other also flows. When one dries up the other also dries up. All this is a play of God. Yes, the kriyas, the activities, of Shakti do come within the boundaries of time. We even talk about experiencing certain kriyas for a certain length of time.

"As long as the basis for kriya is physical or gross in any sense of the term, time will be involved. Kriya cannot manifest without a base, therefore kriyas come within time. However, Shakti remains beyond the limits of time."

46. Sadhana of Music

Dewas is a center of music. It has been adorned with the music of world famous musicians, such as Rajjab Ali Khan and Kumar Gandharva, who made Dewas their residence. Because Kumar Gandharva had built his house adjacent to the ashram, waves of music used to ring in the ashram. In the morning, when Maharajshri and I used to go for a walk, Kumar Gandharva would be practicing. The surroundings would be drenched in the melodies of classical music. Maharajshri's steps also stopped for a little while. We walked silently for some time, then I asked, "Maharajji, is music also a sadhana, a spiritual practice?"

Maharajji said, "Yes, it is a sadhana if it can touch the mind and heart. Music was once part of sadhana for mahatmas, but today it has become a business and a form of public entertainment. Saints and devotees sang not for entertainment, but for humble yearning, for crying out their pain of separation from God, to seek help from God. Their singing came from the heart but the mind would weep, tears would flow from their eyes. This was their sadhana. The purpose of sadhana is to control the mind. If music is an inner expression, only then can it affect mind. The mind becomes more restless and egoistic if the music is an external expression.

"People call the practice of music a sadhana of music. Perhaps they do not understand the difference between practicing music and the sadhana of music. Practicing notes, beats, tunes, ragas, and so forth, is not sadhana. When you get lost in the deep sentiments of the heart while singing — that is sadhana. The basis of musical practice is the vocal chords and the head, but the basis of sadhana is the heart. Practice does not affect the mind and heart, but sadhana wrings out the heart. The boundary of practicing music is art, but the boundary of sadhana is the boundless God, who is free from art. Musicians must be respected because they keep the art alive, which is part of sadhana, but it is not necessary that all musicians are sadhaks. For a spiritual aspirant the study of music can be a sadhana, a spiritual practice. It is a tool for his spiritual pursuit, not the goal. An artist is definitely a practitioner.

"Swami Haridas, the Guru of the famous musician Tansen, must have been a practitioner once upon a time, practicing notes, tunes, beats, ragas, and so forth, but he became a sadhak eventually. His music crossed the limits of practice and took the form of an unfathomable ocean of sadhana. Now he sang only for God. He did not need notes and beats for his music. Notes and beats became his obedient servants and followed his singing. In the temple or in solitude, he used to open up his heart to God. His mind would surrender at the feet of God. This was his sadhana. Through music he connected his mind with God. In other words, he gained control over his mind through the medium of music. Music is secondary and sadhana is primary. Sadhana does not last where music becomes primary.

"After Haridasji passed away his disciples separated into two groups: devotees and court singers. The first group sang only in temples, before God. However some changes did take place. Haridasji sang alone in the temple, for God, but his students sang in temples followed by large crowds of listeners. The singers began to be somewhat distracted. Even if the singer faced God he was aware of the large group of listeners behind. At times they would focus on pleasing listeners instead of expressing their devotion. As soon as there is a desire to display artistic talents sadhana is lost. Devotion is a thing of the heart and not for show. In reality, art is not displayed; it is the ego of the artistic talent that is exhibited. There was a day when King Akbar had to go in disguise and hide in order to listen to the singing of Haridasji. Haridasji did not want to exhibit his art and ego. Slowly the number of listeners grew, and the ego of Haridasji's disciples grew as well. Now the singers started to pay attention to the listeners sitting behind. The sweet melody, feelings, yearning for God, humble requests to God, and so forth, began to disappear.

"The second group of Haridasji's disciples comprised court singers. They left God and went straight to the kings and nawabs. There they received wealth, importance, a position in the court, and everything else.

While singing in the court they faced the king and would be surrounded by the royal members of the court. The position of God was taken by an arrogant person. No one had any devotion. All were only involved in appreciating art. The singer also proudly focused on displaying his mastery.

"Today all types of music are only for audiences, whether it is classical, popular or devotional. God is nowhere to be seen. The earth is never devoid of sattvic qualities, so it is possible that someone, somewhere, may be singing for the Guru or for God. Usually, while practicing, even the musician thinks about the audience. The practitioner remains engrossed in notes and beats and the ego remains intact. Can this be called a sadhana of music?"

Question: "But a common man cannot begin by singing with devotion. Is it not true that one will have to begin with practice?"

Answer: "I do not deny that. There may be exceptions but, generally, one has to start by studying and practicing music. The problem begins when a person becomes entrenched in the art form and the ego and spiritual feelings remain secondary. He wants to hear praise, and his life is spent in singing to please his audience. Today even great musicians sing for money and name, but without any feelings. The lives of how many singers are ascetic and devotional? How many of them have reached spiritual heights? Can anyone come to the level of Haridasji? This means that such art has slipped from the hands of spirituality. If a devotee begins to learn music, he nourishes his ego so much that his devotion is impaired. His admirers fill the remaining deficiencies in this process. He cannot remain a devotee, even while following the path of devotion."

Question: "What can one do, Maharajshri? This age is like that. Which subject, which branch of knowledge, is not commercialized? Why blame music alone? Teaching, raising cows, performing rituals, even social service and spirituality — all are in the same state."

On hearing this Maharajshri laughed loudly. He said, "Yes, this age is like that. Actually, human beings and and all their attitudes are commercialized, and that influences everything. Who can stop the effect of this age?"

47. Dreams

The subject of dreams had internally overshadowed my thoughts. One gentleman told me that he first had a vision of Maharajshri in a dream, and then he met Maharajshri in real life. There were a few similar examples, in which people had premonitions in dreams. I was thinking that the basis of dreams is accumulated impressions, which were mere collections of memories of past experiences. How then can dreams give indications of the future? Dreams can only give shape and form to past impressions. I presented my dilemma to Maharajshri.

He explained in the following manner: "It is true that dreams are based on samskaras. They arise during the sleep state and create the world of dreams. But remember that samskaras are of two types: prarabdha [ripened to give fruits in this life] and sanchit [accumulated impressions from the past]. Sanchit samskaras can only bring memories of past experiences. They may recreate things that have been seen, but they cannot give any indication of the future. Prarabdha samskaras are different. A dream based on prarabdha may give an indication of future events. The prarabdha that is ripe and ready to give results may be expressed as an event in a dream. There is nothing surprising about that. Sanchit samskaras are related to the past only, whereas prarabdha can be related to the future as well as the past.

"There was an American lady whose son was a pilot in the Air Force. This lady had a dream one day. She came to an open field surrounded by mountains. The sky was cloudy and a few raindrops were falling. An airplane came flying in the sky. The weather was not clear, and the airplane hit a mountain peak and fell. People ran to the spot where the airplane had crashed. She also ran to the spot. She saw the dead body of her son lying there. The dream was over. The woman woke up.

"At first she was very extremely worried and scared. She started praying to Jesus for her son. Then she convinced herself that it was only a dream and dreams come and go. They are not related to real life. The incident became a thing of the past. She felt relieved.

"After a few days she went to meet a friend in another city. They went out together for a stroll and she saw that they were in the same open field that she had seen in her dream, the same mountains and clouds. It was drizzling and the weather was foggy. She was struck with wonder. Suddenly, an airplane came and hit the mountain and crashed. Both of them ran to the spot where the crashed airplane lay. She saw her son's dead body lying there.

"Without thinking more about the incident, it may be understood that this dream was related to prarabdha. However it is hard to determine whether a particular dream has anything to do with events that are going to happen or not. For some reason, people have very few dreams based on prarabdha. They mostly come and go, like a movie, and as soon you are out of the theater they are gone. The dream is broken and forgotten.

"Just recently I ran into a similar situation. A girl had many dreams of a temple of Lord Shankara. It was a very ancient temple, situated at a height on the banks of the River Narmada. There was a cremation ground nearby, and the place was peaceful and secluded. This dream came to her three or four times. Then one day she dreamt that the temple was close to Badwah, a town near the Narmada River. One day we all went to find the place. The girl recognized the temple as soon as she saw it. The place was peaceful, close to a cremation ground, near the Narmada River. It was about twelve kilometers from the town of Badwah. Whether this experience has any connection with the future or not, no one knows. The temple is known as Vimleshwar Mahadeva."

I am reminded of an episode from my earlier life, before I came to the ashram. Only a few days had passed since India received independence. India was divided into two parts. Hundreds of thousands of people were coming and going between India and Pakistan. We all came to Kurukshetra [in India], except for my father, who was still in Lahore [in Pakistan]. On both sides of the border, in India and Pakistan, many people were being killed. One day my mother dreamt that some people were running after my father with knives. My father was trying to save himself and someone stabbed him with a knife.

In those days refugees were coming loaded in trains. We did not have any work to do, so we used to go to the station and check every train to see whether any relatives or friends had come. One day three or four relatives arrived on the train. My father was expected to come with them, but he did not. We were told that he was killed outside the Lahore railway station. Here, again, the role of prarabdha may be clearly seen.

Question: "What is the relationship between dreams and spirituality?"

Answer: "Dreams are our best example of the impermanence and transient nature of the world. They seem real when we see them, but they are false as soon as we wake up. This is what happened to King Janak. He lost a war in a dream. He was wandering in the jungle, tired and hungry. As soon as he woke up the dream was gone, and all the royal luxuries were surrounding him. He asked whether this was real, or the dream was real. Ashtavakra replied, "Neither is this real, nor was the dream real. As long as you are sleeping, the dream is real, but when you awaken everything is false. Similarly, as long as a being is in Maya the world is true, but when he wakes up and gains the right knowledge nothing is real. The world is false."

Question: "The dreams that take the form of prarabdha and become true when you awaken — how can they be called false, specifically when that actually happens in life."

Answer: "How can the reflection of falsehood be real? When an untruth mixes with untruth, it does not become truth. A false shadow of a dream based on sanchit [accumulated] samskaras is not even visible after you wake up. In a dream based on prarabdha, the reflection of a shadow is visible. But it is false, just as the dream was false."

Question: "Some people claim that they can interpret every dream and tell its significance. They may say that you were a leader of a gang of bandits in a past life. 'You used to rob travelers. Once a young couple was traveling. The woman was loaded with jewelry. You caught both of them, tortured them, and took all her jewelry. Now you must suffer the consequences of your action.' "

Answer: "Who has seen whether someone was a bandit or not in a past life? Whether one had tortured a couple or not? People believe these things because of blind faith. Thus the spiritual significance of a dream is secondary."

48.   The Mischief of the Mind

One sadhak pronounced, "The mind is troublesome and mischievous. It makes everyone dance. The entire world is troubled by the mind." What Maharajshri said about the mind in his response to this is as follows:

"The world is an extension of the mind. The world extends as far as the mind extends. The world becomes as the mind is. Where the mind starts to shrink, the world also begins to shrink. Where there is no mind, there is no world either. Where there is a mind, there is also the world. Where there is sorrow in the mind, the world also becomes a source of unhappiness. Where there is happiness in the mind, the world becomes the source of happiness. Where the mind is restless, the world also dances with restlessness. Where the mind is peaceful, every place is filled with peace."

(1) Whatever desires and tendencies exist in the mind, the world develops accordingly. With the growth of vasanas in a person, his world also grows with them. Due to this new hopes and worries continue to tighten their grip around him. The chitta of a human being has been so infested with vasanas [mental modifications] that he expects from everyone, he doubts everyone, he is ready to plead in front of anyone, and, if the occasion arises, he is ready to get angry with anyone. Once the wheel of vasanas begins to turn it shows no signs of stopping. It makes the man go around with it.

If the expansion of the mind is extroversion then its contraction is introversion. Once it starts to contract, or shrink, it goes on shrinking (although expansion may introduce obstacles intermittently). It begins to give up the root causes of its expansion: the desires and vasanas. It seems as if a lost traveler has found his way home. At that time his mind dances with joy. He throws away all the unnecessary baggage he was unnecessarily carrying on his head.

(2) The mind is like a pair of eyeglasses through which the living

being sees the world. The world appears to be the same color as the shade of the spectacles it wears. The mind wears the spectacles of vasanas, hopes and feelings, and thus the world appears like that. A sensuous man will only see physical beauty everywhere. The world is like an ignited oven for an angry man. A hateful person will see enemies everywhere. A devotee will go to a temple to worship, while a thief will go to steal. Someone considers his father equal to God, and another wants to swallow his wealth. The virtues and vices in our own mind are reflected in the world. The person who finds faults with the world has a storehouse of faults within himself. A virtuous person sees virtues everywhere, and starts to observe his own faults when he sees those of another.

An introverted mind closes the window that opens towards the world. When a devotee looks at the world he sees love everywhere, because his heart is filled with love. He does not see likes and dislikes, jealousy and desires, and selfishness and suspicion anywhere because his eyeglasses are colored with love. He can only see love. He sees everyone moving towards God. Even if someone has wandered off the path he is still searching for God. No one appears bad to him. He never says a single word against anyone. He is neither angry with anyone, nor disappointed with anyone. His attention is turned inwards, even when he looks at the world.

(3) When the mind begins to contract, hopes and desires begin to fall away. Although the world exists, it seems to be dissolving. Its importance ends. The world exists due to vasanas, the mind exists due to vasanas, and the connection between the mind and the world is also due to vasanas. In the absence of vasanas there is no world, no mind and also no connection between the mind and the world. This is sham-dam [quieting and controlling the mind]. This is pratyahara [recoiling the mind within]. This shrinking and folding-in of the mind is the doorway to spiritual progress. The secret to freedom from the miseries of the world is hidden in this. Expansion of the mind brings nothing but restlessness and turbulence. Withdrawal of the same mind from the world emanates nothing but peace.

(4) The existence of this world [the perception of it being real and

eternal] is felt only by the mind. It is the mind who imagines happiness in the midst of the miseries of the world. The mind brings the soul to the world, and imagines the soul where it is not. The mind imagines eternity and stability in this momentary world. The feelings of purity and impurity, pious and impious, arise in the same mind. They first arise in the mind and then spread in the world. For a mind that is empty of these feelings, the existence of the world and itself is nothing else but the lila, the divine sport, of the Lord.

(5) The world cannot make anyone happy or unhappy. The world is Maya, a show and a fraud. It is the mind who wanders around in the world in order to find the cause of its misery. The mind that is restless and unhappy spreads unhappiness in the world. The world cannot make the mind unhappy, but the mind can certainly inflict pain on the world. At some places it destroys nature, at some places it cuts trees, some places it gravely bleeds, it injures mountain peaks, and at other places with harsh words it disturbs the peaceful minds of others. The world is charged with the live, blissful nature of God. God's sovereign consciousness dances in each and every particle of the world. Unfortunately the unhappy mind sees only unhappiness all around. All this is the play of the mind. With the same mind one can experience light everywhere, or the darkness of unhappiness. The world is what it is. There is light and darkness in the mind. There is unhappiness and contentment, as well as peace and restlessness, in the mind.

(6) The question is whether the mind is steady or restless. Restlessness is the world; peace is spirituality. Restlessness consists of likes and dislikes, anger, greed, desires, vasanas, ego and selfishness. Steadiness includes love, equanimity, compassion, generosity, contentment and profundity. These are opposite states of the same mind. Fickle-mindedness is extroversion and steadiness is introversion.

Question: "How is it that one and the same world, made by God, is a source of misery for some and joy for others?"

Answer: "A living being does not become happy or unhappy due to the world made by God, but by the world of imagination created by himself. If he is not satisfied with the world made by God, pride creates its own separate world within God's world. He divides the world — my home, my family, my language, country and religion, my wealth, fame and success or failure. In this manner his own new world is created that makes him happy and sad."

Question: "Then this feeling of mine and yours causes the trouble, not the mind. This feeling of mine and yours accelerates the unsteadiness of the mind. Is there any way to be saved from this?"

Answer: "Yes, there is a solution. It is the experience of the universal consciousness that is beyond mine and yours. It is awake and alive in one and all sadhaks. However this feeling of mine and yours does not end as soon as the experience of universal consciousness begins. As long as accumulated samskaras of the past are strong, this feeling persists. To weaken them an aspirant must do continuous sadhana for a long, long time.

"We must control our own mind. We must eradicate vasanas, samskaras and perversions from our mind. The world will appear as we want it to appear. If we fall in our mind then we fall in the world, as well. If we rise in our mind then we will rise in the world, as well. First cunning arises in our mind, then we start to walk crooked in the world. As is the mind, so is the world."

49. Jyotirlinga

Maharajshri usually stayed in Dewas for four months during the monsoons. At the end of the monsoons, for the Simolanghan [the ceremonial rite of crossing the boundaries after staying at one place for an extended period of time for a spiritual purpose], he would go to a famous temple of Lord Shiva in the village of Bilawali, about two miles away. This time the plan was to go to Omkareshwar. Eight or ten people were going. A small bus was to be used. The rainy season was not completely over. A hill had to be crossed along the way. It was a mountainous area, there was greenery all around, and the winding road and everything around was beautiful. About fifteen kilometers from Badvah the Narmada River had to be crossed. After that the road ran parallel to the river. In three hours we reached Omkareshwar from Dewas. It was about ten o' clock in the morning. On the way, in the bus, there was a conversation regarding Shivopasana [worship of Lord Shiva].

Maharajshri was saying, "The worship of the Shivalinga [an emblem of Shiva] is a combination of nirguna [without attributes] as well as saguna [with qualities] worship. It seems that people who wanted to worship nirguna Bramha [the attributeless Supreme Self], and wanted a symbol of that, were advised to worship the Shivalinga. Worship is not possible without any basis. Bramha [the Supreme Self] has to have some form. Shivalinga gives Bramha a form. There is no simpler form than this. It is oblong like the sky. The sky is compared with Bramha because it is infinite; it has no shape or quality, and yet it looks round. The same oblong round shape was taken to form the Shivalinga, and its worship began.

"Some Shivalingas are stones that are not shaped; for example, the one at Kedarnath. It is just a bump in a stone. A temple was built over it and faithful devotees have worshiped it for centuries. People must have anointed the stone with many thousands of tons of ghee [clarified butter]. This is worshiping a form of the formless.

"Symbol worship started with natural things like the sun, moon, river, ocean, mountains, and so forth. With the commencement of the age of the Puranas, man-made statues came to be used as symbols. These statues became the basis for saguna worship. Shivalinga worship became popular between these two periods. Not only did Shivalinga worship begin during that time, but also Goddess Bhagawati was worshipped in a linga form. Even today, in some old temples in the Himalayas, the Goddess is present in the form of a linga. Thus the ages may be categorised into three parts: the Vedic Age [formless and natural things], the Linga Age [symbolic], and the Puranic Age [idols].

"Shiva means 'propitious' and attainment of the state of samadhi is most propitious. Hence the samadhi state is also called the Shiva state. Times have changed now, and you can find many pictures of Shiva influenced by movie posters. In the past, Shiva was depicted only in the samadhi state with his eyes half closed."

Comment: "Lord Shiva is shown drinking bhang [an ancient, ayurvedic elixir prepared from hemp leaves]. Near Shiva a grinding stone is always shown, and bhang is called 'the herb of Shiva.'"

Answer: Maharajshri started to laugh, and said, "Do you think Lord Shiva is a human being who will take drugs to get intoxicated? Not only a stone grinder is shown, but a wife and a son are also depicted next to Shiva. His residence is shown in Kailash, and a bull on which he rides also appears. But one who reaches the state of samadhi is always in solitude. Then how come Lord Shiva possesses all this? He is shown carrying the Ganges River on his head and a trident in his hand. All these are shown to explain to mankind through symbolic means.

"Shiva and his consort, Parvati, symbolize Bramha — the Supreme Self and its Shakti. The intoxication of bhang is the intoxication of sadhana in a devotee for attaining Shiva and Shakti. Sadhana is the grinding stone on which the mind must go through a grinding process to gain the intoxication of meditation. The residence on the peak of Kailash is the highest spiritual stage. The bull is a symbol of prana, the life-force, and the Ganges River symbolizes the dissolution of all sins. The confusion takes place when Shiva and Shakti are taken not as symbolic representations, but as deities in bodies like humans."

As we listened to this we arrived at Omkareshwar. In those days one had to cross the Narmada River by boat. Now there is a bridge. The temple of Omkareshwar is on a small island in the middle of the Narmada River. Omkareshwar is on the island, and Mamleshwar is on the other bank. Both claim that their linga is the Jyotirlinga [literally: "the emblem of light"].

After offering his prayers in the temple Maharajshri sat on the riverbank and started to talk about Jyotirlinga. "There are twelve Jyotirlingas: Kedarnath and Vishwanath in Uttar Pradesh; Mahakaleshwar and Omkareshwar in Madhya Pradesh; Grishneshwar, Vaidyanath, Nagnath and Tryambakeshwar in Maharashtra; Somnath in Gujarat; Mallikarjuna in Andhra Pradesh; and Rameshwaram in Tamilnadu. There is a temple of Vaidyanath in the Kangada district of Himachal Pradesh and another temple of Nagnath in Gujarat. They also claim that their temples are Jyotirlinga. The Vaidyanath temple in Bihar also claims to be a Jyotirlinga. Each of the Jyotirlingas has a mythological story behind it. Either a devotee was in great difficulty or someone did severe penance and God manifested to him and then settled at that spot in the form of a jyoti [flame]. Today the jyoti is not visible anymore, but there are huge temples and Shivalinga. The temple of Pashupatinath in Nepal and the temple of Amarnath in Kashmir are not Jyotirlingas, but they command very high faith."

Question: "What is the difference between Jyotirlinga and Swayambhoo linga [a self-manifested linga or emblem, not man-made]?

Answer: "Usually the first thing that happens is that a desire to build a temple arises in someone's heart. Then he builds a temple and procures a Shivalinga and establishes it there. The Swayambhoo linga, on the other hand, manifests from the earth on its own. A temple is built for it, and then it is installed. There is no shortage of Shiva temples in India. With the passage of time, temples, too, disappear. The idols and the Shivalinga lay buried in the earth. When someone excavates them, a Shivalinga is unearthed. This is the scientific description of the

Swayambhoo linga. I already told you about Jyotirlinga."

Question: "Are the sadhanas of Shiva and Shakti different?"

Answer: "There is no difference, but there is a difference of senti-ments and faith. Since Shiva and Shakti are not separate, how can the sadhana be different? The concept of differentiation has rooted so deeply in the minds of people that they look for it. I agree that for understand-ing the subject, it has to be analyzed. An attempt has to be made to understand the different limbs of a philosophy independent of each other. But, finally, the essence is one and the same. An individual soul tears apart the basic elements, but usually he does not have the ability or the inclination to combine it together. Shakti is Shiva's. From Shiva, it manifests within Shiva on the basis of Shiva. While remaining one with Shiva it becomes active, then dissolves back into Shiva. When someone worships Shiva, he is worshipping the Shakti of Shiva."

Question: "Some people believe in Shakti alone and not in Shiva."

Answer: "That is their own perspective, but Shakti cannot exist without any basis, If Shakti exists then so does its basis. Shiva is the basis."

It was around three o' clock. It was time to return. We all sat in the minibus and departed. Sometimes the road was straight and at other times it was winding. Now we had to climb the hill. We reached Dewas at about seven o'clock in the evening.

50. Hope and Despair

Along with the inner flow of thoughts and emotions, a continuous rise
and fall goes on in the inner realms of the mind. One moment the mind
is riding the horse of hope; the next moment it may be in the abyss of
despair. The whole world swings in such a mental state. I was not an
exception to this mental weaving and unweaving. My mind kept on rising and falling continuously.

In a discussion on this subject Maharajshri said, "From hope to
despair and then despair followed by new hope. A new despair following
new hope and again new hope. Thus the mill of hope and despair keeps
on turning. Life passes by in this grind. A human being nurtures a boundless storehouse of hope and despair within. Hope surfaces sometimes,
and despair at other times. Life may end, but hope and despair never do.
At the time of death, too, a human being passes away with the hope of
living.

"Usually the basis for hope in a human being is the world. The
world keeps changing its form and hope changes its form with it. By the
time hope is fulfilled, the world has already changed its form. This hope
has been called an unholy vasana [mental modification] by the authors
of the scriptures because this mental modification keeps a living being
entangled forever. It is as if someone strikes another person until he is
seriously wounded, then he treats him and gives him food. As soon as
the victim is little better he starts to beat him again. In the same way
hope kills the person by making him yearn. Life passes by in despair.
Still the flame of hope keeps burning.

"Just as night follows day, waves in the ocean rise and fall, and one
is repeatedly tormented by hunger even after eating again and again, in
the same way hope and despair keep chasing each other. Sometimes hope
is visible and at other times one experiences despair. Hope does not die,

nor does despair go away. Life is just an other name for hope and despair.

"A worldly person is a slave of hope and despair. He cannot let go of either one, even if he wishes to. If he could give them up he would not be what he is. His life is like sunshine and shadow. As soon as the rays of hope are visible, darkness descends. The life of a sadhak is different from the life of a worldly person. He has hopes, but no despair. He remains hopeful until he meets his beloved. Only a devotee or a sadhak can keep hope alive and never, ever let despair approach him, because his hope does not depend upon the transitory world but upon the unchangeable God. His mind is not focused outward, but inward. Hope from the world and vasanas makes the mind fickle and restless. But the life of a sadhak is just the opposite. Once his hope of union with God is fulfilled he transcends hope. Then new hopes do not arise. Hence the hope of uniting with God is called a holy vasana.

"An aspirant never gives up the path of love for God in despair no matter how adverse the circumstances. The path of love is always filled with difficulties. Obstacles are presented by the world. Inner impurities rise up as roadblocks. The one who can face these difficulties while upholding the torch of hope is a true sadhak. Were Mirabai and Tukaram not tried enough by circumstances? Did Kabir and Narsi Mehta worry about poverty? Did Jnaneshwar bow before the tortures of society? Did any of the saints get mentally agitated and let despair even sprout? A true aspirant does not know how to despair. It would mean mistrust of God. An aspirant can give up the world. He can endure miseries, insult, defamation, but he cannot give up faith in God. Hence the question of despair just does not arise. The so-called aspirants who harbor the pride of being aspirants must look within and see whether the fierce dance of hope and despair goes on in their mind. If the answer is yes then how can they join the ranks of sadhaks?

"A devoted sadhak cries in front of his dear God. He pleads, blames his mind, and expresses his sorrows, but does not give up hope. He never gives up hope for God's grace. He believes that someday his life will certainly bloom when worldly desires release him, and he will meet his

God. 'Perhaps my mind is still attracted to worldly pleasures but one day I will surely be free from them. Now my mind is filled with nothing but darkness. There is not a single ray of hope visible. But I am not despairing. God will surely listen to my cry one day.' To keep this type of hope alive while waiting for God is devotion.

"The essence of this is that there is nothing wrong in maintaining hope if it is not for the world, but for God. This birth and death is only a lila, a play, for a devotee. It is like going backstage to change one's costume and returning to the stage in a new one. This is why death and rebirth is not relevant for him. He maintains hope for life after life. He comes to the world with the hope of meeting God. If he does not find God he goes away holding on to his desire. All the rest is the lila, or the divine play, of the Lord. If the flow of hope turns toward the world then he is caught in the whirlpool of hope and despair. If the flow of hope turns toward God or the inner-self then he becomes a devotee, a sadhak. There is nothing wrong with hope if it is not tied to despair."

51. Ego: A Problem

I went to Indore for two days with Maharajshri. We stayed with a gentle-man. There was discord between him and his brother. Narrating his story, he said he was very unhappy about this. "He is my neighbor as well as my brother because he lives in half of the building. He fights everyday."

Maharajshri said, "I understand your difficulty. A brother on the one hand and a neighbor on top of that. It is going to be difficult if discord persists. Think about the following seriously:

(1) This is the trend of this age. There must be countless families like this in which quarrels occur between brothers. One of the reasons for this is narrow-mindedness; the other is the distribution of the inher-itance. As the era itself is such, you are not alone. Quarrels between brothers have taken the form of a national problem.

(2) Because you are a sadhak you will understand the situation in relation to sadhana. Your brother is not a sadhak so he cannot under-stand this point. I frequently talk about prarabdha. Prarabdha has the central role in whatever situations, convenient or otherwise, come in front of a human. The only way to deplete prarabdha is to endure the effect of prarabdha without becoming disturbed. You can also explain to your brother that there is no benefit in causing distress to both families. If you live cohesively, both families will be happy and both will gain strength."

Question: "Even among the members of the same spiritual family [organization], where all are sadhaks and do sadhana and understand the issue, enmity still exists there?"

Answer: [In a serious tone] "Quarrels also take place between Guru-brothers [those initiated by the same Guru] because they do not under-stand the essence of sadhan in spite of being sadhaks. Their ego makes them fight. They become sadhaks but their ego does not disappear at once. If someone tries to crush one's ego, his ego also tries to make him fall from his sadhan by retaliating with an equal and opposite force. Whoever attacks with greater force is successful. It is clear that many sadhaks are in the primary stages of their sadhan, and at that time ego is very powerful, hence its attack also will be strong. This is the root cause of all fights."

Question: "Can't a Guru control these situations?"

Answer: "First of all, the Gurus of today are themselves in the primary stages of sadhan. It is not their spiritual progress, but their ego that has made them a Guru. They fundamentally lack depth, generosity and tolerance. They themselves are involved in different kinds of fights, so how can they pull someone else out of it! Even if the Guru is capable then the question that arises is, 'What is the capacity of the disciple's mind to absorb the instructions of the Guru?' If the sun is shining but the doors and windows of your home are shut, how can the sunlight enter? A person may deprive himself of the sun that is shining outside. The same thing is true for the teachings of the Guru. If the disciple has shut the door of his mind, how can teachings enter his mind?"

Question: "When they listen to the teachings of the Guru they are influenced by it at that time, but who-knows-what happens, the disciple forgets all his teachings and behaves as he did before."

Answer: "During a satsang [spiritual discourse] the ego temporarily is suppressed. The mind appears as if it is influenced by the teachings. A wave comes and drenches the mind. Everything dries up in a little while. The water of love evaporates and ego raises its head again. The teachings do take the disciple into the land of God on a temporary basis. He can only see a glimpse and then he forgets everything. He remains where he was.

"A satsang is definitely called a 'Sat-sang' [in the company of Sat, the true being, the Universal Self], but, in reality, it is association with holy men. If, even once, a true association [sang] with the Universal Self, the true being [Sat], takes place its effects are limitless. Sat is either the Universal Self, or it is the power of the Self. A real glimpse of that would change one's whole life. But that kind of satsang does not occur. What is the use of a discourse if it does not give any experience of the land of God? This is a thought-provoking question for those who give discourses. Now let us look at the disciples. It is true that today one may be able to find a real Guru, but it is even harder to find a real disciple. A real disciple is one who is sincerely eager to find the truth. Who is hungry for spirituality? Who is restless for self-realization and is ready to give up everything to attain his goal? Do you see anyone like that among those who are busy fighting? A real disciple does not have time to get involved in fights and arguments. Fighting means the focus is the world, and that implies indifference toward spirituality. Those who are not focused toward the soul — what more can be expected from them than fights and strife, jumping and bouncing?

"The behavior, perspective and speech of a spiritually-oriented true disciple are totally different. A true disciple is favorable toward spirituality and adverse to the world. He is compassionate, sympathetic and a personification of love. Humility and simplicity are his nature. Even if he wants to fight with someone he cannot."

Question: "If one looks from your point of view, hardly anyone will qualify as a true disciple."

Answer: "Yes. There is a lot of noise about spirituality but it is not seen anywhere. A true Guru and a true disciple — both are extremely hard to find. In the name of religion there are many power plays, but religion is in a bad state. A brother fights with a brother, a husband with a wife, neighbors, and so forth. No one gets along. Everywhere selfishness and ego rule. In the middle of this a real sadhak is crushed, but that is his sadhana. He is peaceful even then. If he sees the world running, he laughs. If he sees the world sad, he feels sympathy. If he sees that the world is absorbed in pleasures, he prays to God to protect it. He blossoms in all sufferings. The more difficulty he faces, the more he shines."

Question: "Such an aspirant is impossible to find!"

Answer: "Such sadhaks are not available everywhere like the stones on the roadside. Even if someone is like that the world does not recognize him. The world looks at the external form of a person, the pomp, worldly wisdom, and style of communication and skill in worldly affairs. Forgetting the sentiment in the heart the world remains engrossed in the ragas and the notes, the melodies and the beats. The world pays greater attention to artistic aspects of an art."

Question: "Even God does not take care of his own world?"

Answer: "All this is a divine sport for God. He lets the sinful get puffed up and takes them to the mountaintop. Then he drops them to the ground with force. They are unable even to get up. A sadhak climbs the mountain of spirituality slowly, carefully, clinging to rocks and, at times, skipping over things. His speed is slow like the turtle but he keeps climbing constantly. How can someone who is involved in quarrels and fights climb this slope? He does not even turn in that direction."

52. The Upheaval of Succession

It was the beginning of 1964. Winter was just over and spring was coming. New foliage was sprouting on the trees. Flower buds had started to come up. It was very pleasant when Maharajshri went for his morning walk. A light fragrance had spread all around. The sky was partially cloudy. A few drops of rain were coming down. Both of us had umbrellas.

We had reached the road. I started the conversation. "Since you have chosen and announced a successor would it not be appropriate to publish it? The successor will be satisfied and it will make him aware of his responsibilities, as well. He still seems to be in a dilemma."

Maharajshri said, "Does this mean you have made up your mind not to accept being my successor?"

Seeing that the subject of my succession was resurfacing I became somewhat nervous. I said, "Maharajji, I have explained several times that I consider myself to be totally unworthy. I neither have the knowledge, nor have I done enough austerity, nor do I have the right personality, nor the desire. I do not even know whether my primary stage has begun or not. When I look inside I see only darkness. It is your divine grace that you give me the opportunity to serve at your feet. I feel that succession can increase my ego. And you tell us that ego is the biggest obstacle on the spiritual path."

Maharajshri said, "If I tell you something repeatedly, I must surely understand something. If you are talking about worthiness then that can be known only when the right time and opportunity come, whether someone is deserving or not. If everyone in the world believed they were undeserving then no work would be undertaken. Is it not enough that I wish it so? Do you not believe that it is your duty to respect my wish?" Maharajshri became quiet after that but I went into deep thought. Both of us were thinking deeply.

It was correct that my duty was to respect Maharajshri's wish. It was also true that there is little difference between wish and command. But my lack of faith in myself was even stronger. My attention kept going toward my state of mind, which seemed totally incapable of carrying this burden. I had no knowledge and no strength, not even the strength to do austerities. At the time I could not understand what I was to realize later, after Maharajshri had merged with the Absolute: that everything is being accomplished by Guru-Shakti, the power of the Guru. Now I know that it was my ego saying that "I" will have to run the ashram. However at that time this ego stood before me as a great obstacle. "It will be my responsibility, I will have to do everything." My ego was interfering with my duty. I did not understand that human beings are only toys in the hands of God. No one knows what lila he wants to do, or when. This was my lack of understanding. But what was I to do? I was like an ignorant child plagued with ego.

I checked myself again and again. I evaluated myself again and again, and finally came to the conclusion that the job was very big and my shoulders were very weak. "I am totally incapable of shouldering such a great responsibility." I decided not to respect Maharajshri's wish because at this time my ego had become much more important than Guruji. The ashram seemed like a blazing fire pit lit with a flame of problems and complications. I had run away from the heat of this world and sought refuge at my Guru's feet, and Maharajshri, with his infinite grace, gave me that shelter. Why then was I being thrown into the fire of ashram affairs, greater even than the affairs of a family? I did not understand then that one must burn in order to shine. Impurities of the mind do not turn to ashes without burning. Perhaps Maharajshri was throwing me into the blazing fire for that purpose, but at that time I was unable to comprehend this.

Once in a while I started to feel slightly angry towards Maharajshri. "Why does he urge me repeatedly when I am refusing again and again. Is he determined to show my failure to the world, or does he want to disturb my mental peace?" At that time I even forgot that the Guru never wants to harm the disciple. It is possible that the disciple might find the path difficult and slippery, but travelling on that difficult path would be for his own benefit.

How cunning and crafty a human being can be! He finds so many schemes and excuses to escape. He hides beautifully what he has in his mind and shows something else on the surface. In truth I was afraid of being the successor. I saw my weaknesses. I wanted to save myself from jumping into the fire, but I covered all that creatively under the camouflage of Guru-seva, serving the Guru. Service rendered to the Guru as a shield to protect oneself is not Guru-seva at all. I was also such an egoistic and hypocritical devotee of my Guru that I had no hesitation in putting on the mantle of Guru-seva. I told Maharajshri, "My mind is extremely satisfied in doing service at your feet. This is my succession; this is my sadhan. Besides, you have announced someone else to be your successor anyway. It is my request that I remain at your feet."

Maharajshri said, "All right. I will never, ever again ask you to be the successor. I had thought it was for your benefit only, but your mind did not accept it. You want to be free from activities, but it is better for you to be involved. You accept the fact that your mind is still impure. It cannot be purified by retiring, but rather by walking a path full of activities. It cannot be burned by the workings of prarabdha either. For that one must face circumstances, one must taste joys and miseries, one must swallow fame and insult. The activities of the world are like a fire pit that burns impurities to ashes, and you are trying to save yourself. Some time or the other you will have to burn."

With the very first sentence that Maharajshri spoke my move seemed to be successful. I did not pay much attention to what he said afterward. I was very happy and started to feel light, as if a heavy load had been lifted from me. In my excitement I grabbed his feet, but he did not respond.

With the passage of time I realized how accurate Maharajshri's evaluation and conclusion was. He was an advanced master, a mahapurusha, with extremely subtle perception. Along with his own chitta, he was capable of peeking into another's chitta. But disciples hinder their own progress on the spiritual path due to their ego and ignorance.

The irony is that the disciple does not even realize he has lost the true path. He is intoxicated by a favorable outcome. This is the sense of individuality. The ego changes his direction, his sadhan and his destination so much so that he forgets his real Self. That is what happened to me.

53. A Mental Dilemma

I used Guru-seva as a shield and temporarily became happy, but this event had scarred the face of my sense of service. I performed my services as before, but the enthusiasm, joy, love and surrender were missing. My service turned into heartless, mechanical work.

Tenderness of the heart and sweetness were replaced with inertness and dryness. Although Maharajshri was so close, it felt as if some distance had been created. The intoxicating and uplifting joy of the mind had disappeared. It was the same ashram and the same work, but life had become flavorless.

I would go to the cave for meditation as before, but the force of kriyas had stopped. It felt as if kriya-Shakti was displeased. I started to grow tired of sadhan in a short time, and I would give it up, get up and go away, to the extent that I felt like hiding my face even when I saw smiling flowers. Now I started to hate myself. Unnecessary and bad thoughts came like storms into my mind as if someone had pushed me from heaven into hell.

Maharajshri had almost stopped talking during the morning walks. Most of the time he would end a conversation with a yes or a no. Sometimes we returned from our walk without a single word. Maharajshri began to stay more and more in a meditative state and the storm of the dilemma kept on rising in my mind. During the morning walk one day, I had to ask, "Have I made a mistake that you have created a distance between you and me? May I know the reason for your displeasure so that I can correct my mistake?"

Maharajshri said, "I have told you many times that a Guru is never displeased with a disciple. He may not remain pleased, but he is never displeased. You must understand the difference between not being pleased and being displeased. If the Guru does not remain pleased with the disciple the natural flow of love and blessings stops, but a Guru's displeasure would be a misfortune for the disciple. A Guru does not wish misfortune for a disciple under any circumstance, so the question of the Guru's displeasure just does not arise. If God wishes he may punish someone, but a Guru prays to God to forgive his disciple. Thus my displeasure is your misconception.

"It is mentioned in the Skanda Purana that the sun gives light during the day, and the moon during the night. A lamp removes only the darkness in the house with its light, but a Guru keeps a flame of light ablaze in the hearts of disciples at all times. The Guru destroys the darkness of ignorance within the disciple with the light of his knowledge. The Guru is the holiest water for the disciple. How can he even imagine misfortune for a disciple? It is the function of holy water to impart purity."

I said, "Maharajshri, my sadhana has slowed down. My peace of mind has disappeared. My mind feels totally empty."

Answer: "If one wishes to, one can very well understand his own mistake. Since you have asked I am telling you this. Sometimes the matter may be small but its result can be deadly. The significance of anything is understood only by its effect. A small event can bring a great change in life. A short-lived earthquake or storm can destroy thousands of lives. You just turned your face and the scenery changed. One wave of water may drown a huge ship in the bottom of the ocean. In the same way one small thought in the mind can change the flow of an entire life.

"Whether you realize it or not, you have been serving me for certain but you were proud of this service. This ego has continued to grow inside. Then there was another pride within you. You believed that those involved in activities lag behind in spirituality, and that you are moving toward nivritti [abstinence from activity]. With this pride about the goal of abstinence from activities you have shown disinterest in managing the ashram. You did not even consider that this was the Guru's wish. Is it not Guru-seva to respect and act according to your Guru's wish? You have lost track of the fact that Guru-seva is selfless. You have missed the essence of Guru-seva in the pride of serving the Guru. Your secretly nourished ego finally bursts out one day, just as a dam across a huge lake becomes weak and breaks creating havoc and a flood. Your ego understood neither your duty, nor the sanctity of the Guru-shishya [Guru-disciple] relationship. The Guru always wishes the best for the disciple, so his mind is not influenced. The one whose mind is influenced is not a Guru, but Shakti may tolerate the Guru's insult or it may not. Perhaps Shakti did not tolerate it, became upset with you, and retracted the kriyas.

"On the one hand the relationship between the Guru and disciple is beneficial to both. But on the other hand it is very delicate as well. The relationship of many years can encounter difficulties in a second. The Guru has kind affection for the disciple, and the disciple has faith and surrender toward the Guru. As soon as the slightest doubt or ego arises a crack may develop in the relationship. In my insistence there was only affection and no selfish interest, but your surrender had a flaw. Therefore you were incapable of respecting my wish. I detached my mind from this thought and decided never to talk about it in the future, but perhaps Shakti was upset. Feelings and thoughts in the mind can make or spoil situations. A person knows what is in his mind, so look inside your own mind."

Maharajshri was quiet after saying this and I started to slide into a deep valley of thoughts. We did not talk about anything else on the road. In the afternoon when Maharajshri got up after his rest, finding an opportune moment, I asked, "Perhaps I have a sense of ego regarding service to you, but it was more about worthiness. Otherwise I am ready to do anything at your slightest indication."

Maharajshri said, "I read a book. I do not remember its name now. Someone went to a Guru for initiation. Guruji asked, 'Would you jump into the fire of Hell if I asked you to do so? If you are ready to jump without even saying yes then talk to me.' The responsibility of the ashram looked like a burning fire and you started to run. This is your unworthiness. That is it. Now this topic is over. I will not start this subject again. But get rid of the thought that I am displeased with you."

The subject of succession was closed for the time being.

54. Proposal for Sanyas

My state of mind started to improve after a few days. I was happy like before and kept watching the lila of the world. I saw that everyone was looking at each other's faults, but no one was looking at their own weaknesses. Everyone was sneaking around looking for flaws in others, even those that might be imaginary. Perhaps God created the world to watch this show. I saw that everyone was stiff with ego. Everyone was proud and praising himself, but when you searched their hearts there was unhappiness. I watched and was struck with wonder at God's play. I once read in the newspaper that there was a robbery in a temple. The thief even removed and stole God's garments. When I told that to Maharajshri he laughed a lot and said, "The thief does not care whether those things belong to a person or to God. He just wants the loot."

Whenever I looked within I was ashamed of myself. Here, also, the condition was the same. The same ego and anger. What weakness was not there? But on my head was the mark of a sadhak. I also had an appetite for praise. Without knowing, I used to praise myself. If the food was flavorful, I would eat a few extra bites. Is this the reward of sadhana? Is this what I grasped from the company of Maharajshri? Where was Maharajshri's pure personality? Here I was filled with filth! Then my mind would be sad.

Often I tried to console myself by thinking that this was the condition of the whole world. "You are not alone." The very next moment I would realize that this is not the way a sadhak should think. If the world has weaknesses it does not mean that your own weaknesses do not matter. Let the world be what it is. Just be concerned with your own mind. Then, suddenly, I would remember great personalities. They lived in the same world but they did not let the world influence their minds. How much hardship they must have faced! Kabir has said, "Observe your own actions, even if your hut is in the hands of people who slit throats." Why do you get sad? Every one receives according to what they have done. You reap as you sow.

My mind was such that sometimes it would watch and laugh to see the world jumping and bouncing. At other times it would be drawn into this activity. This caused a dilemma. I wondered why my mind was getting affected. Always it was due to impurities of the mind. "How do I clean my mind? I am doing sadhana and I am doing seva." The next moment I would be assailed by the thought, "This is your ego talking. Who are you to do sadhana? Are you doing seva? It is Shakti that is awakened within you doing sadhana. This Guru-Shakti is performing your seva [service]. This ego of yours is interfering with the purification of your mind." Then I would relax.

These controversies kept returning to my mind. I would be filled with hope sometimes, and with despair at other times. As I sat in the cave I would hear the sounds of the sadhaks' kriyas and my mind would be happy and hopeful. But when I saw their behavior and listened to their conversation, hopelessness would engulf me. My mind was still absorbing impressions of the world around. The flow of hope did not spring from within me. I was still oscillating in this dilemma when another event took place that completely shook me.

We were on our morning walk when suddenly Maharajshri stopped and said, "You must take sanyas [join the monastic order] now."

I was stupefied. Maharajshri said this so suddenly. I did not say a word for quite some time. Maharajshri also became totally quiet after speaking. I came to my senses after a while and said, "If this is your wish then it is a command for me. But, with your permission, I would like to say something. It is the same question of worthiness. Am I worthy of sanyas? In my opinion I am not ready. Your wish is my command, but would it be appropriate for me to take sanyas without deserving it?"

Answer: "Do you think that I am saying this to you without thinking? I know what your weaknesses are. No one can deserve this if they have such weaknesses. Still, why did I recommend sanyas to you? Think about that.

"It is a common belief in society that sanyas must be taken, or should be taken, after becoming a siddha [a perfect being], but this is a false belief. One thing is clear: that there is no other goal for you but spirituality. It is another question whether you deserve sanyas or not, but your goal is defined. The answer is hidden in this framework.

"There are two types of sanyas. The first type is vidvat sanyas. It means, 'I am taking sanyas because I have attained what I had to attain. Now there is nothing more to attain or know, so I take sanyas.' In today's age, one rarely sees such a sanyasi, one who has experienced the ultimate reality, in other words, is a siddha, a perfect being. Some people also say that vidvat sanyas is that sanyas which a person takes by himself, without a Guru. I do not know what the basis is of this understanding.

"The second type is vidvisha sanyas. The goal of this is nothing other than the vision of the ultimate reality. The intellect decides that the world is a house of miseries, hence there is no interest in attaining worldly happiness. 'I take sanyas because now my whole life is dedicated to attaining the final truth.' Most of the sanyasis [monks] today are in this category. How many of them are seriously trying to find the ultimate truth is a different issue. But the goal and meaning of vidvisha sanyas is this.

"Your sanyas will be vidvisha sanyas, and you will try, initially, to be worthy of vidvat sanyas. Once you become deserving of that, automatically you will be established in vidvat sanyas. It is possible this may happen in this life, or it may take more than this life. If you think about it, today you are already a vidvisha sanyasi. Only the ceremony has not been performed. Your aim is already established. I am simply talking about performing the formal ritual."

I had no answer to Maharajshri's logic. But I was stuck, like a person who is entrenched in firm ideas or feelings. No matter how much someone explains and tries to logically convince him, a person who is stuck is not willing to change his ideas. It seems that all efforts to explain touch his ears and return without entering his head. My mind was stuck in a cycle of thoughts about deserving and not deserving. Maharajshri's words were unable to reach my heart. Maharajshri's ideas were not penetrating me. Perhaps my perspective was different, or my mental state was different. But it was Guru Maharajshri's wish, without any selfish motive. He was always wishing the best for the disciple. I was helpless because I had suffered the effects of questioning my Guru's wish. I said, "Very well, Maharajji."

Maharajshri said, "It is the duty of a Guru to assign work to a disciple that is appropriate for him. If he is doing something that is not good for him then the Guru must distance the disciple from that. If the disciple is in a dilemma he should give him guidance; he should remind him if he is ignoring something that he must not. This is why a Guru is required. As long as pure distinction of good and bad has not arisen within, it is best to follow the Guru's instructions. In fact, everyone is proud of their intellect, but everyone is prone to make mistakes. One may repent later, but even then one does not give up ego. A simple way to end this ego is to offer yourself to someone."

55. The Incident of the Journey

Now there were discussions regarding my sanyas diksha [initiation into the monastic order]. One day Maharajshri said that he had never initiated anyone into sanyas. He was wondering who should give me sanyas. I was startled to hear this. I said, "Maharajshri, my faith, my sentiments, my surrender is all at your feet. I cannot even think of another place. Please grace me by not showing me another home. I am happy at your feet."

Maharajshri said, "You are making the same mistake. You are not at all willing to give up your prejudice. The one who sticks to his prejudice is not even a sadhak. Prejudice means that memories are too deep in the mind. A person cannot get out of those memories even if wishes to. You are speaking under the influence of your feelings and intellect. You are trying to undermine the Guru's wish by giving unnecessary arguments."

I became silent. Truly, my respect for the Guru's wish had disappeared. Yet, timidly, I asked a question. "I have heard that the voice of the inner Guru is of greater importance then the external Guru."

Maharajshri said, "Definitely. But only if it is the voice of the inner Guru. Often what is believed to be the voice of the inner Guru comes from the impurities, feelings and prejudices of the sadhak. Do not talk about the inner Guru now. That state is too distant. I have thought that you should take sanyas diksha from my Guru brother, Swami Narayan Tirth of Kashi [Varanasi]."

I was very familiar with Swami Narayan Tirth Maharaj. I had been in his service for two or three months in Uttarkashi. His smiling, affectionate face is in front of my eyes even today. His simplicity and gentleness had captivated my mind. I was satisfied to hear his name. He also was gracious to me. It was decided that we make our request through a letter. A letter was sent and his approval came. We decided to go to Kashi to discuss everything and finalize the arrangements.

Our plan was to go to Jagannathpuri, Calcutta, Gaya, Vaidyanath and Kashi. After making the arrangements there we were to proceed to Rishikesh. The program was such that I would be away from Dewas for quite a long time. Maharajshri and I went to Bhopal, Sagar, Jabalpur, Bilaspur and Raipur. One day we went to see the steel plant in Bhopal. A couple from Raipur joined us, and then we went to Jagannathpuri. On the way, during our railway journey, Maharajshri talked about pilgrimage and said that it was a good sadhana for people with an unstable mind. "If one must wander, it is better to wander for God. During the pilgrimage one must face many hardships, which develops the habit of endurance. At times you have to patiently tolerate insults, as well. This is a form of austerity. If rules of the scriptures such as truth, forgiveness, control over the senses, compassion, honesty, and so forth, are followed during the pilgrimage then they may become a part of one's nature during regular life."

Question: "What is the need for a pilgrimage if these virtues can be practiced in regular life?"

Answer: "There is no need. But if the virtues are not natural then it is very hard to develop them in the routine activities of life. This is why scriptures recommend a pilgrimage, so that people can go away for some time, develop the habit of enduring hardships, and take vows of virtue and practice them.

"Right now we, too, are pilgrims, but remember that just by immersing ourselves in the river one does not become holy. Such a bath is merely an external one. You take such a bath every day. The mind should be pure while taking a bath at a holy place. Under the pretext of a pilgrimage sadhaks have an opportunity to practice a few things. Today we do not see any effect of pilgrimage on many people because they do not follow the rules given in scriptures. If a bath is important then the aquatic creatures should be the first ones to be blessed, those who are born and die in the water and spend every moment of their life bathing in this water. Attachment to pleasures is called excreta and detachment from them is called cleanliness.

"If there are impurities in the mind they are not cleansed by mere baths in holy places. If a pot is filled with poison and it is immersed in holy water several times, the poison inside will not be washed away. Yes, if the pot is opened before it is submerged in the water then the water will wash away the poison. Following the rules is like opening the pot. If the feelings in the mind are not pure when you go to a pilgrimage site then all the donations you give, the fire ceremony you perform, and the prayer you recite are all wasted. The visit to holy places is a pretext for filling the mind with sacred feelings, and these spiritual feelings are what purify the mind. In reality, the feeling is the holy entity.

"A person who has control over his senses, harbors truth, contentment, compassion and dharma in his heart, and is without attachment, hatred, anger or sins, and is always engrossed in serving God — his master, the country where he lives, becomes his holy sanctuary or place of pilgrimage. The greatest is manas-tirtha, the pilgrimage of the mind. If the mind is filled with the water of knowledge, love and devotion, bathing in these will wash away the impurities of the mind. A pilgrimage provides the opportunity to look within our own mind."

Question: "Very often the main goal of a pilgrimage is the sight of a deity such as Badrinarayan, the temple of Jagannatha, Rameshwaram or Somnath, or a place devoted to Bhagawati, Ganesha or Dattatreya, but you are talking simply about a holy bath?"

Answer: "Tirtha means holy waters. By drinking this water, by taking a bath in this water or by seeing it, the mind is cleansed and purified. To please the eyes people build temples of deities. These also have elements of a tirtha. To gratify the ears people have developed spiritual singing, discourses, bells, and so forth. All these are like tirthas. They all can be a source of purification. But only that person whose mind is devoted may attain this purity. True tirthas, deities, discourses, bells, and so forth, are within."

We arrived at Jagannathpuri. A gentleman had made arrangements for our lodgings very close to Govardhan Math, which was established by Adi Shankaracharya. The following day we went to Swargadwara and bathed in the ocean, then went to the temple of Jagannatha for darshan.

The temple must have been about a mile and a half from the sea. Beggars were sitting on both sides of the road. I had never before seen so many beggars in one place. The road was so crowded that it was hard to walk. The temple was swarming with pandas [pilgrimage guides].

Maharajshri spoke about the temple of Jagannatha. "Once upon a time King Indradyuma ruled over the land of Malwa. He heard that in Utkal Pradesh there was a statue of Neel Madhava [Krishna] that was worshipped even by heavenly beings. He began to search for the place and eventually found it. Before he could go there heavenly beings took the statue to heaven. Then the King heard a voice from the sky telling him, and also felt in his heart, that he would see the same God in wooden form.

"King Indradyuma started to live near Nilanchala mountain, where the statue of Neel Madhava had been installed. He liked the place very much. One day he saw that a huge piece of wood had been washed up on the shore of the ocean. He decided to have it carved into a wooden statue. A wood carver agreed to do the work, but he demanded that, until he had finished the statue and informed him of its completion, no one could open his door or enter his house. The wood carver took the wood and closed himself up in the building. After a few days there was no news about the craftsman, so the queen became worried. She went to the king and said insistently, 'Who knows whether the craftsman is okay or not? How can anyone survive for so long without food and water?'

"At the King's order the door was broken. They went in and saw that there were unfinished statues of Lord Jagannath, Balrama and Subhadra. The craftsman was nowhere to be seen.

"This is the popular story about the history of the temple, but I see messages for the world in those incomplete statues.

(1) First of all, a sadhak runs out of patience. He worries about so many different things. He is in a hurry to see God, and the result is an incomplete vision.

(2) All the idols in all other temples may be very beautiful, but they are incomplete because no artist can ever depict the real form and qualities of God in a statue. All the instruments in the world are short-lived.

How can they give form to the image of the eternal God? However high one may fly with their mind and intellect they cannot reach God. Yes, a statue can certainly be the basis for efforts to find God. That basis can be anything — an image, book, statue, mountain, river, moon, sun."

After seeing and worshipping we went back to our room. Maharajshri stayed in Puri for fifteen days. It was our daily routine to take a bath in the sea and visit Jagannatha. Once we visited Govardhan Math [monastery] also. Swami Niranjana Tirth Dev Maharaj was the Shankaracharya there in those days. Swami Shankar Purushottam Tirth Maharaj had taken sanyas diksha there from Shankaracharya Swami Bharati Krishna Tirth Maharaj. Shankaracharya gave Maharajshri a gift of a compilation of lectures given by Swami Bharati Krishna Tirth Maharaj in the United States.

A couple of Sun temples have been built in India recently. However during those times I was not aware of any other Sun temple; possibly the only one was situated at about fifty-five miles from Jagannathpuri, the famous temple of Konark. We went to Konark by car. The temple there is surrounded by four walls and is built on slightly lower ground. There is a huge temple of the Sun god in the center, shaped like a chariot. The chariot has wheels and there are places for the horses and the charioteer. The temple had been quite high in the past but its pinnacle had broken and fallen. The original temple does not exist anymore; only portions of the front canopy are still standing.

When we went there the temple was filled with stones; the doors were locked to protect the statues carved into the walls. When I went a second time, after Maharajshri attained oneness with God, the stones were being removed. The temple has deteriorated badly, but what remains is impressive.

One thing I could not understand was why the temple was so full of indecent statues, as if indecency were merely dancing. I saw a few similar statues in other temples as well. What is the use of this in a temple? This is seen not only in Orissa, but all over India, especially in the ancient temples of the East. I have not been to Nepal, but I have heard this is true there, as well. I asked Maharajshri about this in order to hear his thoughts on the subject.

Answer: "In different ages, ideologies and the ways of doing sadhana change. It is said that this was done for protection from unexpected natural calamities, but I do not understand how it is related to natural calamities. It appears that when Tantra sadhana [the practice of Tantra] was devalued, and practices of vaam-marg [a school of thought in Tantra that professes the consumption of liquor, meat and other things] were popular, such temples were built, and such statues were built in the existing temples. In its original form vaam-marg was spiritual, but with the passage of time it became perverse. The indecent statues in the temple can also mean that spirituality is surrounded with attractions, desires and hopes, but that one has to cross those to reach God. When a devotee goes into the temple, many different attractions and vasanas are scattered around, but he must focus on the central statue of worship. I have heard that in some places indecent statues exist all the way up to the innermost sanctuary of the temple. Even here indecent statues are all the way up to the pinnacle of the temple. This implies that worldly desires chase a devotee over a long way and he must ignore them."

From Konark our car left for Saakshi Gopal temple. After reaching the temple and seeing the deity Maharajshri said, "I will not go into the details of the folklore about this temple. I will only say that a devotee needed a witness and there was no witness around. At that time Gopal [Lord Krishna] manifested and became the witness for the devotee. Since then he has been worshipped here as Saakshi [witness] Gopal.

"When I look at this from a spiritual perspective, 'Go' means the senses. The Shakti makes the senses active. It makes one talk, walk, stay and leave. It makes the mind think good and bad thoughts, and it is also the witness of all good and bad actions. This Shakti is Saakshi Gopal. The Gopal who gives Shakti and saakshi [witness] is worshipped here through the statue. This Shakti deserves respect, and is worthy of worship and attainment. This is why it is named Saakshi Gopal."

We returned to Jagannathpuri. It is a great place for a pilgrimage, but for us it was of the highest importance because the founder of our tradition of Shaktipat, Swami Gangadhar Tirth Maharaj, did his sadhana here. On the shore of Chandan Talab [lake] he lived in a small cottage. He lived a quiet peaceful life. He did not meet anyone, or go anywhere. He continuously did his sadhana. He laid the foundation of this lineage by giving Shaktipat initiation to Swami Narayan Tirth Dev Maharaj. One day we went to see Chandan Talab.

There had been great change in the landscape of Chandan Talab since the time of Swami Gangadhar Tirth Maharaj. At that time there was a jungle all around with huts of renunciate sadhus [ascetics]. Maharajshri began to walk around the area where Gangadhar Tirth Maharaji's cottage used to be. Maharajshri was walking in front with his cane, and we were behind him. He went along one small street, and then a second, and then a third. His face changed as soon as he entered the third street. He walked a little distance and stopped. He stood there for a little while and then said, "Gangadhar Tirth Maharaji's cottage was right here."

There was a wood and charcoal vendor's stall there. Maharajshri kept on saying, "It was here. It was right here. Spiritual rays of his sadhana are still vibrating here. The poor people selling wood and coal here do not know that they are doing their business in such a sacred place."

We returned to our lodgings. We had come to know some local people by now. Some of them had started to come regularly in the evening. The couple from Raipur that had accompanied us left after a week. Only Maharajshri and I remained. The schedule continued as before. First, a morning bath in the sea, after that the darshan of Jagannatha. We went out in the evening, after which we hosted visitors. Dinner came from the temple prasad [food offered to God in the temple].

Maharajshri addressed the visitors. "The first man in our lineage, Swami Gangadhar Tirth Maharaj, used to live in this city, seventy or eighty years ago, on the shore of the Chandan Talab."

After inquiring about directions and understanding exactly where the location was, he said, "I have a feeling that his cottage used to be where a stall of wood and coal is now located. Can any of you go and check the old records in the municipal office to find out what was there?"

The next day a gentleman said, "Maharajshri, there used to be a cottage of a Bramhachari named Karali."

Maharajshri jumped up. "Okay, okay. That's it! The cottage was in the name of Bramhachari Karali. He was Swamiji's bramhachari, and he gave it to Swamiji to live in while he went and lived at a dharmashala [a free lodging place for pilgrims]. The bramhachari used to bring alms for Swamiji Maharaj."

Now Maharajshri began to wonder if, somehow, that place could be made available. Then a holy place could be established and an ascetic could reside there. Maharajshri talked to a few people, but no one was ready. I requested, "If you instruct me, I would be happy to stay here."

Maharajshri said, "First we will have to try to acquire the place through local people. This is not a task for you." Consequently this idea of Maharajshri ended without any result.

Maharajshri and I went to Calcutta from Jagannathpuri. An ar- rangement was made to stay with a marwadi [a caste] family. Their house was very big, and many families were living in it. They lived on the third floor and we were given a room on the ground floor. The street was very filthy. The sewer was blocked and, as a result, it was stinking everywhere. We stayed there for three days. Our idea of Hell became a reality. We visited Dakshineshwar, Belur Math, Kali temple, and the botanical gar- den.

Dakshineshwar — the world famous Ramkrishna Paramhansa used to live here once upon a time. Queen Rasmani built this place on the banks of the Ganges River. Along the river there are temples of eleven Shivalingas. Right in the middle of them is a temple of Kali Mata. On one side of it is the room in which Paramhansa used to live. There is a verandah near the Ganges. Often Ramkrishna Paramhansa used to sit on a khatiya [a wooden bed frame woven with jute], look at the Ganges and meet his devotees. In his room, his bed and other memorabilia are pre- served. Samadhis [tombs] of his wife, Shardadevi, and Queen Rasmani are outside the temple. The banyan tree under which he used to meditate is still there."

Maharajshri said, "Spiritual rays attract seekers for a long time to the place where a highly-evolved spiritual being once lived. The resi- dence of Paramhansa has made this place a holy place. While sitting here he spread the light of spirituality with which the world is gleaming today. We believe that Ramkrishna Paramhansa was a Shaktipat acharya [master]. The experience he gave to Vivekananda and his other disciples was nothing other than Shaktipat. He gave an experiential message of generosity and clemency. He was devotion, jnana [knowledge] and yoga personified."

The following day we went to see Belur Math, established by Vivekananda on the banks of the Ganges. It is a majestic temple, with the shrines of Ramkrishna Paramhansa and Vivekananda. This is the main center of the Ramkrishna mission.

I asked what the difference was between Ramkrishna Paramhansa and Vivekananda. Maharajshri said, "It is not appropriate to compare them. Both Guru and disciple were great. Vivekananda has said, 'While I stood on the shore of the ocean counting the waves, my Gurudeva Paramhansa was diving deep in the ocean.'"

Next we went to see the botanical garden, which has a collection of all kinds of trees and plants. That was not our area of interest. Our interest was limited to seeing one particular banyan tree. That one tree was like a jungle in itself. At that time it had more than 1,350 trunks. Its roots, referred to as "the beard of the banyan tree," were hanging from its branches. They would go into the ground and take the form of a new tree. All the trees are connected with each other. I do not know how many trunks the tree has now. We went to the Kali Mata temple afterwards.

From Calcutta we went to Gaya. On the way we crossed a rail bridge many miles long named Deri Aan Sone. After reaching Gaya we stayed at a dharmashala [guest house] belonging to Bharat Sevak Samaj. Maharajshri brought me here because he wanted me to do pindadana [the tradition of making offerings to departed ansectors] to all my ancestors. The master of the dharmashala contacted a brahmin priest and made all the arrangements. It was a day-long event. I arranged for a bath, bed and lunch for Maharajshri because he would be alone all day. I then went with the Brahmin and returned in the evening.

The next day we went to see Bodh Gaya. It was about seven miles from Gaya. It is a very large temple of Buddha. In the back of the building there is the bodhi tree with a platform around its trunk. While meditating, sitting on that platform, Lord Buddha achieved enlightenment. How could the Bodhi tree still be there? A new tree must have been planted in its place.

Many revolving drums were there in the temple. People were turning them. I expressed my curiosity about their purpose. Maharajshri explained. "This is their rosary. They keep turning it and repeating and chanting their mantra. Perhaps they believe that by doing mantra while turning the drum they will free themselves from the ever-turning wheel of reincarnation. Everyone has his or her own belief about the tradition of sadhana. We must respect all traditions."

We went to Vaidyanath from Gaya. On the way Maharajshri said, "Vaidyanath temples are in three places. All of them claim to be Jyotirlingas: Vaidyanath in Bihar, Parali Vaidyanath in Maharashtra, and Vaidyanath in Kangada, Himachal. This is the intellectual exercise of the temple priests and spiritual teachers. Devotees care only about Lord Shankar."

We wanted now to go to Kashi [Varanasi], where the head of the Siddha Yoga Ashram, Swami Narayan Tirth Maharaj, lived. This was my first visit to Kashi. Now I do not remember how long we stayed there, but it must have been about ten days. Of the places we traveled during the pilgrimage Maharajshri was happiest here. Bathing in the holy river Ganga and a visit to Kashi Vishwanath became a daily routine.

With the passage of time, the process of destruction and reconstruction of temples goes on. It is said that Shankaracharya himself re-established this temple after it was destroyed. It was destroyed again, and Maharani Ahalyabai of Indore had it reconstructed. This is one of the twelve Jyotirlingas. Kashi is a city of temples. Among them, Dundiraj Ganesh, Annapurna, Kala Bhairva, and Bindu Madhav are the main temples. The Ganges is always there.

Maharajshri said that it is believed that Kashi could never be destroyed because it rests on the trident of Lord Shiva. Another belief system regards Kashi as a special, inner spiritual state. The mind is fickle.

Modifications of the mind keep changing, hopes and feelings change, but the Kashi-state remains the same all the time. The tradition that one attains liberation if one dies in Kashi means, if someone dies in this particular Kashi-state, he does not take another birth. Kashi has always been the center of India's spiritual convictions and learning. There are hundreds of temples, ashrams and religious schools in Kashi. An average resident of Kashi is the best of pundits in other places. We made our arrangements with Swami Narayan Tirth Maharaj. Swamiji agreed to come to Rishikesh in April and to give me sanyas diksha in May. With Maharajshri I went to Allahabad, where the three rivers come together. It is a great tirth and every twelve years the Kumbha Mela [Kumbha Fair] takes place here. Millions of people go to the Kumbha Mela. During this time the city blooms with satsang [spiritual discourses]. The ancient culture of India develops, is controlled and grows through its mela [fairs]. In this mela, religious meetings are held, satsang and holy baths take place, religious organizations meet, and decisions taken here reach millions of devotees in every corner of India. Kumbha Mela is the largest of fairs. A foreigner who saw so many people at the Kumbha Mela once asked, "Who sent invitations to all these people?"

We arrived in Rishikesh. The Ganges is in Kashi and Allahabad, but Maharajshri was not as happy seeing the Ganges there as he was to see her in Rishikesh. I do not know what relationship he perceived between the Ganges and Rishikesh. This time we stayed in a vacant building of a devotee at Triveni Ghat. There were two rooms on the ground floor and two rooms on the second floor. We stayed for six months in this building.

56. The Story of Rishikesh

Rishikesh and Haridwar must be regarded as one pilgrimage spot. Rishikesh is like an extension of Haridwar. Haridwar can be compared to a
doorway to heaven because from this point onwards is the land of spirituality: the Himalayas and the Ganges. It is studded with many ashrams
and cottages of many spiritual masters. The scenery is very beautiful and
peaceful. In the lower part of Haridwar the Ganges flows in the flat
meadows, and in the upper areas it is surrounded by the lovely ranges of
the Himalayas. The main place for a holy bath in Haridwar is Har ki
Paudi. There are many other places, such as Chandidevi, Dakseshwara
Mahadeva, Bhim Goda, and so forth. Many ashrams now have beautiful
temples.

After coming to Rishikesh Maharajshri's desire to live near the
Ganges was rekindled. He already had thoughts of giving up his body
here. Every year, for two to three months, Maharajshri would come to
Rishikesh. Every time new arrangements had to be made for his place of
stay. So the thought was to build a small place here. The search for a
place in Rishikesh and Haridwar began. Finally a faithful devotee of
Maharajshri donated a piece of land in the area of Muni Ki Reti, of
Maharajshri's choice. This happened in 1965. Construction started. This
is where the Yogshri Peeth Ashram is today.

A few people came from Indore to stay with Maharajshri. It was
the custom to visit Garuda Chatti every year. We crossed the Ganges in
a boat. A retired judge used to live in Swargashram. He was a disciple of
Yoganandji Maharaj. Yoganandji used to live in a cottage next to his
home. Maharajshri's initiation had taken place in the judge's house. We
saw the room in which the initiation was performed. We also saw the
cottage in which Yoganandji used to live, and then proceeded to Garuda
Chatti.

We resumed our journey along a beautiful, winding road beside the

Ganges — high mountains decked with greenery on their slopes, playful monkeys all around among peaceful and beautiful surroundings. There was no change in Garuda Chatti: the same old tea stall, a deserted dharmashala, a temple of Garuda, and one small pier leading to the Ganges. We cooked a meal and ate there. Once again we had a spiritual discussion in the courtyard of the Garuda temple.

Maharajshri was saying, "It is said that some sages were fed-up with their troubles with demons and took refuge in God. God was moved. He killed the demons and gave this land to the sages. It was named Rishikesh. It is the entrance to the Himalayan spiritual land, lying just inside the gate. A sadhak needs to live in a pure and sattvic environment as long as he is prone to be influenced by the world. In reality, our mind is Rishikesh, and our mind is the land of demons, as well. The mind is the world of desire, and the mind is the land of spirituality. As long as the mind soaks up worldly influences one feels that he needs to stay in spiritual places.

"Every corner of India is a tirth [holy place] because in every place some great being or the other has spent time in spiritual pursuits, spread spiritual rays, made the place sattvic and sacred, and made it holy. As time has passed demonic attitudes have negatively affected these places and their spiritual vibrations have vanished. Because of this people regard one place as spiritual and another as worldly, but everywhere in India spirituality is sprinkled, either in manifest or in hidden form.

"A human being has a doubting nature. That is his greatest obstacle. Doubt can give birth to many fantasies. Spiritual aspirants are not untouched by doubt, and worldly people suffer with doubt totally. Doubting minds not only nourish doubt in their own minds, but they pour doubt into the minds of others, as well. Faith and doubt are at opposite ends. Doubt cannot grow where there is faith. A faithful person will see every place in India as a holy place. He will look for God in every person, see God's work in every action. But a doubting person will sense negativity everywhere. He will see tricks and deceit in everything. This thinking turns a holy place into a common place.

"Doubt is the worst of all feelings among humans. It turns even

God into a demon. Sometimes one begins to question the existence of God. Doubt creates discord among happy families and destroys them. It shakes the foundation of happy, prosperous and strong sovereign nations. It can poison the loving and sweet relations of a father and son, Guru and disciple, and between friends. Doubts have ruined holy places in India more than anything else. It has cracked the faith of devotees and made them worldly, and made holy places unholy.

"In earlier days faithful devotees came to Haridwar to enter the land of penance of the Himalayas. They arrived in Rishikesh and began their pilgrimage at Garuda Chatti. This was the first stop on their inner journey. From here an eagle [Garuda] flying in the internal sky, with its wings extended in the form of life-force [prana], took them on the pilgrimage flight through Badrinath, Kedarnath, Gangotri and Yamunotri. Human beings befoul the Ganges, which descends into the plains from the winding passes and peaks of the Himalaya – the matted locks of Shankar's hair. The inner journey took a pilgrim back to the source of his being where he could find pure nectar, happiness and bliss. One saw Kedarnath, steady in its natural, formless state; Badrinath, where Narayan rests happily in the ocean of milk; and Garuda Chatti, the symbol and first stop of this inner journey.

"These days this journey of the northern area is completed comfortably, in cars and so forth, within eight days. A person does not even have an opportunity to move away from the world and get lost in the joy of inner beauty. In older days the pilgrimages were externally difficult but internally blissful. Now the first stop of Garuda Chatti is not even part of the pilgrimage. There are neither external symbols, nor an inner state. Neither does a Garuda extend its wings of prana and fly upon the air, nor does any pilgrimage take place. Only entertainment and travel remain."

Question: "According to you, the significance of Garuda Chatti in the external pilgrimage is the same as the mooladhar [the first chakra, located at the base of the spine] in the internal journey."

Answer: "Haridwar is the symbol of the mooladhar, where Shakti enters sushumna [a channel leading up the spine]. Outside the doorway is the world, and inside is infinite and limitless spirituality. If you take one step outside then you are in the world. With one step inside you are in the spiritual world of Rishikesh. Haridwar is also known as Gangadwar, the door to the Ganges, because it takes one to the source of the Ganges. Just as the river Ganges flows into the low-lying fields, it flows into the lower spiritual planes as well, suppressed under worldly influences. The pathway to its origin starts in Haridwar/mooladhar. This is why Haridwar is a symbol of mooladhar.

Garuda Chatti is the swadhishthana [the second chakra, located near the reproductive organs] of the inner journey. After crossing the entrance of Haridwar the first step inside is Rishikesh. And when you take the second step you are in Garuda Chatti, the symbol of swadhishthana. Swadhishthana means 'one's own place' or 'home.' This is why the temple of Garuda is not in Haridwar or Rishikesh. From here Garuda, or prana, is ready for the inner flight with the help of air. The real pilgrimage starts from swadhishthana."

Question: "What is the relationship between the inner and external pilgrimage?"

Answer: "In the form that pilgrimage has taken these days there is no relationship. The main objective of pilgrimage has lost its significance today. There may be some pilgrims who still value the inner pilgrimage. In earlier days the pilgrimage was made to endure the hardships of travel, to rise above honor and humiliation, to be in the company of ascetics and saints, to purify the mind, and to fill the mind with love for God. All this was done to prepare oneself for the inner pilgrimage. Everything else was secondary. Today the inner journey is secondary, and comfort and honor have become important.

"The external pilgrimage was made as a symbol to become detached from the world, to develop devotion, and to prepare the mind for the inner pilgrimage. This used to be a preliminary preparation, where one learned about generosity and tolerance. During the journey one used to do japa, visit different temples and holy places, and spend time with ascetics and saints. Slowly the sadhak would pass through the entrance at Haridwar, meaning mooladhar, go to Rishikesh, and then reach Garuda

Chatti and get established in swadhishthana. Then only would the purpose of his external pilgrimage be fulfilled."

Question: "This pilgrimage would sometimes result in time being wasted. Would it not be utilized better in sadhan?"

Answer: "I never said that a pilgrimage is essential for everyone. If someone is able to sit in sadhan then he does not need to go on a pilgrimage. He can sit in one place and do sadhan. But if your mind is not stable and it is hard to steady your mind in sadhan then the question of a pilgrimage arises."

Now we started our return trip to Rishikesh. On the way Maharajshri said, "Those who live in Haridwar, Rishikesh or Garuda Chatti do not pay attention to these things because they do not fall into the category of pilgrims. They live on the banks of the Ganges but do not bathe in the Ganges. They do not realize where they are standing. Those who live in Garuda Chatti are not established in swadhishthana. This is the condition of everyone in holy places. A temple priest spends his whole life in a temple but his attention is on the gifts people offer. People who sing religious songs spend their whole life singing but their attention is focused on notes and beats. Pilgrims also think that their main purpose is to visit all these places but they are unaware of the true purpose. Today the result of all this is before us."

57. Gita Knowledge

Usually Maharajshri would bathe in the Ganges at the place where the Chandrabhaga and the Ganges meet. After bathing he would go to the temple of Shankar, situated in the Chandrbhaga, and then return to his lodgings. During the evening walk he would go to Muni Ki Reti, where the new ashram was under construction. People asked Maharajshri to talk on the Gita. Maharajshri accepted the request happily. The talk was scheduled one evening.

Maharajshri said, "The Gita is such a great and mystic scripture that it is not easy to understand and explain its real meaning. What is its purpose? What are its principles and traditions? Different scholars of the Gita have interpreted the Gita differently and written commentaries on it. It is possible that there is no other book on which commentaries have been written in so many different languages. On the one hand Shankaracharya calls it a scripture emphasizing advaita [non-duality]; on the other hand teachers of bhakti call it a book of devotion and love. Scholars enamoured of the Guru call it a book illuminating the Guru-disciple relationship. According to Tilak Maharaj [Bal Gangadhar Tilak], the Gita is a book on Karma Yoga. From the sixth to the ninth chapter it seems as if it is all about yoga. Those following the path of Shaktipat believe it is book on Shaktipat, and say that the rajvidya rajguhya [the king of knowledge and the king of mysteries] is nothing other than the path of Shaktipat. This shows that the Gita is filled with so much that one can find whatever he is looking for in it.

"This is the only book in which vishaad [dejection] is called yoga. In dejection one is unhappy. How can that be yoga? This is the genius of the Gita. Usually books ask one to give up dejection, to get out of it. But the distinctiveness of the Gita is that it says giving up dejection requires the help of dejection itself. To overcome some impediment, can the obstacle itself be used as a device? If a high mountain stands in front of you, it can be crossed by climbing over. The obstacle helps one in getting beyond the obstacle. To cross an ocean, a boat has to sail with the support of the water of the ocean. In the same way, if you want to give up the world then dive into the world and swim to get out of it. The pathway to renounce the world goes through the world itself. To fight with an enemy it is necessary to have an enemy. If the enemy is not in front of you on the battlefield then how can the enemy be killed? If you run away from the battlefield then how will you drive away the enemy? Who will kill them? Who will drive them away?

"If someone makes the world the means of rising above the world then the world does not remain an obstacle. It becomes a device to remove the obstacle; a path opens up. This dejection is the foundation upon which Gita jnana [knowledge] stands. The path of devotion described in the Gita does not mean ringing bells and cymbals in front of God. It is not a path of taking vows and fasting. It is, rather, a way to live in the world so that you are not influenced by the world, and so that the world is not affected by your ways. The Karma Yoga [the yoga of action] of the Gita is not just a way of doing karma. It is, rather, a Karma Yoga in which you do work while remaining free from it. While performing your duties and fulfilling your duties you remain free from obsession, greed, hatred, illusion and jealousy. Real Karma Yoga is a technique for becoming free from the bondage of karma while performing karma. The knowledge given in the Gita does not end with the turning of pages. It is not a path of Jnana Yoga [the yoga of knowledge] in which you keep on arguing and developing new principles day-by-day. The knowledge rises from within. As long as illusion persists no amount of book knowledge will prove beneficial. The signs of jnana, knowledge, must manifest in your behavior. Knowledge pervades everything in the world but, due to illusion, only ignorance is visible. If the world is a cause of ignorance for some then the same world will be the cause of the removal of ignorance and of kindling knowledge.

"To grasp the knowledge of the Gita one must understand the difference between vishaad [dejection] and vikshep [distress]. Lord Krishna took dejection as the basis, not distress. In distress, the mind

becomes restless when it is disturbed about worldly comforts and pleasures. The immediate causes of this restlessness are desire, anger, greed,
ego and selfishness. The psyche is dominated by rajas [disturbing quali-
ties] and tamas [inertial qualities]. The mind keeps on flying around in
worldly pleasures. When these pleasures are not available, or situations
develop so that they may be lost, then the mind is perturbed and agitated. Such a state of mind is not appropriate for grasping the knowledge of the Gita.

"The mind of Arjuna was not perturbed; it was sad. And it was
dominated by sattva [harmonious and good qualities]. It was not hungry
for worldly pleasures. If it were then he would have been ready to kill his
relatives, but it was not like that. He did feel attachment to his relatives,
but the attachment was of a mind filled with a willingness to renounce
everything, and not of a mind deep in desire for sensuous pleasures.
Therefore Arjuna said, "I will not kill them for the kingdom of
Hastinapur, not even for the whole universe. I will give up my arms.
Seeing me without arms they may kill me, but I will not kill them. I will
tolerate the insult of being called a coward because I ran away from the
battlefield. I will accept the ascetic life of the forest, and I will beg alms
for survival, but I will not kill them." All this shows his detachment.
Only then, when the mind attains such a state, does a Guru like Krishna
come and cut and throw away the ignorance of attachment with the axe
of knowledge. This is when one becomes worthy of the knowledge of
the Gita.

"The relationship between the Guru and disciple has become impure these days. Neither can you find Gurus like Krishna, nor disciples
like Arjuna. The relationship of the Guru and disciple has become a
game. How can a Guru who is still attached free a disciple from bondage? And disciples are no better. The truth is that one meets a Guru
depending on his own mindset. If the heart is filled with worldly happiness and pleasures then he will find a Guru who will show a garden
decked with those pleasures. Arjuna said, *'Shadhi mam twam prapannam.'* 'I
have come to you for refuge. Please give me wisdom.' It is essential that
the disciple surrender to the Guru. The Guru should not give lectures

before the disciple has expressed his desire for knowledge and surrender. In such a situation the objective would not be to benefit the disciple, but rather to catch the disciple and keep him under control. The disciple, for his part, says whatever he pleases, but he also keeps his ego intact instead of surrendering to the Guru's feet.

"Teachings must be given at the proper time. Lord Krishna and Arjuna were friends and relatives. Thousands of occasions must have arisen when Krishna could have imparted knowledge, but neither was the relationship of Guru-disciple established, nor had Arjuna sought refuge, nor was his mind ready to receive and grasp knowledge. The iron was not hot at those times. It would not have changed its shape no matter how hard it was pounded. Such a situation took place only on the battlefield of Kurukshetra. At that time the Guru-disciple relationship, surrender and Arjuna's mental state were all in the proper state. The iron was hot. Lord Krishna hit it, and the knowledge of the Gita was revealed.

"When Arjuna saw Dronacharya [Arjuna's Guru in the art of war] and others in the enemy camp he was filled with attachment. Within the same mind feelings of detachment and allegiance arose at the same time. This was most unusual. On the one hand he recoiled from war due to his attachment, and at the same time he declared that he would renounce the world and lead a life of an ascetic. His mind was faced with a dilemma, a dilemma of detachment and attachment. He was unable to decide right from wrong. In this type of situation a Guru is needed most. This is when he surrendered as a disciple to Lord Krishna. The Lord accepted him in his grace. Then the knowledge of the Gita was revealed. Surrender and discipleship are two important conditions under which knowledge manifests. Arjuna was a worthy disciple. He had control over his senses, he was not attached, and he had surrendered. He was lost because his mind was clouded by the delusion of love. He was not distraught, but he was dejected.

"This subject deserves serious thinking, both by the Guru and the disciple. A disciple must consider, before requesting initiation, whether he deserves what he is asking for. A Guru must also consider what the person deserves. I am not saying that the Guru should refuse, regarding a person as unworthy. But the disciple should be directed to do the sadhana of which he is capable. And when he is ready he must be initiated. Because he is a Guru, the Guru cannot refuse anyone, but he also cannot overlook the fact that someone is worthy or unworthy. Generally a disciple comes to a Guru when he is disturbed. His detachment is momentary due to a passing disturbance. As soon as the cause of the disturbance disappears the intoxication of detachment also passes. But dejection mostly takes place due to a dilemma of right and wrong. One thinks about spirituality and not about worldly pleasures.

"Lord Rama also had the same kind of dejection. When he returned from a pilgrimage his mind was dominated by a strong sense of detachment. He had no desire to do anything. He wanted to go to the forest and do sadhana. That was when knowledge was imparted to him by Sage Vasishtha. He showed him the falseness of the world, and involved him in the work of the world with a sense of duty.

"Some people believe that the Gita really starts with the second chapter. They say that the first chapter only provides the background. But, in reality, the first chapter is the foundation of the Gita. It describes the prerequisites for attaining the knowledge of the Gita. In the very first chapter Arjuna's mind is filled with despondency. The dejected and detached state of mind of the disciple is as essential as the discourse of the Guru. Scriptures on Tantra say that initiation must be given at the time when there is an equal balance between the samskaras of sins and good karma. In Arjuna's mind false attachment and detachment were vibrating equally and simultaneously. He surrendered and became a disciple, and then the knowledge of the Gita was revealed.

"Today people want to gain the knowledge of the Gita without becoming an Arjuna and without bringing out Krishna. Gita-jnana is revealed only when Krishna and Arjuna meet as Guru and disciple. If one of them is absent then it cannot take place and the knowledge remains hidden. Often the disciple is not like Arjuna and the Guru is not like Krishna. How, then, can the Gita manifest? Gita-jnana cannot be attained from books and commentaries, from lectures and discourses, from contemplation and meditation. You have to awaken the sleeping Arjuna within. You have to discover the Krishna that is hidden. Then only will the knowledge of the Gita be revealed."

The next day Maharajshri and others went for a bath in the Ganges and sat on the sand on its banks. Someone asked, "Only one sentiment can be in the heart at one time: either anger or love, generosity or miserliness, discernment or illusion. How can both contrary feelings arise at the same time?"

Answer: "It can happen. If there is only one feeling, that is fine, but everyone is in a dilemma at some time or the other. A dilemma means that two contrary feelings arise at the same time. It means you do not know which one to accept and which one to give up. Is it good to go toward the world or toward spirituality? How do you express this condition? You say, 'One mind says this, and the other mind says that.' But the mind is only one, and two feelings have arisen at the same time. A person in such a dilemma needs a guide. When there is a conflict between sin and virtue, that is the best time to give initiation. People face dilemmas in worldly affairs as well as in their spiritual path. On one side the world pulls, and on the other side spirituality attracts. It often happens that a person wants follow a path of spirituality, but he cannot decide what his duty is. His attachment comes in disguise, puts on a cloak of discretion and makes him wander."

Question: "At some point the dilemma is resolved and the mind makes a decision. Where is the difficulty?"

Answer: "The difficulty is making a decision that is correct and beneficial. The mind may make improper decisions. The sadhak wants someone to help him in this process and take him forward on the spiritual path. The difficulty is that, although the sadhak wants to go in the direction of spirituality, delusion intervenes to change his direction. Arjuna was not hungry for worldly pleasures; he was detached from them. His path was not toward pleasures but he did love his relatives. Delusion took advantage of this weakness. Arjuna was overcome by delusion, which resulted in his dilemma."

58.   The First Chapter of the Gita

The next day a gentleman opened a discussion of the Gita with this question: "Who deserves to receive the knowledge of the Gita?"

Answer: "Only that person deserves to receive the knowledge of the Gita who is in vishaad [dejection]. I have already discussed the differences between vishaad [dejection] and vikshep [distress]. In theory, all desires going toward spirituality are worthy, but real worthiness comes after one becomes detached. To understand worthiness according to the Gita, we need to understand Arjuna's state of mind because he deserved and received the knowledge of the Gita. Lord Krishna did not give these teachings to Duryodhana because his mind was perturbed. When Lord Krishna went to Hastinapur as a messenger of peace he tried to reason with him, but this had no effect. It is true that not even the Lord can make those understand who do not want to. Arjuna was sad. He wanted to understand, and therefore he came to take refuge in Krishna's guidance. He was detached, he had control over his senses, and he was prepared for the teachings. The land was tilled and soft, so Lord Krishna planted the seeds."

Question: "Other brothers of Arjuna [the Pandavas] were also detached and had control over their senses. Why was the knowledge revealed to Arjuna only?"

Answer: "Only Arjuna was in dejection, no one else."

Question: "Does this mean that all the commentaries written on the Gita are useless? If the knowledge manifests from within then what is the need for the Gita?"

Answer: "The state of dejection comes into many people's lives but they cannot take advantage of it. When there is a dilemma toward duties they slide toward the world. Constant study of the commentaries written on the Gita, other sadhana and religious undertakings, and constant practice of Karma Yoga will help develop the mind to take advantage of dejection. I have written a verse on each of the eighteen chapters of the Gita. The verse on the first chapter is as follows:

Vishaadeapisthito yogi, Gitaadhyayan tatparah;
Muchyate shoka santaapaat-shaantimaapnoti shaashvatam.

If a yogi is in the state of dejection and becomes an eager
    and ardent student of the Gita,
He will be released from his suffering and attain eternal peace.

All the knowledge has been interlaced in seven hundred verses — twenty eight hundred aphorisms of the Gita. It is hard for an average person to understand. Therefore scholars have tried to make it simple and understandable by writing commentaries. However some scholars have expressed contradictory opinions and raised confusion. People remain entangled in scholarly debates. Generally they wander in literary and verbal interpretations. They forget to study their own mind, for which the knowledge given in the Gita is like a pillar of light. If people first read the Gita on their own in order to understand it, and then read commentaries and accept what feels correct, then their life can turn around. In this verse a yogi or a person with detachment is said to deserve the knowledge of the Gita."

59. The Accidental Beginning of Kriyas: The Second Chapter of the Gita

There was a retired colonel from Dehradun, a normal, worldly person with no involvement in spiritual pursuits. One day, as he was seated, he suddenly began to have very forceful kriyas. He tried hard to stop them but his efforts were futile. People said he was having fits of madness. The colonel told people that, while it was happening, he was aware of everything around him. How could he be mad? Doctors could not find anything wrong with him. He had a friend in Rishikesh whom he told about his condition. The friend understood everything and advised him to write a letter to Maharajshri in Dewas. Maharajshri replied, saying that he was travelling to Rishikesh and that the colonel must come and meet him there.

The friend informed the colonel that Maharajshri had come to Rishikesh. He came to see Maharajshri one day. After introductions he explained his problem. "Maharajshri, I do not understand what happens. I may be just sitting and suddenly a force comes. I start to dance and jump, cry and quiver. I try to control myself but I cannot. People say I am getting bouts of madness. I am afraid."

By then Maharajshri understood that there was nothing wrong with him, that these were symptoms of awakened Shakti, and that people were unable to understand. It was natural that they did not understand because they did not know about Shakti.

Maharajshri said, "Colonel Saheb, this is not a disease. It is your good fortune. These are signs of the awakening of the Shakti. This is the fruit of pious karmas of some past birth. You are afraid of these signs, but yogis, devotees and ascetics thirst for them. I assure you that you have no disease. Physically and mentally you are totally healthy. Your Shakti has turned inwards and has become active. You are confused because you do not know these things."

Question: "But people say this is madness. Doctors have also confused me because they talk in a roundabout manner."

Answer: "This is not a subject for doctors at all. They can examine things at the physical level only. What do they know about inner samskaras and the activities of Shakti? People also speak out of ignorance. Awakening of Shakti is an important turn on the path of spirituality."

Question: "But Maharajshri, spirituality has never been a part of my life. I have preferred to eat, drink and have fun. I have never done any worship, studied scriptures, recited prayers, or done anything else that is spiritual. How did this spirituality manifest then? I do not even have a Guru."

Answer: "This present life is a part of a continuous cycle of life and death. In one life the individual soul may be totally indifferent toward spirituality, and in others spirituality may be very strong. You must have done intense austerities in some past life. Your Shakti must have awakened in that life, and you must have had strong kriyas. Then your sins arose and you became uninterested in spirituality. Your kriyas became latent. You became a purely worldly person. This continued into this lifetime. Sixty years of your life have passed. The condition of your samskaras has changed again. The signs of awakening of Shakti and violent kriyas have started to show again. With changes in samskaras, life also changes. Even though all this knowledge is within you, you are unaware of it."

Question: "Does this mean that this is not a kind of madness?"

Answer: "Not in the least. In madness the force of mental defects arises. When that takes place the person does not know what is happening or what he is doing. You do not have an upsurge of mental disturbance. This is a surge of Shakti and your mind remains stable. Because of the strong force of Shakti you lose control over it, which should not happen. Still, you remain aware of what is happening and what you are doing. This is the difference between kriya and madness."

Then Maharajshri gave him two books, *Devatma Shakti* and *Shaktipat* [written by Vishnu Tirth], and asked him to buy a copy of *Mahayoga Vijnana* [written by Sri Yogananda Maharaj]. He said, "Study these books and you will know that these things do happen. You will also know why they happen and what their purpose is. Then your confusion will disappear. Then you can decide what to do."

It was evening. Maharajshri had returned from his walk. It was time for his discourse on the Gita. This satsang continued for many days. Discussion on the discourses would take place at other times, as well. Some memories have become hazy and some concepts were very difficult, so I have made efforts to simplify them. Some of them are not included in this book because the book is written with the average aspirant and reader in mind.

Maharajshri said, "The verse written by me on the second chapter of the Gita, goes like this:

Karmanaa badhyate jivaha, karmanaa muchyate hi saha
Karmasu kaushalam yogam, saakhya tatvam bhaje sadaa.

It is true that karma puts an individual soul in bondage, and
    only karma releases one from bondage.
Yoga is to do karma competently. For this an individual must
    always remember the essential knowledge and do karma
    competently.

"First, it is necessary to understand what it means to do karma [actions] competently. It is to do karma in such a manner that, even while doing the karma, you are not bound by it. Competence here is to remain free from karma even while performing karma; not to accumulate impressions while doing karma; not to get attached to what you are doing. Not to get happy or unhappy from the results of your actions is competent karma. To do only correct things and not do inappropriate things is karma with competence. To give up one's own benefits to benefit others is competent karma. To maintain balance of mind even in adverse circumstances is competent karma. To be free from ego in favorable situations is competent karma. Generally, doing something well is called competent karma, but the Gita's ideas about competency are different. Generally, in the world, competency is decided on the basis of the world, the body, the way of working, and the results of karma. The physical body is present in the visible world. On the basis of the workings of the body competence is decided. The world does not realize that the body and the mind are only the medium, not the doer. The body becomes active on the basis of thoughts and resolves in the mind. Competence ought to be measured on the mental level. Happiness and misery, honor and insult, are experienced by the mind only. Attachment and passion, hatred and avarice, take place in the mind. Surrender to God is also through the mind. Only the mind can be attached or detached from karma or action.

"Incompetent karma is a cause of bondage. It is the sense of doership and the cause of accumulating impressions; it is the influence of the fruit or result of the action; it is not duty and it is selfishness. Incompetent karma addresses the world. It is contrary to spirituality and gives birth to vasanas. It is only harmful and damaging. This is why Lord Krishna says that karma done with competency gives liberation, and incompetent karma causes bondage.

"The cord that establishes the relationship between the world and the jiva [individual soul] is attachment. If this link of attachment does not exist then the jiva, even in the middle of the world, can be free of the world. He appears to be doing karma, but in reality he is free from karma. A knot in the form of attachment binds the two ends of the cord. Even when the two ends are tied they are separate, but a feeling develops that they are one. The feeling of oneness of the jiva and chitta [psyche], oneness of the body and mind, oneness of the mind and the world, and oneness of the body and the world are due to this knot. These feelings come and go, other feelings of oneness take their place, and the knot remains intact. The jiva remains lost in these feelings. He goes on doing karma [action] with incompetence, and Shakti goes on flowing in the direction of the world. This is the mockery of the jiva. For peace and happiness the jiva must go home. He has to turn within.

"The journey toward the real home begins only when Shakti begins to flow inward. Karma Yoga, or the yoga of action, doing karma with competence, and all other spiritual practices are preparation for that. The biggest obstacle in the inward flow of Shakti is prarabdha, which creates favorable and unfavorable circumstances. An individual soul is also influenced by attachment, does karma with incompetence, and misses the opportunities for a break in the sequence of the formation of prarabdha. Competent karma is the beginning of a break in prarabdha. This is Karma Yoga, this is a sense of duty, and this is selfless service.

"Competent karma is the means of attaining the state of sthitaprajna [the state of steadfast wisdom], or Buddhi Yoga [the yoga of intellect]. Incompetence does not mean that the being lacks competence. By nature a being is competent, but he has put on a cover of incompetence. For regaining competence one does not have to perform any practice, but he must remove the layer of incompetence. Competence is in the nature of the being and incompetence is unnatural. To do karma with competence is only letting the being's natural quality come forth.

"The ability to bear and maintain a balanced mind through joys and miseries arising out of prarabdha is imparted by competency. It is the cause of the depletion of prarabdha. Forbearance, contentment, forgiveness and generosity are all deeply related to competency. If these qualities are lacking then a person cannot attain competence. If someone is too strong then he can never be forbearing and forgiving. Anger and revenge are hindrances to competence. Due to these a person loses balance of the mind.

"A suspicious nature also affects competency. A suspicious person looks at everything — people and situations — with doubt. His mind always remains fearful, fickle and inclined towards the world. By turning away from competency and becoming attached to the world, he develops incompetence.

"The union of the world that exists within, in the form of the samskaras in the chitta and the visible world, stifles the competency of an individual soul. The world is compared to a river that has five origins, five tributaries and five whirlpools. The five origins are the samskaras of the pleasures of sound, touch, appearance, taste and smell. The five tributaries are the actions performed through the five senses, and the five types of sensuality are the five whirlpools. The person caught in a whirlpool is an incompetent person. He goes on sinking in the waves of desires, anger, greed, infatuation and indulgence. If he wants to come to the bank he cannot, because by the time he even wishes to do so a new wave sweeps him into its current. Competence means the ability to swim across the river and reach the shore.

"True knowledge will arise from within over time, and will release the individual soul from the cycle of birth and death forever. The first encampment of the inner journey is Buddhi Yoga [the yoga of intellect], sthitaprajna, a balanced state of mind. For attaining this, intellectual understanding is helpful. This knowledge can be acquired through study and recitation of scriptures, contemplation, satsang, prayers and spiritual songs. These give guidance and new enthusiasm to the heart and faith in God, and remove doubts. This sadhana is included in anvopaaya. If the aspirant grasps the technique of not getting involved in the bondage of karma then he can be released from a huge load of miseries. This involves efforts to bring one's mind into a special state that enables one to go further on the inner journey. When the mind is balanced, this means that the significance of the world has come to an end. This state of mind is essential for concentration and meditation. That element that remains eternal and stable behind every happening in the universe can be found only after acquiring this mental state."

On one side of the building the Ganges was flowing. On the other side was a road with more buildings on its opposite side. In those buildings people were fighting with each other loudly. Some were using harsh words. Then they began to fight with canes. They began to scream and yell as if a riot had started. The discourse had to stop. In a little while dogs started barking. Possibly a dog from another territory had entered.

Question: "Why do human beings fight over little things?"

Answer: "The question is not whether it is a small matter or a big matter. The question is how important the matter is for a particular person. A small matter can be big if it is made important. Then ego rises and anger mixes with it. Thus a fight starts. Most fights take place due to a lack of tolerance. A person cannot tolerate something because of his ego, and things get blown out of proportion."

Question: "Do animals also fight?"

Answer: "Fights between animals are usually related to food. Animals do not have feelings of ego and insult. They do not think much. Their greed is usually limited to food. They fight for that. Birds and animals are also naturally attached to their offspring. When a bitch gives birth she gets very hungry and eats two or three puppies. She becomes attached to those that remain. If she feels that someone is likely to harm them she prepares to attack."

60. Qualities of a Sthitaprajna, I

The next day Maharajshri described the qualities of a sthitaprajna [a person of steadfast wisdom or intellect; the perfect yogi] as presented in the last eighteen verses of the second chapter of the Gita, which describes doing karma competently.

"When prarabdha is completely depleted by doing karma competently, when all desires and deep-rooted tendencies are cleared, when the world appears to be God's play and joy constantly fills the mind and the heart, then it is a clear sign that the intellect of that person is steady. His joy does not depend on any external factors and his contentment comes from within.

"It is hard for a worldly person to understand this inner joy. He cannot think of joy without external pleasures. He believes that only worldly pleasures can give joy. He does not know that what he considers to be real joy is only its shadow. But as long as the external door is open the inward door cannot be opened. The way to open the inward door is to perform karma without attachment.

"A sthitaprajna is not perturbed when unfavorable circumstances develop. He does not wish for favorable, happy or desirable circumstances. A person free from attachment, fear and anger is called a sthitaprajna. Otherwise what would be the significance of purity of the mind? To get angry when upset and to feel fear at the possibility of losing something are signs of impurity. Stability develops with purity of the mind.

"The senses of a sthitaprajna withdraw from pleasures in the same way that a turtle withdraws his limbs. This is called pratyahara [retraction of the senses] in the path of yoga, that is, the senses give up their pleasures. In this state the aspirant's mind turns away from the world. That is when real hunger for spirituality arises, and one feels the pain of separation from God. This is when the inner spiritual journey starts.

"This state of sthitaprajna should be natural and effortless. If you force the senses to abstain from pleasures then externally and only temporarily will they give them up. Interest in those pleasures will remain latent and will arise again as soon as favorable situations occur. As long as the samskaras of pleasures are alive only temporary control can be achieved with suppression. But when the mind is totally purified, then on the one hand the desire for worldly pleasures dies, and on the other hand spirituality is achieved."

The next afternoon the Colonel Saheb returned from Dehradun. He had finished studying the books, reading them thoroughly day and night. He said, "Maharajshri, after studying the books all my doubts have vanished. Previously I did not know that such things were possible. The surprising thing is that I am developing control over my kriyas. Before now I did not understand what a kriya was. Now when I feel like sitting in sadhan I sit and strong kriyas take place. When I feel like getting up my kriyas stop. Now my relatives are wondering what this is. They are sure that this is not insanity. But what is it? They are unable to understand."

Maharajshri said, "How can they understand? They have no knowledge or experience of the subject. How can you expect them to understand? You cannot give them the experience, but you can explain it to them. That will remove any remaining doubts, and they will stop disturbing you while you are doing your sadhana. You can give them the books to read."

Colonel Saheb said, "From reading these books, I understand that God's divine Shakti becomes active and, on the basis of samskaras, many different kriyas in the mind and body arise. But I do not have a Guru."

Maharajshri replied, "I told you that you had samskaras of an awakened Shakti from a past birth. For some reason its activity had stopped. It had become active again and was without control. You believe that you have developed control over those kriyas by reading books. When you came to me last time my Shakti extended, established contact with your chitta, and brought your Shakti under control. Perhaps you did not experience this but I did. Is this not the work of a Guru? Our Guru-disciple relationship was established when you came last time. A formal initiation has not taken place yet."

Question: "Then please bless me a formal initiation."

Answer: "A ceremonial initiation is only a formality now. If you still desire it then I will find an auspicious time and let you know."

61. Qualities of a Sthitaprajna, II

The discussion of the Gita resumed in the evening. Again the subject was the qualities of a sthitaprajna.

"We may say that these are qualities of a sthitaprajna, but they are the same for a devotee, a jnani, a yogi, or a person beyond the gunas. All of them have the same qualities, but they have been narrated differently. It seems that the objective of Lord Krishna in the Gita is not to unite the individual soul with God, but to free him from worldly attachments. This is absolutely appropriate. God is always available, but if one is still attached to the world how can God be experienced? One does not have to attain God, but to attain the experience of finding God. Perhaps this is the mistake that an aspirant makes: He sets the goal of his sadhana as the attainment of God and not the removal of attachment towards the world. How can a spiritual aspirant climb the heights of spirituality when his feet are shackled with deep-rooted tendencies and desires and the path is full of stones, thorns and weeds, and wild animals roam all around? This is why Lord Krishna emphasizes ending the influence of the world on the mind.

"Lord Krishna further says that an aspirant must be very cautious, even if he is very intelligent and discriminating, and control his senses with full attention. It is possible that with the slightest attraction to pleasures of the senses he may fall for them. With the slightest slackening, sensuous pleasures will be ready to attack. This is why the Lord talks about remaining totally cautious and absorbed in yoga. One never knows from which side worldly pleasure might raise its head. For stability of the mind and intellect, the senses must remain in control. An aspirant should never think that now he is a siddha [perfect] and need not be concerned about worldly pleasures.

"The person whose mind keeps on thinking about pleasures becomes attached to them, and then desires arise. When desires are not fulfilled, then anger arises. The distinction of good and bad is lost and memory is destroyed. Thus his life is wasted. Whichever pleasure a human thinks about, he gets dyed in its color. Thoughts about these things come continually, while sleeping or awake, thoughts about desire, sometimes of obsession and, at other times, of anger. If you must meditate on something then why not think about the futility and transient nature of the world, so that the mind desires renunciation of the world? Why not think about the qualities of God, so that you desire to develop them? Why not concentrate on the purity of the minds of the saints, so that the mind of an aspirant can also be purified by their contact? If senses move the intellect then the intellect also guides the senses. The one whose senses are free from likes and dislikes will be able to remain balanced even while enjoying the pleasures of the world."

Maharajshri went on talking and I listened quietly. My mind was, as it were, divided into two parts. One was listening attentively to the discourse of Maharajshri. The other was churning my heart. "I have given up my home, taken initiation, taken bramhacharya initiation, and now I am preparing for sanyas diksha. Still, I am so far away from real spirituality. I do try to remain free of likes and dislikes, but my mind is filled with them. I may not listen to gossip about others, but my attention does turn toward the vices and weaknesses of others. Externally I do not live in the world, but the world is deep within me. My mind does get restless. I do think about many things, but my mind does not let me pursue them. What is the use of only thinking about things? First I have to convince my mind, but how? If I try to convince my mind then it escapes me very cleverly. If I scold my mind it gets angry with me and starts to jump even more.

"Am I the only one in this world who is tormented by this dilemma, or is the whole world in the same condition? My problems will not be solved by others' problems. The person who faces a problem must find his own solution. I must solve my own problem. When I used to have an interest in gossip, I noticed that the people I criticized would turn out to be much better than myself. As I criticized others I did not realize that I was unaware of my own vices. When my attention turned toward myself I realized that the weaknesses of others were nothing compared to my own. Still I was indifferent toward my weaknesses and felt proud about my virtues."

My intensity did not leave me alone either. On the surface I appeared very quiet but inside I was very intense. I used to boil over at small provocations. Strong feelings would erupt and I would want to do all kinds of things. Those whose intensity was expressed openly appeared to be very bad, but the force of their intensity would be released. I was being eaten up by my intensity and I was forced to bear its heat.

At one point I even began to wonder whether I should take sanyas or not. I was witnessing many weaknesses within myself. I had a full load of vices and weaknesses. When and how would these vices be exhausted? I could not see an end to them. Would it be appropriate in this condition to accept the staff of a sanyasi, to put on the garbs of Narayan and make people bow to me? Always I heard "No" coming from within. But what will happen then to Maharajshri's wish? He must have some thoughts as well. He must not be unaware of my mental state. In spite of that he has proposed that I take sanyas? Once again my mind started to oscillate in the dilemma. "Is it good to take sanyas or not?" Finally I thought it was better to submit to the Guru's wish. Maharajshri had told me that my sanyas would be vidvisha sanyas [renouncing worldly life in pursuit of the ultimate truth].

The next day Maharajshri spoke further on the Gita.

"It is okay to make efforts and one must make efforts, but it must be done with a sense of surrender to God. The state of shitaprajna is attained not by efforts, but by the grace of God. There is the fearful possibility that the ego will arise if you believe it to be the result of your own efforts. Thus everything a person can attain is due to God's grace. In spirituality, the attainment of worldly pleasures is not God's grace; their renunciation is God's grace. The real attainment is inner renunciation. Peace of mind is contained within inner renunciation. The individual soul is freed from all miseries and remains joyful. Consequently his intellect becomes stable. The one who is not committed to yoga cannot have a steady intellect and the yearning for spirituality cannot arise in him. How can a person who is empty of spirituality attain peace?

"The essence of all this is that people wander in search of peace, but how can they find it where it does not exist? The world goes through constant change. There is no stability in the world due to that. Peace is in stability, thus there is no peace in the world. Peace is not a thing of the world, it is a state of mind. If the mind is peaceful then the whole world is at peace.

"If senses are fickle then the mind wanders with them. This robs the intellect just as a boat in strong winds is dragged upon the waters. Consequently he whose senses are unaffected by sensual attractions, his mind and intellect also remain steady.

"Lord Krishna explains the importance of control over the senses. Just as control over the mind is important, control over the senses is equally important. Sometimes the mind makes the senses restless, and at other times the senses make the mind restless, hence control over both is necessary. The Lord has compared the mind absorbed in sensuality to the night. For a mind attached to pleasures, attraction towards worldly objects means being awake. Just as the world disappears for the person who sleeps, spirituality disappears for the mind absorbed in sensuality.

"Things are exactly the opposite for a person with control over his senses. For him the attraction of sensual pleasures is like night, and being conscious of spirituality is like being awake. In other words, desire for pleasure is darkness, but a worldly person considers it light. For a self-controlled person, desires are like a dark night. He maintains interest and awareness about spirituality, remains conscious of his mind, and keeps marching forward toward the light of spirituality. The ocean does not exceed its shores even when all the rivers of the world keep flowing to the ocean with their waters for thousands of years. Similarly, for a sthitaprajna, worldly pleasures come and strike his mind and are destroyed, but his mind is always steady and his intellect always unshakeable.

"The person who has given up desires and expectations, has no attachments, is free from the feelings of 'mine' and 'yours' and performs his worldly functions without ego attains peace. Lord Krishna calls this state brahmisthiti. Bramha, while doing everything in the world, is doing nothing. In the same way a sthitaprajna, free from ego while performing actions in the world, is free from action.

"This is called Karma Yoga, Buddhi Yoga, Seva Yoga or competence. This is the foundation of all spiritual practices [sadhana]. For depleting prarabdha there is no better practice than this. The aptitude for inaction comes only after continuous Karma Yoga. The secret of being in the world, yet performing all worldly duties while being detached from the world, is Karma Yoga. This is the entrance to all kinds of sadhana. This Karma Yoga gives strength to sadhana, depletes prarabdha, and annihilates itself when its job is done."

62. The Invisible Master: The Third Chapter of the Gita

It was about three o'clock in the afternoon. Maharajshri had risen after a short rest and was sitting on his chair. I do not remember which book I was reading, but my mind was not able to focus on the book. Maharajshri had said that invisible masters live in the mountain range of Vindhyachal. He used to see some of them now and then. "Are there such invisible masters in the Himalayas as well? Do people see them here also? Maharajshri has not said anything about this so far. Does Maharajshri want to keep these things a secret? If that is the case then why does he talk about this in Dewas? Why can we not see those great beings? Perhaps we do not deserve to see them." Numerous such thoughts were going through my mind. Finally I asked Maharajshri.

At first he laughed loudly and then became very serious. "Invisible masters are also present here. They dwell at great heights. They have independent cottages and ashrams as well. Their places are invisible just like them. When they are gracious to someone they appear before him, and also take many of them to their dwellings. Some stay at the same place and do sadhana and others go about. Their movements are very fast. In the blink of an eye they go from one place to another.

"These great masters have many supernatural powers [siddhis], such as the ability to become visible or invisible, astral travel, and so forth, which they use only for the benefit of spiritual aspirants. It is definitely a great power to become invisible and reappear at will, but it is highly astonishing that they can also make their dwellings invisible and visible at will. This is their natural state. They do not have any ego about that. If they had any ego they would not remain in seclusion, and they would display their supernatural powers. To show off one's powers and to make good use of them are two different things. They use their powers to find spiritual seekers, to learn and help solve their spiritual problems. Such great masters are discovered through true good fortune because they do not travel much. They mostly remain absorbed in the state of samadhi. Their siddhis are not like black magic or spells. This is just a specific stage in the spiritual process."

Question: "What are their cottages and ashrams like?"

Answer: "Their cottages are natural caves. There are no material comforts because they do not need comforts. There is no kitchen, bathroom or living room. For relaxing there is no better means than samadhi [meditation]. They do not need a kitchen because they do not eat anything. Everything is made of the five basic elements, and they take energy directly from those elements. Scientists would not understand this. This is a yogic process, related to yogic science. These processes take place at very subtle levels. Their ashrams are large caves where five or more great beings are absorbed in their sadhana."

Question: "How did you come to know about this?"

Answer: "In this physical body I have not been to such places. But I have had an opportunity to go to such places in the subtle body. Once I was traveling in the subtle body and saw two or three caves. In each cave one great soul was dwelling. Then I entered a big cave that could be called an ashram. Six great beings were deeply absorbed in samadhi there. I could not talk to any of them because they were all in samadhi."

Question: "Doesn't the fear of wild animals trouble them?"

Answer: "If a wild animal enters the cave they lose their killing instinct due to the effect of spiritual vibrations. Another thing is that these great beings cannot be seen with physical eyes if they do not want to be seen. The animals have only physical eyes so they cannot see them."

Question: "I have heard that sadhaks have no problem with birth and death. If they leave one body, in the next body they are eager and ready to begin their sadhana. These great beings have tremendous longevity and remain absorbed in sadhana for thousands of years. Do they fear death and get attached to their body?"

Answer: "This is a way of thinking. They have no attachment to the body or fear of death. In one long life they experience birth and death again and again. What an average person experiences only through birth and death these invisible masters experience in the same lifetime. They can witness birth and death experiences occurring separately from themselves, and they rejoice in it. A common being experiences an obstacle in his sadhana with death, then he is reborn and has to go through childhood. He also experiences that he will someday face death. If he has done good karmas then he may be born as a human being and progress spiritually. For these masters, sadhana goes on incessantly.

"Sometimes a great being has to take birth into the world for some specific purpose. These great men have totally surrendered to God's will and command. Without any thought in their minds, they follow God's command and return to their place upon completion of the mission.

"The prarabdha of some of these great beings is not fully depleted yet. It may be good prarabdha, but it is still prarabdha. In spite of attaining so many supernatural powers, at some time some samskara of some lifetime may arise and he may have to come back to the world. Because their inner state is so high they do not accumulate new samskaras. They behave according to prarabdha, deplete prarabdha, and go back to their place."

Question: "These concepts would not be acceptable to the modern and, so-called, progressive and scientific world."

Answer: "There is no need for convincing anyone. These things cannot be discussed with an average person. Common people are not ready to hear this, and even if they heard it they would not understand. Their minds are so polluted that they cannot see anything other than the world of their desires. For them spirituality is nothing other than an indulgence, or a pastime, since it encourages one to do nothing else in life. If such people do not believe in these things what does it matter to us? Even if you falsify a truth thousands of times it will remain the truth."

Question: "You talked about these things in Dewas. Does that mean that people there are worthy of this?"

Answer: "I would not have talked about this in Dewas, but letters from the devotees of Agasha were coming there and the secret was divulged so it had to be mentioned. I had to talk about that a little. I never talked at length about invisible masters in Vindhyachal. When any sadhak had related experiences I would confirm that there were a few invisible masters in the area."

People waiting in the lower level of the building had come upstairs now. Maharajshri also stopped talking on the subject. I also did not ask any further questions.

The evening program of the lecture on the Gita resumed, and Maharajshri read his verse on the third chapter:

Yasyaanukampayaa buddhihi karmapashairvimuchyate,
Yogeshwaram rishikesham pranamaami punaha punaha.

I bow repeatedly to that king of yogis, Rishikesh,
by whose grace and compassion the intellect is freed from
    the shackles of karma.

"In the second chapter Lord Krishna shows that sthitaprajna, or Buddhi Yoga, is the first goal to be achieved. Listening to this, Arjuna had a natural question as to why was he being pushed into to this horrific war if Buddhi Yoga, stability of the mind, was the best objective. This problem is faced by most sadhaks. All of them are trying to achieve stability of the mind by ignoring responsibilities and work, but Lord Krishna gives a direct answer, saying that if you do not perform your duties and do work, how will you achieve steadiness of the mind? Favorable and unfavorable situations keep arising due to one's destiny. Facing those situations, you must do your karma with detachment and with peace of mind in order to deplete prarabdha, or destiny. This alone gives rise to the state of a sthitaprajna. If you do not face your circumstances then neither will the mind be purified, nor will the intellect become steady. Elsewhere in the Gita Lord Krishna explained this by saying that that nivritti [freedom from action] comes from pravritti [performing karmic duties].

"Without doing karma one cannot attain freedom from karma. If you give up karma then how will you attain the desired state? The only way to exhaust prarabdha is to endure the fruits of your destiny. No one can exist without doing karma. The individual soul is bound to take action depending upon the proportion of qualities — sattva, rajas and tamas — in the mind. If a lazy person sits inactively then he will wander in the kingdom of his mind. The person who continues to do his work without attachment to the results, one day, with God's grace, will become worthy of Buddhi Yoga.

"Just as ignorant people do karma with attachment, the enlightened person must do karma to give guidance to others for their spiritual benefit. The jnani must do karma without attachment, but not advise Karma Yoga to those who cannot be detached due to their mental state. Otherwise those people, unable to give up attachment, may give up action and become lethargic."

Question: "Why do people commit sins?"

Answer: "The force of qualities [gunas] makes people commit sins or do good deeds. The whole universe contains the three qualities. It is controlled by the qualities and impelled by the qualities. When the influence of tamo guna or rajo guna becomes dominant within, then the person surrenders to lust, anger and attachment.

"The desire of lust is never satiated. The fire of lust keeps burning inside; in fact, it will not be an exaggeration if we say that it keeps growing. As long as such samskaras and the predominance of rajo guna and tamo guna persist, this fire will not be extinguished. Anger flares up when desires are not fulfilled, an obstacle arises, or things do not go according to one's wishes. Just as the flame of desire flares up, the fire of anger may flare up at any time. In his anger and lust a person loses control over himself, the sense of discrimination of good and bad dwindles away, and a person blinded by desires and anger may do anything harmful. You must regard desires and anger as your greatest enemies. Try to protect yourself from them. Put an end to their root cause, which exists in the form of samskaras in the chitta. The sure way to this is to endure with a peaceful mind, to be detached from the fruits of your actions, and to practice Karma Yoga. You can do all this. Remove all doubts and misconceptions from your minds. You are the master of your inner spiritual power. Nothing is impossible for you. God's gracious hand is on your head.

"Just as a mirror gets dirty with smoke from fire, the mind gets dirty with the fire of vices. From attachment arises desire and from aversion arises anger. Expectations arise out of attachment and, when hopes are not fulfilled, anger bursts out. For overcoming lust and anger the only way is to get rid of attachment and aversion."

Question: "Is this path separate from Shaktipat?"

Answer: "No. This must be practiced simultaneously with following the path of the sadhan of Shaktipat. Spirituality is not at all possible without the awakening of the Shakti. Karma Yoga is nothing other than efforts to exhaust destiny. So far Lord Krishna is only giving intellectual wisdom. Later he will use Shakti and give inner experiences. The scripture develops slowly, step-by-step. The inner journey starts from outside. One can only imagine the inner journey while he remains outside.

"It is the fundamental duty of a man to have self-control, fulfill his duties, drive away anger and desires from within, and open up the path to spirituality."

I used to find time alone with Maharajshri after he rose from his afternoon rest. I resumed the conversation from the previous day about the invisible masters by asking, "Yesterday you were telling us about Karma Yoga without attachment and that it was a necessity from an aspirant's point of view, but those invisible masters do not do anything besides sadhana. Is that correct?"

Maharajshri said, "You should understand this. Spiritual discipline changes with time, place, condition, and the state and level of a person. Things that are essential in the beginning become superfluous with progress. There will definitely be some differences between an aspirant languishing in this world, having an impure chitta, troubled by desires and tendencies, and an aspirant with a pure mind who has risen far above the world. The rules and discipline for a worldly sadhak are unavoidable, but an evolved sadhak has left the circle of this discipline. The subject of detached Karma Yoga was not mentioned with the invisible masters in mind. People in the shackles of the world are innumerable. How many invisible masters are there? These commandments are for the individual souls in the world."

Question: "Have you ever touched these invisible great beings?"

Answer: "I understand what you are asking. You wonder whether the vision of these invisible great men is real or simply an experience in meditation. Do they have any physical power and existence or not? The reason for this doubt is that the individual soul dwells so much in a physical realm that he wants to gauge everything from a physical perspective. He wants to bring God also down to the physical level. He does not want to give up gross materialism, and also wants to experience the subtle realm on the basis of gross matter.

"No, I have never tried to touch them. It is also inappropriate to do so. I have only bowed to them and that, too, from a distance. Just a short time had passed after my initiation when I first had such an experience. I had arranged to stay in a room in a dharmashala. Because it was winter very few pilgrims used to come. I was alone in the whole dharmashala so there was ample opportunity for sadhan. I was experiencing forceful kriyas of Hatha Yoga. I would often stand on my head, stretch my legs and roll around. Perhaps there were samskaras of Hatha Yoga from some lifetime. I was sitting in sadhan one day. The room was locked from inside. Suddenly my eyes opened. In the air a tall and well-built old master appeared. His eyes and face were shining with divine light. He was naked and totally intoxicated with spirituality. At the time I did not even remember how the master had entered the room, locked as it was from inside! I stood up and bowed. The only sign of old age was his white hair. He stood quietly and looked at me. With his hand, he gestured toward me, indicating that I should sit down. Once I was seated he slowly came to me and placed his hand on my head. Thus I did not touch him, but he touched me. I experienced the touch of his fingers on my head. My eyes closed.

"My first experience of the subtle body leaving the physical body took place then. This was due to the grace of that master. My physical body was sitting with legs crossed and eyes closed. I was watching the body. The master stood opposite me, looking at the body. Then he turned toward my subtle body, raised his hands and blessed me without saying anything. Then he disappeared into the air as I watched. Thus at first I saw him with my gross eyes, then I saw him with my subtle body, then he disappeared in front of the subtle body. This means that his state was subtler than the subtlest, but when he wished he could be seen with gross eyes. In other words, he manifested on the physical level. If he wished, someone could see him in subtle form with their subtle body, but when he rose to an even more subtle level, no one could see him, either with physical eyes or with the subtle body."

Question: "If his level is so subtle then how could he take the form of a physical body?"

Answer: "A common person can neither generate a gross body, nor leave the body at will. His physical body is his home as long as he is alive. Whether he likes it or not, he is helpless. This kriya of the invisible master is under the control of his will. Whenever they want they can manifest in a physical body from a subtle body. When they wish they can fold the physical body into the subtle body. And whenever they want they can fold in both, the physical and subtle bodies, into a much more subtle form."

Question: "Are their physical bodies similar to those of all other physical bodies?"

Answer: "Yes. They are similar to common bodies, but they have much more of the prana [life-force] element. It can be said that even in the physical state their bodies are closer to the state of pure knowledge, or consciousness. Those who have the power to travel in space must increase the percentage of the air element in their bodies prior to space travel, so that their bodies become light enough to travel in space. These masters do not need any such special technique. Their bodies are made up of consciousness from the beginning. They become invisible as soon as they merge their physical bodies into the subtle bodies.

"Even *Yoga Darshan* describes the siddhi, the miraculous power, of disappearing. For this the yogi concentrates on the form of his body and paralyzes the vision of the viewer. Thus he stops the viewer's power of sight from operating. As a result the knowledge of his presence is not acquired. But the technique of becoming invisible of these masters is different. He merges his physical body into the subtle body and thus his body goes beyond the grasp of the gross senses. The body of the yogi who practices the siddhi of invisibility remains present, but cannot be seen. The bodies of these masters fold into their subtle bodies and merge with them."

Question: "That is possibly why they do not feel hungry."

Answer: "Yes. When prana is working on the basis of the physical body, then the body needs food to function. When the body asks for food it is called hunger. But when a siddha [a perfected being] primarily dwells in the subtle body, which consists of only consciousness and manifests only occasionally in the physical body, why does he need to eat and drink?"

Question: "What happened after that master became invisible?"

Answer: "For a while I stood near my physical body and then involuntarily started to fly. I crossed the banks of the River Ganges, went around Swargashram and reached Dev Prayag, flying over the mountains. I took a bath in the Ganges and returned the same way, flying. The door was locked. The physical body would not have been able to enter. But this was not an obstacle that would stop the subtle body. My physical body was sitting in the same cross-legged position. It cannot be said that it was in samadhi because at that time there was no ego in the body. It was in the subtle body, and the subtle body was watching the physical body. The physical body did not see the subtle body because the senses were non-functional. Even otherwise the subtle body is beyond the reach of the physical senses. I re-entered my physical body."

In the meantime we heard the sound of people coming up the stairs; the subject of the invisible masters could not progress further. The subject of our satsang was changed and a gentleman asked:

Question: "Is it not the sole meaning of all that you said yesterday that, without performing action, one cannot deplete destiny?"

Answer: "That is the meaning. Still, although all perform action their destiny is not depleted. On the contrary it keeps growing because people do not perform actions with the goal and feelings with which they must be done. They do not want to give up attachment and ego.

They do not want to let go of impurities. They do not want to perform the action for God. No one wants to understand the real form of service and duty. No one has the patience, enthusiasm, seriousness and tolerance needed for sadhana. How, then, can destiny be depleted? Everyone performs action [karma], but with attachment. People do not understand the meaning, nature and feelings of selfless action. Even when they give donations and do good deeds they are bound by them. Even while doing service and sadhana, their ego continues to grow."

Question: "Maharajshri, please talk about something higher than worldly matters."

Answer: "It is you people who do not rise above worldly affairs. There are many topics of a higher level to talk about, but that can be done only when you are free of worldly matters. You have grabbed worldly affairs as if you will never give them up. How can the subject move higher?"

Question: "Does this mean that until worldly behavior is purified, sadhana cannot even commence?"

Answer: "No, it does not mean that. Efforts for wholesome worldly behavior and sadhana must continue simultaneously. But you cannot go within until you have established purity in your behavior in the world. Pure worldly behavior means to push the mind inwards from outside, and sadhana means to pull the mind inside from within. Both have the same objective: to pull the mind inwards. But if the mind remains extrovert, towards the world, and shackled in worldly affairs, tied in attachment and attractions, it will not be possible to push it inwards or pull it inwards from within. Karma Yoga purifies one of worldly activities and breaks the chains of attachment."

Question: "From what you are saying, it sounds as if this path of sadhana involves effort, and there is little room for spontaneous kriyas of Shakti and surrender."

Answer: "No. That is not what I want to say. As long as the ego is strong there must be effort to perform action, but there should be surrender of the fruit of that action. Finally, as long as you are protecting the ego of the mind, you have to start from there. The baggage of destiny that you carry on your head will have to be thrown away sooner or later. The miracle of destiny is that if you do not start to throw it away, it keeps growing. Karma Yoga is the name of the solution that weakens ego and reduces prarabdha [destiny].

"Awakening of Shakti is most important in any case. With the awakening, on the one hand personal knowledge of the falsehood of ego is gained, and on the other hand hidden samskaras in the chitta are dug out and thrown away so they do not take the form of future destiny. But the difficulty is that the experiences of sadhan are forgotten during worldly activities and one is filled with ego again. As long as a sadhak cannot maintain the state of an observer while performing worldly actions he has only one way out: to change the nature of worldly activities done with ego."

Question: "On the one hand you talk about the high state of the invisible masters, and on the other hand you talk about purifying common behavior. This is causing some confusion."

Answer: "There is no nothing confusing in what I said. This is about the level and state of an aspirant. The sadhan of each person will be appropriate to his worthiness. With continuity in sadhan the state of the aspirant and the form of his spiritual practice — both change. All aspirants are not at the same level, even after Shaktipat. The knowledge of the Gita starts with vishaad [despondency], passes through beautiful passages of knowledge and devotion, and ends with surrender. The final goal of the Gita is not self-realization or God-realization, but surrender to God. God-realization is the fruit of surrender, but its first and foremost goal is Buddhi Yoga [yoga of the intellect]. After narrating the whole Gita, the Lord says,

> *Sarva dharmaan parityajya maamekam sharanam vraja.*

Give up all other duties and take refuge in me, surrender to me.

"The awakening of Shakti is important to understand the feeling of surrender and to gain experiential knowledge of that which the Lord has called rajvidya gudhvidya [the king of all knowledge, the secret mystic knowledge]. The Gita ends with the direct experience of surrender to this king of all knowledge. One can reach the peak of a mountain only by climbing one step after another.

"The final teaching of the Gita is that a human being cannot do anything. He can only nurture ego, and that ego contaminates the psyche. The individual soul who surrenders to God, God will purify his chitta. The essence of the Gita is to surrender to God."

Question: "But you were asking us to make efforts and perform action."

Answer: "Whether someone says it or not, as long as the ego exists in the mind the individual will depend on his own efforts. The ego of the individual soul is shattered while doing karma, and only then is he ready to surrender. Lord Krishna also, in the Gita, at first teaches that one should take action. Then he shows what the results are when one takes action on his own. 'Give up all efforts and ego and take refuge in me. After you take refuge I will free you from all the sins.' "

Question: "This means the basic problem is giving up ego. Then what is the necessity of awakening the Shakti?"

Answer: "Awakening of the Shakti is essential, especially for giving up ego, because only after that does one gain the knowledge of the witness-state through personal experience. And after that one realizes the hollowness of the ego and the feeling of surrender arises. Surrender is a state of mind. It is not just a blank and transient feeling. Temporary feelings may arise from reading books and listening to lectures. But steadfast surrender can arise only after the awakening of Shakti.

"Subsequently, when Lord Krishna says, 'I will free those devotees from all their sins who have a full sense of surrender,' it means that God's Shakti will awaken within the devotee, and with its workings it will free him from all his samskaras. Karma with a sense of surrender is real Karma Yoga. Surrender gives Buddhi Yoga. Surrender is the ultimate teaching of the Gita. The Gita ends with the counsel of surrender. There is nothing more to say after that."

Question: "Why did the great Sage Vyasa write the Gita as a part of the Mahabharata? He could have made it an independent scripture."

Answer: "In my opinion, writing the Gita in the middle of the Mahabharata is more appropriate because the complete background of the Gita is the Mahabharata. The knowledge of the Gita was imparted to Arjuna, but he was not the main character of the Mahabharata. The main character was Grandsire Bhishma. The Mahabharata begins with the narration of his birth and it ends with his death. If you want to see the highest embodiment of the knowledge of the Gita, it can be seen in the life of Grandsire Bhishma. For the happiness of his father he gave up his own happiness and accepted the responsibility of protecting the royal throne. For the sake of his vow he had to give support to adharma [divergence from the moral law, injustice], and also had to bear the intolerable act of the disrobing of Draupadi. His heart and blessings were with the Pandavas but he had to go to war on behalf of Duryodhana. As a result of his blessings the Pandavas emerged victorious, but he had to lose his life for taking the side of injustice. He himself showed the Pandavas the means to his death.

"The Gita is the heart, or the center, of the Mahabharata. The fuller elaboration of the knowledge of the Gita is known as the Mahabharata. The Mahabharata is the basis for the Gita. If such a deep and serious subject is presented without any basis then it becomes impossible to grasp. It is difficult to understand the Gita in spite of such a basis, but it is easier to understand because of the story and the qualities of the characters of the Mahabharata. It is certain that each and every character and every event in the Mahabharata is meant to provide a deeper understanding of some spiritual instruction. Some characters reflect demonic qualities and some represent divinity. Vyasa took the trouble of writing such an enormous book in order to explain the Gita.

"Vyasa presented the human mind as the ground of dharma [duty], and the human body as the Kurukshetra [the battlefield for the great war of the Mahabharata]. The Pandavas were to represent divinity and the Kauravas demonic tendencies. The limits of demonic attitude can be seen in the character of Duryodhana and Shakuni, and divinity is represented in Vidura and Yudhishthira. The role of someone blinded with infatuation is given to Dhritrashtra. In the midst of all these, Grandsire

Bhishma is a sattvic spiritual aspirant. The cause for the manifestation of Gita-jnana [the Knowledge embodied in the Gita] is Arjuna's despondency. These painful scenes and events of inner conflicts and dilemmas are presented as the principles in the Gita. The same thing is expressed elaborately in the Mahabharata with innumerable examples. Thus the Mahabharata and the Gita complement each other."

In the meantime voices from the ground floor were heard informing us that the evening tea was ready. All of us went downstairs. As the time was right, I resumed the conversation about invisible masters. I asked, "You were saying that the invisible masters live in caves in the Himalayas. Are there similar caves in Vindhyachal, although that range is not so high?"

Answer: "Caves are merely a pretext for lodging, otherwise they do not need caves to stay in. They can stay anywhere — in the open, on riverbanks, on mountain tops or in dense forests. Densely populated or solitary, both are acceptable to them. Neither do the changing seasons affect them, nor does the hustle and bustle of the world. They have no problem living in Vindhyachal or anywhere else in the world. However there are caves in Vindhyachal, as well."

Question: "I am struck with wonder as I listen to all these amazing things."

Answer: "Yes. This is amazing for worldly people. By remaining in a state of samadhi most of the time they receive many akalpita siddhis [non-artificial and unexpected powers]. One such siddhi — I have not read even the slightest mention of this in the books of yoga — is that they experience birth and death without giving up their body. Thus they go through many species while staying in the same body."

Question: "How many such great beings exist?"

Answer: "It is hard to say how many of these great beings exist, but one thing is certain: They are not innumerable like the creatures that wander on the earth. Only once in many ages does one odd great master reach such a high state."

Question: "Will each and every sadhak go through this stage?"

Answer: "I do not think so, but one thing is certain: The spiritual journey is very long. Who knows how long a particular being has been wandering at the gross physical level? He does not have even the slightest idea or hint about his journey through the subtle spheres. According to the scriptures, Kak Bhushundi has been observing the creation and dissoluton of universes for a very long time, whereas these invisible masters, while dwelling in subtle spheres, are still drifting and wandering in the gross physical world.

"The objective of a sadhak is to attain that state which is beyond the subtle and physical, as well as within the subtle and physical. All aspirants have their own experiences, their own stages, and their own spiritual goals. All of them cannot be guided with the same stick. A sadhak dominated by yoga and a sadhak dominated by devotion will be very different in their feelings, thinking and levels. The path of the person following jnana will be very different. As long as aspirants have a heart and a mind their feelings and thoughts will differ."

63. Sanyas Diksha

Swami Narayan Tirth Maharaj had arrived from Varanasi. He expressed a desire to go on a pilgrimage to Badrinath and Kedarnath. Maharajshri instructed me to accompany him and serve him, so I was deprived of listening to the rest of Maharajshri's thoughts on the Gita. I went on the pilgrimage with Swamiji Maharaj. In those days buses and cars had started going up to Kunda Chatti, the place of Agatsya Muni. On the way to Badrinarayan, ahead of Rudra Prayag, car travel was possible up to Joshi ashram. I felt the same joy in serving Swamiji Maharaj that I felt in serving Maharajshri. We returned in about ten days.

The preparation for my sanyas diksha [initiation into the monastic order] began upon our return. A cottage was arranged for on the banks of Ganga River, where I could stay while performing the rituals and fast. A priest was assigned to perform the rituals. On the day of the initiation Swami Narayan Tirth Maharaj showered me with grace by initiating me as a sanyasi, a monk, as I stood in the Ganga River. After we returned to Dandiwada my new name as a monk, Shivom Tirth, was announced.

The next day a meeting of great souls took place where Maharajshri gave a discourse. Maharajshri said, "First I bow to the revered Bhagvadpad Shankaracharya, who instituted the tradition of sanyasis, which is continuing until today. This tradition has continued for the last 1,300 years. He introduced the goal of advaita [non-duality] and obligated the human race. The revered Bhagwan Shankaracharya included all paths and practices in the path of non-duality. He accepted the practice of worshipping five deities [Shiva, Bhagawati, Sun, Vishnu, and Ganesha] and showed the way to attain non-duality through this practice. He composed *Yoga Taravali*, and emphasized the need for yoga in order to be an authority on the Vedanta. He offered *Saundarya Lahari* to the world, and also gave formal acceptance to tantrik spiritual practices. The final goal of life was non-duality. To attain that goal a person must follow some spiritual path or another, purify his psyche, and be worthy of non-duality. His non-duality was not opposed to any spiritual practice, rather it was the foundation of all. It was an ocean in which all kinds of waves would rise, and into which rivers would flow from all directions. It was like an infinite sky where innumerable small and big stars would spread their own light.

"It is cause for great sadness that today the literature of Shankaracharya is used for comparative analysis and to disprove other spiritual paths. We want to jump straight to the non-duality state, ignoring the spiritual paths of bhakti [devotion], yoga and karma [action]. We also ignore detached karma, which weakens prarabdha and prepares the foundation for the experience of non-duality. We ridicule devotion, which fills the heart and gives rise to an ardent desire for non-duality. We believe that yoga that brings control over the mind, purifies the power of discretion, and makes one worthy of grasping the Vedanta is superfluous. Standing at the window of duality, looking at duality, while being influenced by duality, we talk about non-duality. Even when fully besieged by Maya [the grand illusion], we say that Maya is false. It is true that, in principle, Maya is not real, but its falsehood must be experienced. As long as one is influenced by the illusory world it is a mistake to call the world an illusion.

"We have wandered away from Shankar Bhagavadpad's coherent perspective and are lost in comparative analysis. Bhagavadpad included all spiritual paths in non-duality, whereas we oppose all paths, put them aside, prove them inappropriate by comparative analysis and try to establish non-duality. We forget that comparative analysis itself involves duality. Comparison is only possible between two, and hence non-duality can never be proven with comparative analysis.

"Authority over the Vedanta is achieved only after the study of Karma Yoga [an action-based spiritual path], Bhakti Yoga [a devotion-based spiritual path], and so forth, wherein the awakening of the Shakti plays a key role. The system of the fourfold Vedanta sadhana is a kind of yoga, but today we have turned a blind eye to it. Listening, thinking and contemplating are our areas of focus today. Many people wander around as sadhaks in the absence of inner preparedness. They do not find God; rather, their psyche keeps on getting filled with pride and other vices.

The great saying of the Rigveda is *Prajnanam Brahma*, meaning, Prajnan [consciousness] is Brahma [the absolute]. Has anyone tried to experience prajnan? This cannot be experienced merely by book knowledge and thinking. If someone wants to know prajnan then he must experience prajnan directly. The grand mansion of spirituality can only be built upon the experiential knowledge of prajnan. Dry and heartless discussions without direct experience of prajnan cannot free anyone from the desire-filled darkness of delusion. Direct knowledge of prajnan is the awakening of the Shakti. Only then will one be able to say, 'So ham,' 'I am that.' *So Ham* is not a chant; it is an experience.

"Prajnana is kundalini, Allhadini [Giver of Bliss], directly perceivable consciousness. It sends waves of joy and beauty upon awakening, which is described in *Saundarya Lahari* by Bhagavadpad. The perspective of Adi Shankaracharya was so broad and all encompassing that he was even concerned about the progress of his opponents. He never despised any path, considering it inferior. In fact, he saw all the paths flowing toward the great ocean of non-duality. Today we are becoming narrow-minded in the name of Shankar Bhagavadpad, who was all embracing. We consider others to be inferior, hateful and lost. We try to climb the path of Vedanta, neglecting the need for sadhan and sadhana. Do not consider Shankaracharya's practice of worshipping the five deities unnecessary.

"Sadhan and sadhana are the supporting pillars of spirituality. Sadhana ripens sadhan. Love enhances one's ardent desire for God, and ardent desire makes one worthy of God's grace. The Vedanta state is not a thing to be attained. It shines within on its own. Keep your attention on the peak of the mountain, and keep on marching, keep on climbing. This moving forward and climbing is sadhan. As the psyche becomes purer, as you keep on going, you will be elevated.

"Sadhan is like a lamp in the hand. As you keep moving forward the light will also keep moving forward. It will continue to illuminate the road further. In this lamp the inclination towards sadhan is the wick and sadhan is the oil. If you stop doing sadhan then the lamp will extinguish. If the inclination towards sadhan is removed then the lamp will be turned off. But if you take the lamp in your hand and start moving ahead it will keep illuminating the path ahead. Once you reach the destination, the lamp will automatically be set aside."

One Swamiji in the audience said, "Maharajji, your point is well taken, but my inclination has developed in reading and reciting, thinking and contemplating. We are almost the age of sixty or more. We have passed most of the time of our life; only a little time is left. In this condition it is difficult to change the form of our sadhan."

Maharajshri said, "I accept your point. As one's age progresses habits become strong and therefore it is advised that one must develop a habit of sadhan when one is young. There is nothing wrong with the fact that you have a strong habit of reading and reciting. This also is a part of sadhan. But what I would like to point out to you is that most of your reading and contemplating is thinking about the absolute, whereas until now you have not attained the ripened stage of detachment. It would be far more beneficial for you to think about the difference between temporary and eternal. Then you will see that the whole world is in the category of temporary. This will reduce your attachment to the world, and your desire to know the eternal essence will grow. This will continually strengthen your worthiness for the Vedanta.

"You must be doing some chanting. There is no age limit for starting sadhana. It can be started once one becomes aware. But one thing is certain: that a fickle mind cannot contemplate or meditate on Brahma. With God's grace Shakti can be awakened at any time. God can manifest at any time through the medium of a Sadguru [good Guru]. Chant with this objective in mind.

"Give a thought to whether you have developed pride in being called an ascetic, on becoming an ascetic. If so, then it can be a serious obstacle and appropriate efforts must be made to remove that pride. If you can take up a vice you can throw it away as well. It is not a difficult job. It just needs a firm resolve.

"You are on the spiritual path, the only thing needed is the right direction. All roads lead to God. Some may be direct and others round about. Some may be smooth and others may have bumps and potholes. Expand your mind and respect all the paths and love all spiritual aspirants. Why only all aspirants? Why not all living beings. This is sanyas. The path of an ascetic is very difficult, much more difficult than the path of worldly people. Therefore you must walk very carefully."

A Swamiji asked, "The essence of what you are saying is that sadhana is necessary, but scriptures say that liberation is attained through listening. If one can be liberated by listening then why get involved in the complexities of sadhana?"

Maharajshri said, "Most of you here are monks. You all must have heard the four great sentences [of the vedas] at the time of initiation into the ascetic order. Who is liberated among you? No one. Liberation can definitely be attained through listening but one has to become worthy of that listening, and that comes with sadhana. One can be liberated by listening to the advice of a Sadguru just as Ramkrishna Paramhans was liberated by listening to Totapuri."

64. The Teachings Related to Sanyas

Shri Swami Narayan Tirthji Maharaj said, "Shivom must spend a holy period of four months [after initiation as a monk] in my company and that, too, for the entire four months. In the future he can reduce such holy periods to two months." Hence, with the permission of Maharajshri, I went to Varanasi with Swamiji Maharaj. Before leaving Maharajshri spoke to me in this way:

"Now you are a Swami, but remember one thing: Your mind is the same as it was before. The color of your clothes has turned saffron but your mind still needs to be colored. You have taken on the holy shaft [as is the custom after being initiated as a monk] symbolizing the absolute, but the absolute has not arisen in your mind yet. Desires, anger, jealousy, greed, hatred, and so forth, are not yet extinguished from your mind. This external change can take you forward in your spiritual pursuits, or it can cause your fall amidst false pride. In other words, after becoming a monk you are standing at a crossroad.

"Geru [the soil that makes the monk's clothes saffron] is a soil of special color. Putting your clothes in geru means that the clothing you wear in the form of this body will also merge with the soil. The color of geru represents fire. It means that, from today, you must burn yourself, heat yourself to ashes. Sanyas [becoming a monk] is another word for burning oneself, heating the body, heating the mind, burning the tendencies and accumulated impressions to ashes. If one can do that while being a householder then that person is called a householder ascetic. But it is difficult because, in that case, other members of the family must also burn, for which they are not prepared. Therefore it becomes necessary to give up the family in sanyas.

"After becoming an ascetic the pride of being a great soul can arise. That pride, for the crushing of which sanyas was accepted, starts growing. The spiritual aspirant becomes pitiable in such a condition. He cannot return to being a householder, and nothing is visibly attained by becoming an ascetic. You must remember that initiation to become a monk is only a change in one's ashram [phase of life]. No one becomes a great soul just by taking initiation. For that, sadhan, removal of pride, and God's grace are essential.

Until now only your body has received initiation to become a monk, not your mind. Mind can become agitated and throw into turmoil the body, which has received initiation to become a monk. Scriptures approve physical austerities, but real austerities take place in the mind. The mind remains attached to physical austerities. The mind is disturbed with tendencies and accumulated impressions. The purpose of mental austerities is to purify tendencies and destroy accumulated impressions. This is not an easy job. This is the hardest job in the world. The mind runs externally under the control of tendencies but discriminative intellect pulls it within. Austerity accompanies discriminative intellect in this internal conflict. This requires infinite patience and perseverance. Austerity is a process that goes on continuously until the mind is purified. The resolve to persist in this inner fight is called sanyas.

"At this stage you are not free from attachments and desires. You still have ambitions and desires in your mind. Impurities are still accumulated on the surface of your psyche and intellect is caught in delusion and suspicion . You have chosen the path of sanyas with the resolve that, from now on, the only purpose of life is to be free from attachments and desires. However strong the storms of tendencies may be, face them with courage. You do not want to succumb, irrespective of the number and kind of temptations that appear in front of you. You do not want to leave your path no matter how much success and failure you may have to face. This is austerity. But the resolve of such austerity can be fulfilled only with God's grace.

"The world will throw obstacles in the way. Sometimes it will entangle you in greed, and at other times in fear. Sometimes it will try to trick you with sweetness, and at other times it will show you affection as a well-wisher. These are the tricks of the world. Friend-enemy, mine-yours — all these are imaginations of the mind, wherein the living being becomes deluded by becoming externally oriented towards the world. Keep your mind protected, behave lovingly with everyone, but do not get attached to anyone. Do not feel hate for those who believe you to be their opponent, otherwise your mind will be polluted with hatred. In this way there is a possibility of losing your path. Endure your destiny without any resistance.

"Now for four months you will be physically away from me. Do not worry about me. I am also an ascetic. Whatever circumstances come forth, God takes care. Even if some inconvenience or unfavorable circumstance arises, accept it as destiny or as God's grace. In Dewas there will be many people who will take care of me. Write to me. Keep in mind the things I have told you."

I went with Swamiji Maharaj to Varanasi for the holy period of four months. I was deprived of Maharajshri's company for those four months. The question of any memories related to this period does not arise.

65. The Authority of Succession

Swamiji Maharaj and I left for Dewas at the end of the four months. This was December 1965. Maharajshri appeared to be very happy.

The subject of succession arose again upon our arrival in Dewas. This time the assault was stronger. People from Dewas and Indore were present, and some had arrived from other places. Some of the more influential people had decided to recommend that Maharajshri select me as his successor. Among them was the gentleman who had been chosen earlier for succession.

They all came to Maharajshri and made their proposal when Maharajshri said, "I, too, wish to make Shivom my successor. I have talked about it many times but Shivom is not ready to listen. Finally I told him that I would not talk about this subject ever again in the future. Therefore I cannot say anything. If you wish, you can talk to him."

Those people came to me and explained, "Your life has been offered in service to Maharajshri. Whatever belongs to you has been offered to Maharajshri. You respect Maharajshri's wishes and follow them. If Maharajshri wishes to make you his successor then why do you disrespect his wish? You recommend someone here and someone else there."

I was stunned by their direct appeal. I thought for a while and said, "When the subject of succession has been decided why is it being raised again?"

They answered, "When that same person is sitting before you and repeatedly insisting that you should be the successor, what is the significance of such a decision? The decision was never made; in a sense, you forced this decision on Maharajshri. You and we also know what Maharajshri's wish is. And we all also know that to follow Maharajshri's wish is your life's objective."

I said, "I do not see in myself the strength to carry the load. I do not have an iota of the knowledge, austerity, personality, generosity or endurance that Maharajshri has. I do not have any of the qualities needed to maintain the honor of his position. You do not know what I am. Only I know the state of my mind."

I received the answer, "Whether you are worthy or not we do not know. The only thing we know is that you are Maharajshri's servant. The one who serves does not pay attention to his worth or otherwise, he only pays attention to the wish of whom he serves. Only the one who is served knows why and how the wish arises and in what circumstances. The duty of a servant is to follow the instructions of the master and respect his wishes."

I had no answer to this argument. My belief about service was the same as theirs. Perhaps at some time I had tried to explain this aspect of the duty of a servant to them. My own ideas about the duties of a devoted servant were being presented to me, but the ego within me was rising up again and again and bringing forth my unworthiness. Perhaps this was a tactic of my ego, to lead me astray from my duties as a servant. I was unable to escape the cover of unworthiness wrapped around me. Without any doubt I was unworthy. But my unworthiness was being proven in the strongest way by my refusal to follow Maharajshri's wish. I told them that I would talk to Maharajshri.

When I talked to Maharajshri he said, "I had told you that in the future, I would not talk about this subject. Now you have introduced it. You have known my wish from before, and it remains the same even today. Whether you take up my wish or reject it is up to you."

I said, "But what about the one whom you have announced as your successor?"

Maharajshri said, "When he himself comes along with the others and pleads on your behalf, and also comes to you to convince you, that issue is resolved. We do not have to do anything."

I left Maharajshri's room after requesting to think it over for some time. I was very confused and could not understand anything. I went to Swami Narayan Tirth Maharaj's room. I said, "I want to talk about an important matter." I asked people present there to leave. I expressed my confusion to Swamiji Maharaj.

Swamiji Maharaj said, "You have taken up sanyas now. You are also in the service of Maharajshri. If this is his wish then you have no authority to make a decision. It is Maharajshri's wish and Maharajshri's decision. Your duty is to uphold his wish in your mind. This is surrender."

I said, "But what about my unworthiness?"

Swamiji Maharaj said, "Your arrogance has taken the cover of your unworthiness."

I said, "But people can say that I served in order to take over the ashram."

Swamiji Maharaj said, "Forget about what people will say. Whether you do something or not they will talk. It is their job to talk. A true gentleman does not talk about others. You do not become what someone says simply by their saying so."

Now I had no way out. I went straight to Maharajshri and put forth my consent. Maharajshri instantly sent for people and announced that I was to be his successor. The decision was made to have a ceremony to formalize the succession the following day.

I sank into a deep ocean of thoughts after going to my room. This was a very important turn of events in my life. My entire past began to pass in front of my eyes. I remembered the days that had passed in Nangal and Himachal Pradesh. What peace and joy was there! Today I was entering a field where there would be a crowd all the time, problems and no peace. Until now I had thought I would serve Maharajshri until the end of his life and then return to that peaceful environment, but now arrangements were being made for me to never return to that peaceful place again. A human being faces many helpless situations, but usually the world is responsible for that helplessness. The satisfaction in my helplessness was that its cause was my Guru's wish.

Slowly I took control of my mind. I had never thought that I would be a Maharaj of an ashram one day. I was able to see clearly that this position of Maharaj was filled with so many problems, obstacles, attractions and slippery slopes. It is easy to stay in solitude and do sadhan. But to stay amongst people, to take friends and opponents along, to love them all alike, to serve them, is so difficult. Then I was trying to adopt certain disciplines in my own life and this work was even more difficult. But once the head is between a mortar and pestle, what is there to be afraid of? Having said yes, there is no alternative but to face the circumstances. It would suffice if my mind remained attached to my Guru's feet.

The following day a modest ceremony was arranged to formalize my succession. In the morning I went to Maharajshri's room, bowed, and said, "You are a siddha [a perfect being]. Your dignity, sadhan and vision are incomparable, but I am like an ignorant and unskilled child who does not know anything about himself or the world. Only with your blessings and strength will I be able to fulfill this responsibility."

Maharajshri said, "I know it is not the goal of your life to be the head of an ashram. Neither do you desire this as a reward for serving me, nor am I giving this for that reason. To think or to do something like that would be disrespectful to service. Service is a pious sentiment; attaching a price to it would not be proper. The link between the Guru and disciple is such that the Guru bestows upon the disciple as a grace and the disciple, too, accepts it as his greatest fortune. The benefit of this sentiment and relationship, whenever it is attained, can only be one, and that is spiritual benefit.

"You know, and it is my experience as well, that the ashram is a great facade, much larger than worldly activities. Here the possibilities for attachment, ego and hate are great. A man can get entangled in expectations of adulation and self-righteous experiments of authority. Consequently, day by day, he may get farther away from his real spiritual goal. The ashram is like a frying pan with hot oil that heats and burns an aspirant. I am purposely throwing you into this boiling oil. I know you will burn and I want you to burn. It is necessary to burn to be luminous. Contact with people and worldly activities are essential to deplete prarabdha [destiny]. The fruits of worldly activities bind you only if you are attached to them. Otherwise they deplete prarabdha. The spiritual aspirant must suffer greatly and burn a lot as prarabdha is depleted. This endurance comes without a word of complaint from the mouth and without any resistance. Otherwise prarabdha does not diminish.

"You will have your disciples and your Guru-brothers [disciples of the same Guru]. This is what happens in an ashram inherited through a lineage. It is much easier to build an ashram and then run it because there are only disciples; whatever the Guru's behavior it is accepted. But here you must walk with and support both disciples and Guru-brothers. Your Guru-brothers must not feel that they are being ignored. Some of your Guru-brothers are far more senior than you, and they have seen you work like a servant. You must have even served quite a few of them. Some of them, therefore, will hesitate in accepting you as a Guru. You will have to go on accepting them. I do know that this is not an easy job. Your job is even harder than mine. I had only my disciples, but it will not be so with you. Disciples of other Gurus will also come to you. You will need to give them love and respect without making efforts to bring them under your influence. Otherwise it may cause friction with other ashrams. I know it is not your habit, but remember never to criticize the head of any other ashram. If someone else says something then just bear it without any response.

"You are certainly being given the privilege of succession, but you do not have any rights. I also had no rights here. Talk about rights and authority is appropriate for worldly people, but not for ascetics. The ashram belongs to Lord Shankara and only he has all the authority. We all are there for service. The head of an ashram is the biggest servant. This alone is his right. Whether you give initiation or a discourse, do it without ego as a service to Lord Shankara.

"Houses in the world open only to the world, but the door of the ashram is open to both the world and spirituality. It is up to the individual to choose where he wants to go. If one gets attached to the ashram and develops pride then the door to the world opens and the person keeps getting deeper in the world, much more so than a householder. If the sentiments of service and love prevail then the ashram becomes an entrance to spirituality.

"The ashram is the path to spirituality even while one is involved in worldly affairs. Knowledge of the world is acquired only by staying in the world, therefore life in the ashram is not useless. How can you know the selfishness, likes and dislikes, egoism and duplicity of the world by living in solitude? Also, how can prarabdha be depleted? Therefore you need not be afraid of the ashram. Just keep doing your duty and don't worry about the world."

When I raised the issue with Maharajshri of not being worthy, he said that no person is unworthy in the world. A person has worn the garb of unworthiness, which is his unnatural form. Worthiness is the nature of human beings. If you take off and throw aside the garb of unnaturalness then the natural quality will come out. If a person can put on clothing he can take it off, as well.

I pleaded, "But, Maharajshri, I am worried and frightened. How will I bear such a great responsibility?"

Maharajshri replied, "This responsibility is great as long as you consider that responsibility to be on your own shoulders. But who are you to carry that responsibility? You just keep on doing your duty. The responsibility will be borne by Guru-Shakti."

In a brief ceremony Maharajshri wrapped me in a shawl and performed other rituals of authority, and even signed a document declaring the succession. On this occasion Maharajshri said, "For some time I have been thinking, and others have expressed the same view, that I must name my successor. I am seventy-eight years old now. There is no certainty about anyone's life as such, but with advancing age the end definitely approaches nearer. I am feeling very light and comfortable after the announcement of my successor. This is a continuous tradition. A prince after a king and a disciple after a Guru have always inherited responsibilities. If the successor is announced while the position holder is still alive then many potential problems are resolved.

"The full authority of Shivom will begin after I am gone, but from today, in terms of activities, I am retiring from quite a few responsibilities. Perhaps Shivom will now do the initiation work. Taking care of the ashram also will be his responsibility. The only thing I want to tell you all is to take interest in the ashram just as before and cooperate as before.

"I know that the job of a new Maharaj is very difficult. It will take time to perfect his personality. He does not have the experience of many things, but no one comes into the world knowing everything; all learn after coming into the world. Therefore he will need some time to learn. I am hopeful that your cooperation will always be available."

I went to my room after the function and became lost in my thoughts. So far I had not accepted gifts from anyone, but now, as a representative of the ashram, I would have to accept gifts for and from the ashram. Maharajshri had asked me to give initiation in 1961, but so far I had not done so because I believed that the job of being a Guru as well as a disciple would be difficult for me. I had no interest in becoming a Guru. I believed this to be a trick of inner tendencies. But now that I was the successor I would have to perform the Guru's duties, as well.

I was able to see clearly that my life was changing. I was troubled by the worry that, with this change of events, my attitude would change, as well. I knew how difficult it was to control one's self amidst luxuries and comforts. Then I remembered: "If the head is placed in the mortar then why worry about getting pounded?" During the last five years I had gained quite a lot of world experience. There is no friend or enemy, even if the mind considers someone to be a friend and someone else to be the enemy. I had to get beyond the agitation of the mind even while staying in the center of this agitation. I had to become free of the bondage of luxuries while living in the middle of luxuries.

Then my thoughts turned toward giving initiation. The work that I had been saved from for the last six years would now have to be done. I decided that I would not give initiation at my own will. Maharajshri would give permission for initiation. I would give initiation only to those whom he chose. As long as Maharajshri was physically present, those desiring initiation had to go between Maharajshri and me three to four times. Maharajshri would say, "I am not giving initiation," and I would say, "Maharajshri's permission is required."

Maharajshri had instructed me not to nurture the pride of being a Guru. "You have not become a Guru by your own worthiness, austerities and detachment. You have attained the position of Guru by Gurudev's resolve. Now the Guru's resolve will work through you. If you develop the pride of being a Guru then you will be severed from the Guru's resolve. The work of giving initiation also must be done as a service to the Guru."

I also thought that first and foremost I was a disciple of this ashram. Only as a disciple am I someone's Guru-brother, a successor, and now I am preparing to be a Guru. Therefore I must always remain like a disciple of Maharajshri. I may have become something else for others, but Maharajshri's service should not be disturbed. As long as Maharajshri's body was in the world, I cleaned his cottage, washed his clothes, took him out for walks, and performed other tasks in his service as before.

In the evening Maharajshri was sitting on a chair in the front yard. Disciples were sitting on mats. A spiritual conversation was going on. Maharajshri said, "The journey of life is such that every traveler is lost. Still he claims his own path to be correct, and tries to show the way to others. This journey of life is such that no one knows where he is going. Even then he shows others their destination. This journey goes on through eternity, and no one knows how long it is going to continue. Sometimes the traveler starts to climb icy peaks, and at other times he starts to roll down the slopes; sometimes he gets lost in the greenery of the ranges and forest, and at other times, in the desert enduring the intense heat, he wanders around in the sand. Sometimes there is a high tide of enthusiasm, and at other times hopelessness dominates. At some point he thinks it appropriate and takes a heavy weight upon his head; the next moment he gets scared of the weight and throws it off.

"The journey of life is such that each and every traveler is in a dilemma. He is deluded and in the dark. Each traveler is taking steps in dense darkness without any preparation for the light, without seeing his path. When he stumbles and falls down he realizes that he has made a mistake but does not know where the mistake took place. Because he walks in the dark constantly, he falls frequently, dresses his wounds, gets up and walks on. The journey of life is like a whirlpool, swirling at an intense speed in one spot. The journey of life is like a boat that is tied to the shore while efforts are made to swiftly row the boat.

"When travelers are in a dilemma, one of them becomes a guide. The guide himself does not know the destination and the path; nevertheless he accepts the responsibility. The other travelers believe him to be knowledgeable and experienced, they praise him, serve him and follow his directions. The guide keeps marching ahead, giving guidance, until, eventually, his face shows signs of failure. The travelers become disappointed and another traveler pushes the guide aside and takes over his responsibilities. In this way the guides keep on changing, the journey continues, but no one reaches the destination.

"Many times the traveler gets fed up with the journey. He takes a liking to a cave in the mountains, or a cool river bank, or the shade of a tree. He gives up the idea of traveling and decides to stay at a chosen place. He experiences happiness and believes he has arrived at the destination. But the mind is such that it is not happy to remain in the same place and in the same circumstances. The traveler eventually gets restless and moves on. Then he locates another guide, praises him and follows his directions.

"This journey is very strange. The traveler asks others to introduce themselves, but he does not know his own self. He looks for the way when he does not know the destination. He collects different things for the journey although nothing works. The earth on which he walks slides from under his feet one day. The air that he is breathing stops its movement one day and moves away. The sun, in the light of which he has fought all his life against darkness, sets for him one day. Even his body, which he believed was an inseparable part of himself, leaves his company.

"This is a journey of a lost traveler who is thrown out of his home, with no place to go and no one to give shelter. He is alone under the infinite sky, wandering with the hope of finding support and shelter. His every birth comes with new hope and he leaves the world with every death bringing a heavy weight of disappointment on his head. This poor, helpless and lost traveler keeps circling in the maze of hope and despair.

"For success in this journey the traveler must seek answers to questions such as these from his own heart: If he reaches the door of failure again and again then why does it happen? If he continues to be trapped in the schemes of guides who do not know the path or the goal, why does this happen? Why is he unable to travel in high spirits, free of shackles on his feet? You may read thousands of scriptures and listen to discourses, but the real answers to these questions will only come with independent contemplation within one's own heart. Scriptures are many and multifarious. In every discourse the impressions of the speaker's viewpoint are always present. This may help to some extent in your independent thinking, but real knowledge and light will arise only from your own heart."

Question: "If knowledge arises from the heart, and all doubts are clarified internally then why attend satsangs or read scriptures?"

Answer: "These provide you with material you need to look inside. The Guru also guides one toward the inner journey, he shows the way to go inward, he awakens the Shakti, so that the path to purify the psyche is opened up. Then the traveler can experience light within himself. But it can be done only by that person who has not lost his way. He must be a traveler who is steady on the spiritual path."

Question: "Do you mean to say that a traveler needs a Guru for proper guidance?"

Answer: "There may be some exceptions, but generally everyone needs a Guru to navigate the spiritual path. Once a mountain starts to fall it keeps on falling. In the same way a lost traveler keeps on making mistakes. At last he finds himself alone in the thick forest of sins and desires, suffering helplessly and restlessly, from which he cannot find any way out. Like a sinner who commits a hundred new sins to hide one and goes deeper into the valley of sin — the lost traveler is in a similar plight.

"A lost traveler is like a homeless animal. He has no place to live, no owner, and he keeps moving aimlessly in whatever direction he turns his head. A man is drawn to the attractions of the world and keeps running after them. Sometimes he feels that he has acquired something, and sometimes he feels it has slipped out of his hands. It is as if someone were making futile efforts to tie flowers from the sky into a bunch. This delusion fills the life of the traveler with suffering and imbalance.

"It is such a sad thing that a human being, who has the potential to be similar to God and possesses the possibility of developing all the strengths behaves like an animal, runs around, and wastes his life. If he wishes, he can follow the right path and return to his true self, but he wanders in delusion."

Maharajshri finished his talk for the day but this was the beginning of a new lecture series. I felt as if today's talk was mainly directed at me. Now, after taking sanyas, self-examination had become even more significant. As I tried to go deeper within myself I could see many more faults. During the morning walk I discussed it with Maharajshri. "Maharajji, I believe I am a lost traveler myself. Then how can I have the authority to give initiation? I see many faults inside me even today."

Maharajshri said, "If you are able to see your faults then how can you be lost? You are on your path. A lost traveler is indifferent toward his faults. As far as initiation is concerned you are only a medium, through which I will give initiation. Your authority to give initiation depends on my resolve. This is why I have told you not to entertain the pride of being a Guru. However you still believe it is you who will give initiation."

I said, "Maharajshri, I should not say this, but since the subject has come up I must do so. Does this mean that I will be able to perform initiation only so long as your body exists?"

Maharajshri said, "My resolve will keep working even after I leave the body because my resolve is now established within you."

I said, "Then this means that the lineage will continue as long as my body exists!"

Maharajshri said, "No. After that my resolve, as a part of your resolve, will work through your disciples, but your resolve will be controlled by mine. When the ego of being a Guru arises in you, this chain of resolves will be broken and the resolve will lose its power and disperse."

66.   The Essence of the Teachings, I

A large group of people came today because Maharajshri's talk yesterday had made quite an impression on the mind. People were hoping that Maharajshri would talk more on the same subject and explain even more impressively. In the evening Maharajshri started by saying:

"The greatest contradiction in human life is that a man says life is priceless, and yet remains engrossed in wasteful activities. This age is filled with crooked politics. Every person's head is filled with tricks, dishonest maneuvers and gamesmanship. Every person is deep in pride and selfishness. Every person knows that nothing can be accomplished by bouncing and jumping, and yet everyone keeps on bouncing and jumping. Everyone knows that nothing can be taken along after death, yet all are busy accumulating. Even after knowing well that sensuous pleasures ultimately inflict a lot of pain, everyone pursues them. Even after knowing that they are on the wrong path, everyone keeps marching forward.

"A lost traveler needs a path that will take him to his destination. He needs a ladder that will take him up. He needs a boat that can take him to the other shore. He needs to find happiness that it will end his miseries forever. He needs a companion who will never leave him. He needs grace that will end his obstacles and afflictions forever. He needs energy that has the power to change gross matter into consciousness.

"It is impossible to find such a path and a boat, a ladder and happiness, a companion and grace or energy in the world. The world can only give conflicts and turmoil. It can deceive, violate trust and defraud. It can sink the boat midway, knock one down from the ladder, and mislead one who is on the right path. When the world itself is gross, how can it give the power of consciousness to anyone? But the traveler needs precisely these things. The individual being is entangled in the gross and changing nature of the world. He is fooled by its illusory appearance, and overburdened by the weight of difficulties, sins and miseries. Now he is desirous of relief from all of them. He needs to take the load off his head and rest under the cool shade of a tree. He is tired, sick and miserable. His feet are injured by the thorns and stones on the roads that he has walked. He needs a doctor who can apply the ointment.

"When a traveler feels that he is lost and that this is the cause of his miseries, he tries to find the right path. In this search he goes on pilgrimage, examines books and listens to spiritual discourses, and in this way tries to understand the truth. If he hears of a knowledgeable person he rushes to take advantage of his company. He is like a lost cow that goes around restlessly with its head raised.

"Those who set forth from their house to be misled will be misled. Those who are hungry for worldly comforts and luxuries, those who want solutions to their worldly problems, and those who are attached to the world will find guides who claim to have the power to fulfill all their desires. They are themselves lost and they mislead others more.

"Those lost travelers who find a true guide are very fortunate. One must not rush to accept a guide. Usually people get involved in the guides' outward show, the performance and the skilled talk of the guides. This decision [to choose a guide] is the most important event in the traveler's life, and it is intimately related to his mental state. If one makes a mistake then great mental anguish may be the result. Therefore one must be very careful in this matter. One must also give time to the guide to think and understand. It is not appropriate to insist with closed eyes or under the sway of emotions.

"While walking on the spiritual path one must take each step very carefully. His first job is to attain freedom from prarabdha. He is bound by prarabdha, he is inspired by prarabdha, and prarabdha makes him laugh and cry. Prarabdha nourishes his pride and makes it grow. Prarabdha grinds the individual being in the mill of reincarnation. Prarabdha is invisible but its results are apparent. It is a ghost that dances and makes the being dance. Prarabdha does not allow the being any opportunity to understand and think. It stands as the first and foremost obstacle on the spiritual path.

"As long as the feeling of doership remains prarabdha cannot die.

If one head of prarabdha is cut off then the sense of doership creates another. Somehow you may free yourself from one accumulated impression, but the sense of doership will add ten new impressions. Prarabdha sustains the sense of doership while the sense of doership keeps prarabdha alive. In the city of the chitta [psyche] these two demonic rulers [prarabdha and doership] prevail, and they give rise to whatever resolves they wish in the mind and control the actions brought about by the sense organs. The sense of doership also, like prarabdha, strikes while remaining invisible. How difficult it is to fight a war with an invisible enemy who hides and strikes! The individual soul feels as if some invisible hand is pushing him in some direction.

"By using his discriminative intellect the being can visualize and understand what these demons of doership and prarabdha are like. He can understand their way of working. A person shooting an arrow is not visible, but the arrow, as it approaches, is seen. What gives rise to a resolve in the mind may not be known, but the process of its rise in the mind can be experienced. Prarabdha may not be visible, but its fruits, in the form of happiness and misery, are apparent. Even this provides help to the lost traveler in determining his direction.

"It is the guide's [Guru's] responsibility to turn the help of the discriminative intellect into a real experience. To initiate this experience is called Shaktipat. Shaktipat raises sadhana up from the level of doership and establishes it at the level of an observer. Then all modifications of doership, happiness and misery, the results of prarabdha, are visibly separated from the self. First, samskaras begin to weaken through kriyas [workings of the awakened Shakti]. The process of formation of prarabdha is interrupted and the path to weaken the sense of doership opens. Real sadhana is that which removes the garb of the pride of false doership and takes the traveler towards the spiritual goal of annihilating prarabdha. Self-study and sadhana with effort are means of changing one's attitude, but the attitude changes only when one has direct experience of the sense of an observer.

"One difficulty still remains. How does one utilize the sense of an observer obtained in sadhana in worldly activities? Most sadhaks do not understand how to reap the maximum spiritual advantage out of this. They experience the absence of the sense of doership but are unable to implement it in life. They cannot move forward even after finding the right path. They cannot halt the accumulation of new impressions and the formation of prarabdha. They discover the solution but cannot apply it. They find the key but cannot open the lock. The sky gets cloudy but it does not rain. They find a vehicle but it does not move.

"Initially the traveler had only prarabdha and doership. Now the sense of an observer is also involved. One foot is in the boat but the other is still on the ground. The mind is now confronted with consciousness but the gross state has not yet been given up. It is early morning, light is about to come, but darkness has not yet left.

"One foot has been placed in the boat but to bring in the other foot is very difficult. We think it would be good to find a way in which we can enjoy the boat ride without sacrificing the ground. If only we could continue to enjoy worldly pleasures while making spiritual progress! But as long as you are not fully on board how will the boat sail? How can the boat that is tied to the shore sail on the water? Attachment to the world is so strong that we do not feel like giving it up. The impressions of attachment do not leave even after one gains experiential knowledge as a result of discrimination. They must be eliminated through sadhan, service and endurance. It is a long-term process.

"Generally a sadhak spends his entire time at this juncture of life and leaves. The boat rocks slowly and the joy of its movement is taken to be the ultimate bliss. He does not understand that this is not even the beginning. It is only a glimpse of joy. The boat is still tied to the shore. On the other side of the mountain there is infinite light, and he has seen only a glimpse of it from far away. At present, between him and joy a great mountain of desires, tendencies and illusion stands tall. One foot is still on the land. This sadhak is like a person who visits a palace, is charmed by the beauty of the gate and does not go inside. He takes his initial joy to be the supreme joy and does not feel the need to go any further.

"In the initial phase, similar to a light that passes through a filter

338   CHURNING OF THE HEART

and only a small amount is seen, only a glimpse of the inner light filtering through the chitta [psyche], which is filled with vasanas [tendencies], is experienced. In reality, this is not even a reflection. It is a reflection of a reflection. Just as light from the sun shines on the moon and reflects back from the moon to the earth, so the power of the soul's consciousness shines on the psyche and makes the psyche shine and active like consciousness. Then it reflects on the samskaras in the psyche and makes them active through the sense organs. In the beginning a sadhak experiences the joy from its activity. The initial experiences of the sadhan are mere experiences of the activity of the reflected form of consciousness. But that, too, happens on the basis of impressions. If someone is gratified with only this, what can be said of that person?

"The inner journey of sadhan is very long and difficult. It requires great caution, and every step must be taken very carefully. At the slightest folly you could slip. It is a very steep climb. A man cannot climb on his own strength. If someone takes another up, holding his hand, only then is it possible. For this, total surrender to the inner consciousness is required."

I was listening to all this very attentively. I became frightened upon listening. Now I had a double responsibility. I had to do my sadhan and give guidance to others, as well. Fight the war and save the army, too. How essential it is to observe oneself to attain this! Pride stands behind with a cudgel and many warriors have fallen to the ground. Everyone is handicapped by the tendency to not regard others as equal to the self. Even when everyone has lost the way no one understands that they are lost. All are busy pursuing selfish ends.

When Maharajshri was alone in his room I asked, "Maharajji, I am unable to have faith in myself so far. The psyche is not prepared in any way. There is a lack of sadhan and self-control. If I cannot control my own mind then how can I give guidance to others. On top of that, you have given me the responsibilities of a successor and assigned me the difficult task of giving initiation. How will I be able to fulfill all this?"

Maharajshri smiled and said, "You are still unable to escape the circle of your ego. You still harbor the ego of being the Guru yourself, even though I have explained to you that you are not the Guru at all. You are only a medium for the Guru to do his work. You will certainly be a Guru in front of the people, but the Shakti responsible for the Guru-work is distinct from you. You are like a transformer that does not generate electricity, it only distributes electricity, one that directs the flow of Guru's power towards the spiritual benefit of the world. If someone, by mistake, believes that the transformer is a generator then it is not your fault. Therefore you need not be scared.

"It is essential that the transformer remain connected to the generator, otherwise what will it distribute? If the Guru were to develop the pride of being a Guru then it means a disconnection from the generator. Then the transformer would stop distributing. Pride is an obstacle in the creation, distribution and experience of Guru-tattva [the Guru's elemental power]. Guru-tattva does not have a mind and senses, therefore it shines through a person with mind and senses. A Guru is only a Guru. He is not the Guru-tattva. A Sadguru is in very close touch with the Guru-tattva, but he is only a medium carrying the light of Guru-tattva. He is not Guru-tattva. In short, understand that all those who have a mind and senses are distinct from Guru-tattva. The pride resides in the mind, whereas the Guru-tattva does not have a mind. As long as you are tied to the mind you have fear, doubt and dilemma. If you are connected to the Guru-tattva all these will automatically dissolve.

"This does not apply only to the Guru. Every sadhak is in the same situation. Think about it: What is sadhan? To put an end to separate identity and unite with Guru-tattva is sadhan. Only to attain this goal does one destroy tendencies [vasanas] and accumulated impressions [samskara] and purify attitudes. Only then can a person be free from attachment, hatred, desires, anger, greed, dilemma and doubt. Only a pure mind is capable of turning toward the Guru-tattva."

Question: "So one must not entertain the wish of becoming a Guru?"

Answer: "Holding the title of Guru is not for worship. The Guru gives responsibility to a selected disciple and gives him a chance to serve. The Guru gives this opportunity to whichever disciple he wishes. This certainly does not mean that the one who is given this responsibility is the Guru's best disciple. It is possible, sometimes, that the Guru does not feel right giving this opportunity to his best disciple. In choosing a successor the same rule applies. If the Guru wishes to, he will tell a disciple to do the Guru's work. If a sadhak wishes to be a Guru on his own, that is an obstruction to sadhan."

Question: "But what about the desire not to be a Guru?"

Answer: "If the Guru wishes to give the responsibility of a Guru to a disciple then to have a desire not to be a Guru is also an obstacle. Nothing in the past or the future of the disciple is unknown to the Guru. Hence it is beneficial for the disciple to follow the Guru's wish."

67. The Essence of the Teachings, II

The following day Maharajshri began to talk on the same subject.

"The lost traveler becomes so confused that he has no awareness of who he is or what he has. He chases imaginary pleasures and happiness. The medicine for one sick with the disease of birth and death is always with him, but he never thinks of searching in his own pocket. He forgets that the joys of the world are nothing other than the reflection of his own inner Shakti, and that one day he must return to the Self within because that is the only cure for his sorrows. Two obstacles hinder the inner search. They are prarabdha and a sense of doership. The disease is inside, and the cure is also inside.

"The Guru's work is to remove the inner darkness and illuminate the mind. It is not to make the mind more attached by fulfilling worldly desires and requirements. Whatever is meant to be attained in this world you will get according to your prarabdha. The duty of a sadhak is to work without any attachment. The Guru is essential for guidance, support and removal of doubts during the inner journey.

"If the sadhak has any questions regarding whom to serve, whether he is on the right path or not, he must surrender to a Sadguru because the Sadguru understands the difficulties and helplessness of a being, and is familiar with the complexities of sadhan and the elements helpful in sadhan. A sadhak must present all his faults, mistakes, doubts, dilemmas and thoughts openly to the Guru, and after bringing the mind to a prideless state he must offer all the feelings in his heart to the Guru and listen to the Guru's words with total attention. A real Guru is never selfish or greedy. He always wishes well for his disciples. He is generous, self-controlled and far-sighted. He is capable of saving sinking souls. The only duty of a disciple is to surrender at the Guru's lotus feet."

Question: "Such a Guru is not easily available to all; what can a person do? If a Guru has something in his mind and says something else then what can be done?"

Answer: "I have used the word Sadguru, real Guru. You cannot imagine such impurities in him. It may be possible that the Guru thinks that something is special and must not be told immediately for the benefit of the disciple. He may decide to leave it unspoken. His purpose for this is the spiritual benefit of the disciple only.

"Now as far as the ease of finding a real Guru is concerned, that is why I recommend not hurrying in accepting someone as a Guru. If someone is truly in search of a real Guru he will definitely find a real Guru, because a real Guru is, likewise, in search of a real disciple. The difficulty is for those who, after polluting their mind with worldly desires, look for a Guru to fulfill those wishes and give them worldly pleasures. Frequently truth finds truth and falsehood finds falsehood."

I had taken sanyas. Perhaps people had started looking at me as a mahatma, but I had not yet been able to develop a feeling of total surrender towards Guru Maharajji. I had not overcome the tendency of hiding things in my mind while talking. I did not have the courage to reveal all my inner impurities. Even if I talked I would do so in a roundabout way. It was like being in front of a mirror while concealing a black smudge on the face. Hiding the smudge would not wash it away, but there would be satisfaction that the black smudge was not visible. I would use my intellect more than my heart, as if I had no heart. These things perturbed me and I ran to Maharajshri's room. I was still unable to give up my habit of using my intellect and I wanted to talk only in a roundabout way, but before I could say anything, a gentleman sitting there asked, "Scriptures and saints say that Guru is God. Then how can anything be hidden from God? Also, God is not a person, but the Guru is a person. So how can he be said to be God?"

Maharajshri said, "This dilemma exists due to the fact that the difference between the Guru and Guru-tattva is not clearly understood. In the form of the inner Guru, Guru-tattva resides in everyone. Because we are unable to see that we need to imagine God in a Guru's body. Through that medium we can experience our own inner Guru. Although the Guru-tattva is present everywhere, it is difficult to experience it in all the things. Therefore it can first be experienced through the medium of the Guru within, and then its presence can be experienced everywhere.

"As regards hiding things from the Guru, the issue is whether the disciple goes to the Guru considering him to be a person or God. If he considers the Guru as God then he is concerned with, and focuses on, the God present in the Guru's body. The same God, from the beginning, is present in the disciple's body in the form of Guru-tattva. Then how can anything be hidden from the Guru? Still one may certainly derive satisfaction from the act of hiding."

Question: "If we need to imagine Guru-tattva then it can be imagined in our own body?"

Answer: "Certainly this can be done if one is able. The mind of a human being is extroverted. It operates outwards and finds it difficult to turn within. Therefore it is easier to imagine God in someone other than the self."

Question: "If it is easier to imagine God outside then why not imagine God within a mother or a father?"

Answer: "Definitely this can be done. In that case, if the mother or father becomes the Guru it is one and the same. But parents may have an attachment for their child. They may not be able to look after the spiritual benefit of their offspring. The children also, after reaching maturity, may strongly regard the parents as humans, and that can come in the way of seeing them in the form of God. Still, if someone can do it there is no problem.

"Besides, it is not only a question of the disciple's imagination. The Guru must also be worthy and capable. He must have the experience of Guru-tattva and must be capable of making the disciple have the same experience. Establishing the relationship between the Guru and disciple is the ultimate achievement. There is no attachment or expectation of worldly gains. That is why it is believed that, even when the mother and father are worthy and capable, a Guru must be other than a parent.

"When a sense of the Guru's divinity becomes solid, then the question of hiding from the Guru becomes irrelevant. It is wasted effort to hide from the Guru because the Guru-tattva is a witness to each and every feeling and thought. The Guru-tattva is familiar with impressions and tendencies hidden in the psyche that are unknown to the person himself until they come up and create waves in the psyche."

I had received the answer to my question but still I was very sad, because even after reaching the riverbank I was still thirsty. I was unable to surrender to Guru Maharaj even after taking sanyas. How complete was the surrender of Kabir, Meera, Surdas and Tulsi! These people were my ideals, but only in theory. The devotion for the Guru in the heart of Shankar Purushottam Tirth Maharaj was incomparable. And here I am keeping things in my heart hidden from Guru Maharaj. If this was not pride then what was it?

I did not say anything. I went to my room and lay down quietly. By the grace of the Guru I had received such a direct spiritual path and divine experience, and still the pride in my heart was intact. "When and how will I be free from my pride? What is the shortcoming in my sadhan? I consider myself a great servant. Is this my service? Is this spiritual achievement? Is this a sign of progress?" I was lost in such thoughts for a long time. Who knows for how long?

68.   The Essence of the Teachings, III

Somehow Maharajshri knew the state of my mind. The following day, as he was sitting on the verandah, he said, "Some people get very disturbed about certain things. I have repeatedly said that the spiritual journey is very long, wherein there is a possibility of the sadhak falling again and again. There has not been a single sadhak who has not fallen frequently. The samskaras of attachment and pride are so strong that they keep dragging a sadhak down.

"Man does not have faith in self or in God. He does not have the courage to get up on his own, nor does he have firm faith that God will be gracious and raise him up. Such people become worried on falling. The devotee should have a firm faith that the god by whose grace and strength he has jumped into the ocean of reincarnation is still merciful. I knew that the ocean was very deep, but I had confidence that God would certainly come to save me when needed. Why should one be afraid of small falls when one was not scared of falling into the whirl of Maya? Do not be afraid of falling, be afraid of not getting up.

"If some day you fall do not stay down. To remain down is the task of worldly people. They derive joy from remaining down. An aspirant is one who makes an effort to get up immediately after falling. A person falls only when he falls in his own mind. For that it is essential to have samskaras of tamas and rajas in the mind. Supporting circumstances develop externally and related resolves arise in the mind. The intellect operates accordingly and sights appropriate to a fall appear. God showers his grace by giving rise to such samskaras and giving one an opportunity to destroy them. If a person cannot make the most of the opportunity and stumbles, what can God do? Sometimes a person, while stumbling, reaches the end of a ditch; sometimes he slips and sometimes he falls. What a person will do in such a situation depends on his mental state, his ability to face difficulties and the force of his samskaras.

"The subject of spirituality is very subtle and the human mind is filled with doubts and impurities, deluded and worldly. Spirituality directs one inward, whereas man functions outward. As a result, it becomes more difficult to understand the secrets of karma and the nature of prarabdha. With logic and speculation one becomes further entangled. Once a person starts to fall he continues to do so until he settles into a fallen state.

"God is present in each and every person in the form of his chaitanya-Shakti [energy of cosmic consciousness]. He not only gives life, but also gives the energy to continue life. The intellect could not function if it were not mixed with God's consciousness. There would be no feelings in the heart and no thoughts in the mind. Not only that — God's Shakti is required even to accumulate impressions and experience the fruits of prarabdha. Does a dead man accumulate impressions or experience the results of his past actions? The feeling of hunger, eating and digesting, inhaling and exhaling, the flowing of blood in the arteries and veins, the activities of the senses, hands and feet, the waves of desire, anger and greed agitating the mind – all these are activities of God's Shakti based on accumulated impressions. The human psyche, body and senses are only the vehicle. The scriptures and saints, therefore, say that God does everything. Nothing can be done without Shakti-energy and only God has energy.

"While doing everything God remains a non-doer. God does not have any prarabdha. He does not have a mind, body or senses. Only an individual being has all these. That is why God does not have to experience or do anything. With his infinite grace he only gives energy to live. The mind, intellect and body of an individual being are activated by God according to the being's sentiments, prarabdha and tendencies. But the individual being forgets the power of God's Shakti and puts on the garb of doership. He pretends he has done it all. All other faults follow the pride and prarabdha is formed. The doer is God's Shakti but the individual being feels the false pride of acting. Shakti does not have any ego and, as a result, Shakti does not accumulate any impressions. But the individual soul accumulates impressions due to false ego."

"The first step on the spiritual ladder is to experience the workings of God's energy. Earlier I have elaborated on prarabdha and doership. These begin to dissolve with the experience of God's energy. We fall when our mind descends to the level of ego. That is when we become enveloped in worries. That is when we feel the grip of desire.

"To worry about something means that the attention of the sadhak has shifted away from the workings of Shakti. His sense of an observer has gone and he has become a doer. If the aspirant can return to the observer state then all his worries will disappear immediately and his mental depression will pass.

"The problems of an individual being arise when he does not experience the Shakti of God that works within the chitta [psyche] as distinct from himself. This experience of separateness is called the awakening of Shakti, and the grace of the Guru is essential for that awakening to take place. Along with the experience of the separateness of the Shakti from the chitta, one starts to see the separateness of chitta from the workings of the Shakti based on the chitta: the accumulation of impressions, the formation of prarabdha, the rising of tendencies and attitudes, sentiments and resolve. In this way the sadhak, that is the being, becomes a witness to the chitta, Shakti and all the influences on the chitta. Just imagine how different this state is from that of worldly people. When someone can see worries and problems separate from him, then he observes them as if he is watching a movie. He is free from all worries.

"The difficulty is that a sadhak cannot continuously maintain this state of mind. These feelings arise only at the time of sadhan. At times even during sadhan the samskaras of worries arise and take the form of kriyas [spontaneous workings of Shakti]. The sadhak leaves the state of an observer, accepts himself as the doer, and gets involved in worries. After getting up from sadhan, generally, sadhaks give up the sense of an observer, become totally worldly and behave with attachment. In any case, after awakening the Shakti certainly gives a glimpse of hope, light and true knowledge. Then life starts to shift direction. Darkness is recognized as darkness. Bricks in the wall of prarabdha start to loosen. This is the greatness and the grace of Guru-Shakti."

I was listening to Maharajshri with concentration and simultaneously evaluating my state of chitta. I asked, "When the mind starts to fall, I don't know where the memory of the experience of separateness of Shakti hides. At that time a person merges with his fall and finds himself fallen into a ditch."

Maharajshri said, "I am explaining exactly this. Some have pride of being worthy and others have pride of being unworthy. The forms are different but, basically, they both are pride. In both situations the sense of an observer is absent; the feeling of doership alone is dominant in the chitta. As the feeling of being an observer diminishes, prarabdha becomes more powerful and the sense of doership becomes equally strong. Consequently the individual being experiences more joy and misery."

Question: "What can be done to maintain the sense of an observer?"

Answer: "It is clear that the reason for all the miseries of humans is the absence of the sense of an observer. This absence is called avidya in *Yoga Darshan*. Doership contains avidya, and the sense of an observer holds the seed of vidya. It is impossible to be free from sorrows as long as an individual being has a sense that he is the doer. Now the question is how to attain the sense of an observer. For this, first of all, the awakening of Shakti is essential. Only after that will spontaneous kriyas begin within the psyche. This is the first attack on doership. This is when the separation from the Shakti is experienced. Surrender is the only thing that can give stability to the sense of an observer."

Question: "What is the relationship between surrender and the sense of an observer?"

Answer: "This is a subject worth understanding. There is a strong relationship between surrender and the sense of an observer. When someone sits in sadhan with a state of surrender he watches kriyas taking place as a witness. He does not interfere with them in any way. He sees them separate from himself and is not affected by them. Real devotion enters sadhan only after a sense of surrender arises. In other words, surrender itself is devotion. As surrender grows the sense of an observer becomes stronger. Nothing else except awakened Shakti can give rise to the sense of an observer and surrender."

Question: "Is surrender required only at the time of sadhan and not at other times?"

Answer: "Surrender is essential at all times but its practice begins at the time of sadhan. Shakti awakening takes place within so, at first, surrender during sadhan also takes place within. As the workings and all-pervasiveness of Shakti are experienced the sense of surrender enters everyday life. Without that surrender in the external aspect of life an individual being cannot be free from the joys and miseries experienced in life. Thus both types of surrender, internal and external, are necessary."

Question: "Does this mean that karma [action] becomes totally unimportant when one surrenders?"

Answer: "Karma [action] takes the form of duty once one surrenders to Shakti. Action is for worldly people but a sadhak only performs his duty. After identifying his duty a sadhak gives up the sense of convenience and inconvenience and does whatever is his duty. By performing actions only as duty one does not accumulate samskaras, because while performing a duty the attention is on the fulfillment of the duty and not on the result. This is the true nature of Karma Yoga [an action based spiritual path]. This state persists until one realizes that Shakti does everything and that Shakti is all-pervading. Then it is experienced that all the senses work due to Shakti. Just as a sadhak experiences that all the kriyas in the mind and body during sadhan take place independent of himself, similarly the senses are seen working independent of himself. His preliminary condition reverses and ghat-avastha [a state of discernment] arises. Just as a pot fills with water he experiences his body filling with Shakti."

I became silent listening to this. I had nothing more to say.

69. The Personality of Maharajshri

Maharajshri was a spring of knowledge and experience whose flow never dried. Like the holy river Ganges, the Ganges of knowledge kept flowing while he lived in his body. How much the listener could understand and grasp depended on his state of mind. Maharajshri never tried to avoid any question. If he thought someone had asked a question beyond his capacity to understand then he would offer the listener an appropriate explanation. It was very difficult for a lowly person like me to understand the depth of his heart, the expanse of his sadhan, and the subtlety of his knowledge. He was a straightforward and uncomplicated, innocent and pure personality, without pretense, devoid of pomp. He spoke simply, like a common person. But when a discussion about sadhan or spiritual knowledge began a window would open up within and one gem of knowledge after another would emerge.

There is no question of my knowing the gems of knowledge he doled out in my absence. Those that I could not gather because of my limited intellect, these I could not bring to you. Those gems which I forgot due to the lapse of time also remained untouched. Whatever I could remember I have presented here. In reality, this exercise of recollection has been a reason for churning my heart, a process that has become an instrument for writing this book. I would like to request readers not to regard this as a mere book and make it a decorative piece on a bookshelf. Please try to examine your heart in the light of the teachings of Maharajshri.

One day Maharajshri said that Shri Gangadhar Tirth Maharaj had done a limitless favor to the people of the Kaliyuga [modern age] by bringing the knowledge of Shaktipat out from its concealment and making it easily available to the average householder. This knowledge has spread to such an extent today as a result of the austerity and sacrifice of Swamiji Maharaj. Hundreds of thousands of sadhaks have benefited from

Shaktipat today. Many large ashrams have been built, an abundance of literature is available, and many Gurus are doing this work. But as any knowledge starts spreading, its quality starts deteriorating. Today we neither see the same results of initiation as before, nor sadhaks like before.

This observation of Maharajshri deserves the attention of all sadhaks. Maharajshri mentioned this at least thirty-five years ago. There are no signs of change in that situation even today.

Sadhaks have a duty toward themselves as well as toward their lineage. Hence the plea that sadhaks/readers take their responsibility earnestly. Life is passing moment by moment. An entire life might pass in just thinking. Average sadhaks like us have many difficulties. The world makes all efforts to entice, scare and lead astray the person who is walking on the straight path. The greatest obstacle is impurities of the mind. Extreme caution is necessary. But if the sadhak surrenders, the Guru-Shakti takes him to his destination.

Glossary

Abhinav Gupta — Tantra master, regarded as the greatest Shaivite philosopher of Kashmir. Author of *Pratyabhijnahridayam*.

Adi Shankaracharya — Adi ("first") Shankaracharya (686 A.D. - 718 A.D.) coordinated the vedic spiritual tradition in India at a time of turmoil and dispersion. He gave enormous inspiration, insight and understanding of the underlying truth of life and living, relevant to this day. He is considered the greatest spiritual saint India has ever produced

Advaita — The theory of nonduality. The exponents of this theory believe that God is present in each person.

Akalpita siddhis — Spontaneously manifesting spiritual powers.

Akasha — Literally "luminous"; Ether.

Allhadini — "Giver of Bliss"; term in Bhakti Yoga which corresponds to Shakti.

Anvopaaya — That expedient which is concerned with "anu," a limited being, signifying his mental effort to end ignorance of his true nature.

Asamprajnat samadhi — Seedless meditation.

Ashram — Monastery.

Atma — Soul.

Bhagavadpad — Adi Shankaracharya (see above).

Bhagawati — A goddess who is the form of divine energy — Shakti — created by the confluence of all the powers of all other gods and goddesses. An epithet of Parvati, the consort of Lord Shiva.

Bhajan — Devotional hymns which describe the glory of the Lord.

Bhakta — A devotee.

Bhakti Yoga — Path of Devotion.

Bhiksha — Asking for alms.

Bhogi — A person engrossed in worldly pleasures.

Bhuddi Yoga — Yoga of the intellect.

Bramha — The one, self-existent, impersonal spirit; the one universal soul; the divine essence and source from which all created things emanate, with which they are identified, and to which they return; the self-existent; the Absolute; the Eternal. Not generally an object of worship, but rather of meditation and knowledge. Also: the one, impersonal, universal Spirit manifested as a personal Creator and as the first of the triad of personal gods in the Hindu religion.

Bramhachari — A spiritual aspirant who has taken a vow of celibacy and devoted his life to the practice of spiritual discipline.

Bramhacharya — The practice of celibacy.

Chaitanya — The conscious-self.

Chaitanya Mahaprabhu — (1486-1533). Saint, visionary and poet who revived and formalized the worship of Lord Krishna. Identified with Bhakti Yoga movement in Indian history.

Chakras — "Wheels"; the six chakras situated in the human body are energy centers, the activation of which represents progressive steps on the path to Self-realization.

Chetan — Animate; conscious.

Chetana — Consciousness.

Chitta — Mind-stuff.

Dakshina — Offerings made at the time of obtaining knowledge, usually presented at the feet of the Guru.

Dattatreya — God described in the Puranas, son of Atri and Anasuya. Symbolically represented with three heads, which represent Bramha tattwa, Vishnu tattwa and Shiva tattwa.

Devatma Shakti — Divine power.

Dewas — A city in central India. Swami Vishnu Tirth Maharaj established his ashram here in Narayan Kuti.

Diksha — A ceremony of initiation. It is, in fact, a procedure of bestowing the divine powers of a Guru upon the disciple, by which he progresses continuously on the path of divinity.

Garuda — A divine being, half-man, half-eagle, who serves as the vehicle of Vishnu.

Geru — Soil used to dye clothing a saffron color, indicating renunciation.

Gita — The Bhagavad Gita, also called Shreemad Bhagwat Gita. This is one of the holy texts of the Hindus, which contains the divine discourse given to Arjun by Lord Krishna at the battle of Kurukshetra.

Guru — A spiritual teacher or mentor. According to ancient Indian Philosophy, one cannot attain success in the spiritual field without the help of a Guru or Sadguru (true Guru).

Gurudev — A reverential form of the word Guru.

Guru Purnima — The day of full moon, Purnima, in the month of Ashadh (June/July) is traditionally celebrated as Guru Purnima by Hindus. Also known as Vyas Purnima, the day is celebrated in remembrance and veneration of the sage, Ved Vyas.

Guru-Shakti — Power of the Guru; Power of God.

Guru-tattva — The elemental power of the Guru.

Hanuman — The ever-living (Chiranjeevi) son of Lord Vayu (the wind god) and a devotee of Lord Rama. He is a symbol of devotion and love.

Haridwar — A city situated on the banks of the holy Ganges river in the northern plains of India. Associated with both Lord Shiva and Lord Vishnu, Haridwar is one of the seven sacred cities of India.

Himachal Pradesh — A state in Northern India at the foothills of the Himalayas. It is referred to as the land of eternal snow peaks.

Indore — A city near Dewas, in Madhya Pradesh in Central India.

Japa — Chanting a Mantra.

Jnana — Knowledge.

Jnana Yoga — The science of knowledge for attaining self-realization.

Jnana Yogi — One who practices Jnana Yoga.

Jnaneshwar — Jnaneshwar was a great siddha, mystic and poetic genius of Maharashtra, India who gave up his mortal form at the age of 21. His spiritual roots were in both the nath and bhakti traditions, and his lineage is listed as: Shiva, Shakti, Matsyendra, Gorakhnath, Gahini and Nivritti. At the age of fifteen (1290 C.E.) he is said to have delivered *ex tempore* the nine-thousand verses of his poetic commentary on the Bhagavad Gita; *Jnaneshvari.*

Jyotirlinga — "The emblem of light"; Sacred stones used for symbolic worship of **Shiva.**

Kabir — Kabir was a great musician saint of fifteenth century India, a weaver by profession. The hallmark of Kabir's poetry is that he conveys in his two line poems (doha) what others could not do in many pages.

Kailash Mountain — A Himalayan peak regarded as the home of Shiva.

Kak Bhushundi — An immortal being living in the form of a crow, desbribed in the Ramayana.

Kala — Art.

Kaliyuga — The present Dark Age. In this era there is an abundance of strife, ignorance, vice and irreligion, true virtue being practically nonexistent.

Kalpita siddhis — Spiritual powers developed through personal mental resolve.

Kama — Desire.

Kama-Kala — The art of procreation.

Karma — Action in progress.

Karma Yoga — The science of dutiful action.

Karma Yogi — One who practices karma yoga.

Kashi — Also known as Varanasi, Kashi or Banares; one of the oldest living cities in the world and the ultimate pilgrimage for Hindus, who believe that to die in the city is to attain instant salvation. It is located on the left bank of the Ganges River.

Kriyas — Automatic movements that are observed by an individual after his Kundalini has been awakened.

Kriya-Sadhana — Spiritual practices involving kriyas.

Kundalini — "Coiled"; the power of Shakti residing at the base of the spine, whose awakening represents the first step in the process of Self-realization.

Lahore — Present-day city in Pakistan, it was a part of India before the partition.

Lila — Divine sport.

Lokas — Regions where souls reside according to the level of development of their consciousness.

Lord Rama — An incarnation of Lord Vishnu; one of the most commonly adored gods of Hindus, known as an ideal man and hero of the epic poem Ramayana.

Madhya Pradesh — A state in the central part of India.

Maharajshri — Term of highest respect. In this work it refers to Swami Vishnu Tirth Maharaj.

Mahatma — A Great Soul.

Mantra — Sacred words or sounds invested with power.

Marathi — A language spoken in the state of Maharastra in Western India.

Maya — Illusion; the manifest world.

Mirabai — (1504-1550) Meerabai was a princess from Rajasthan, India who is known for her steadfast devotion to Lord Krishna.

Moksha — Liberation.

Mooladhar — First chakra, which corresponds with the pelvic plexus of the sympathetic nervous system.

Namdev — (1270-1350) A famous saint of Maharashtra. He is regarded as one the pioneers of the Bhakti movement in India, along with Jnaneshwar and Tukaram

Nangal — A town in Punjab state, a Northwestern Province of India.

Narada Bhakti Sutras — An exposition of the path of Bhakti Marg by the great Sage Narada.

Narayan Kuti — Narayan Kuti was the place at the foothills of the mountain in Dewas where Swami Vishnu Tirth Maharaj settled.

Nirguna bhakti — Devotion to God without attributes.

Nivritti — Inward path by abstention from all acts. The path of sanyas is known as "Nivritti Marg."

Prajnana — Supreme Knowledge.

Prakriti — Original nature; The creative principle.

Prana — Life force. Sometimes identified with Shakti.

Pranayaam — Exercises involving breath control whose primary aim is the awakening of the Kundalini.

Prarabdha — Destiny formed by one's past actions.

Prasad — During any form of worship, ritual or ceremony, Hindus offer some items of food to the Lord. After the ceremony, this sacred food is distributed to worshipers as the offering of the Lord.

Pratyahara — The process of turning the mind inward, through spiritual disciplines.

Pravritti — Active participation in life and due discharge of one's duties and obligations to society.

Punjab — A State in Northwestern India.

Puranas — The Puranas are a class of literary texts, all written in Sanskrit verse, whose composition dates from the 4th century B.C.E. to about 1000 C.E.

Puri — A holy place in the state of Orissa in India. Swami Gangadhar Tirth Maharaj lived there.

Purusha — The soul.

Purushartha — Self-effort toward attaining Self-realization.

Rajas (Rajo Guna) — Guna (quality) of activity.

Ramayana — One of the Great Indian epics. The story of Lord Rama.

Ravana — A demi-god, rival of Lord Rama in the Ramayana.

Rishi — Sage. Literally, it means "the seer."

Rishikesh — A spiritual center on the banks of the Ganges in Uttar Pradesh in Northern India. Rishikesh is one of the most popular pilgrimage centers and there are many ashrams there.

Saakshi — Witness.

Sadhak — Spiritual aspirant.

Sadhan — Automatic spiritual practices, as in the case of Shaktipat.

Sadhan Dairy — A diary written by Swami Vishnu Tirth Maharaj describing his experiences in Sadhan after his initiation in Rishikesh from Swami Yoganand Maharaj.

Sadhana — Spiritual practices involving effort.

Saguna bhakti — Devotion to God with attributes.

Samadhi — Super-consciousness; when individual consciousness merges with the universal consciousness; also, a tomb.

Samprajnat samadhi — Samadhi with intellectual consciousness; Samadhi with seed.

Samskaras — Accumulated impressions.

Sanchit samskaras — Accumulated impressions from past lives.

Sankalp — Resolve.

Sanyas Diksha — Initiation into the monastic order.

Sanyasi — A renunciate.

Satsang — The company of good men.

Sattva Guna — Harmonious quality.

Sattvic — Harmonious.

Seva — Service.

Sevak — A servant dedicated to serving his master.

Shakti — Spiritual energy; spiritual power.

Shaktipat — Descent of Spiritual energy. Literally defined as "the fall" of spiritual energy.

Shaktopaaya — A yogic practice of thought only. In this the seeker has to develop concentration upon God-consciousness by means of a special initiating thought unfolded by the master. He does not have to practice pranayaam or any other practice on his own.

Shankara — Another name for Lord Shiva; the lord of destruction and one god of the Hindu trinity. Also, sometimes, Adi Shankaracharya.

Shishya — Disciple.

Shiva — Lord Shiva or Maheshwara. One god of the trinity in Hindu spirituality. He is the God of Destruction.

Shloka — A short Sanskrit verse or stanza.

Siddha — A perfected, realized or enlightened being. One who possesses siddhis.

Siddhi — Spiritual power.

Sita — Consort of Lord Rama.

Spandan — Vibrations.

Sthitaprajna — The state of steadfast wisdom.

Sushumna — A channel flowing up the center of the spine. The movement of Kundalini energy up this channel corresponds to spiritual awakening.

Sutlej — A river that flows through Punjab and other Northwestern states of India and Pakistan.

Swami Gangadhar Tirth Maharaj — Founder of the Shaktipat system of Yoga, he lived in Puri, a town in eastern India.

Swami Muktananda — Modern saint, disciple of Swami Nityananda. Muktananda was to travel widely in the west, attracting many followers in the U.S. and Europe.

Swami Narayan Tirth Dev Maharaj — The only disciple of Swami Gangadhar Tirth Maharaj, the founder of Shivom Tirth's spiritual lineage, who was given the power to initiate other disciples and spread Shaktipat.

Swami Narayan Tirth Maharaj — Disciple of Swami Shankar Purushottam Tirth Maharaj. Sanyas Guru of Swami Shivom Tirth.

Swami Shankar Purushottam Tirth Maharaj — Purushottam Tirth Maharaj was the Sanyas Guru of Swami Vishnu Tirth Maharaj, and a disciple of Swami Narayan Dev Tirth Maharaj.

Swami Vishnu Tirth Maharaj — A preceptor in the Shaktipat order, he was initiated into Shaktipat by Swami Yoganandji Maharaj and was the Guru of the author.

Swami Yoganand Vijnani Maharaj — He was the Shaktipat Guru of Swami Vishnu Tirth Maharaj and a disciple of Swami Narayan Dev Tirth Maharaj.

Swaroopa Darshan — Seeing one's own embodied form separate from one's Self.

Swartha — Selfishness.

Tamas (Tamo Guna) — Guna of rest, passivity, inertia.

Tantra — Tantra, or more properly Tantrika, is a diverse and rich spiritual tradition of the Indian subcontinent. A system of spiritual beliefs and practices said to be derived from Sanskrit roots signifying: "body" because of its emphasis on bodily activities; "stretch" because it extends the faculties of humans; "rope" because it secures the devotee to the deity; "harp" for the music and beauty of its philosophy; "interiorness" for the secrecy of its doctrine; "loom" suggesting the two cosmic principles, male and female, that make up the warp and woof of the woven fabric of the universe.

Tapas — Austerities.

Tattwa — Elemental power.

Tirth — Holy place, pilgrimage site.

Tukaram — (1608-1649) Great seventeenth century saint from Maharashtra. Spread the bhakti movement in India. Tukaram was a Vaishnava bhakta, a true man of God.

Ujjain — A historic capital of central India in Madhya Pradesh. A venerated pilgrimage center enshrining Mahakaleshwara, one of the Jyotirlinga manifestations of Shiva.

Uttarkhand — The north Indian towns of Nainital, Almora, Pauri, Tehri and Dehradun make up this land of Uttarkhand. It is full of temples.

Vasanas — Mental tendencies formed from past experience.

Vedanta — The word Vedanta is normally read as a combination of two words: *veda* and *anta*, end. The Upanishads are sometimes called Vedanta since they are seen as the end and the fulfillment of the Veda. The Vedanta viewpoint is a family of philosophical schools which take up the issues discussed in the Upanishads: the nature of the self, the relation of the Ultimate Self to Ultimate Reality, Atman to Bramhan, the status of the world given inexperience, the relation of the world we experience to Bramhan.

Vidvat sanyas — A vow of renunciation taken by a person who has already attained Self-realization.

Vidvisha sanyas — A vow of reununcation taken by a person prior to Self-realization, formalizing one's intention to devote themselves to the attainment of that goal.

Vidya — Knowledge.

Vishaad — Dejection.

Vishwamitra — A great Hindu sage and scholar who is referred to as the Bramharshi; Incidentally, he was born a king and, due to penances, he acquired the status of a Bramharshi.

Vrindavan — A town in Northern India that is another major place of pilgrimage. It was the sacred abode of Lord Krishna.

Yoga Darshan — Written by Patanjali, this is the basic treatise of the philosophy of Yoga. Considered the most authoritative text on the school of Yoga.

Index

Dronacharya, 280
effort
  and ego, 26
ego, 28, 77, 78, 79, 84, 96, 100-104, 110-
  115, 120, 123-128, 131, 143, 145,
  146, 153, 157, 158, 159, 164-169,
  175-179, 184, 191, 208, 213, 214,
  215, 229, 230, 237, 246-260, 279,
  280, 287, 290, 291, 297, 298, 300,
  308-311, 324-327, 333, 338, 346,
  347
  a heightened, 22
  began to sprout, 21
  eclipsed by, 110
  false, 16, 35
  mind and, 22
  must be given up, 37
  of a living being, 15
  of doership, 125
  rise of, 13
  source of, 22
  strike at, 74
egoism, 23, 59, 70, 102, 111, 124, 142,
  159, 328
Egypt, 44, 167, 168
endurance, 324
Fickle-mindedness, 133
food
  becomes tamasic, 14
  sattvic, 14
forbearance, 74, 92
Galav, 168, 169
Ganeshpuri, 160, 162
Gangadhar Tirth Maharaj, 180, 184, 266,
  267, 350
Gangotri, 90
Garud Chatti, 41
Garuda, 188, 192-195, 204, 220, 275
  delusion of, 220
Garuda Chatti, 272-275
Gauri Kund, 89
Geru, 23, 320
Gita, 34, 35, 54, 102, 143, 181, 199,
  277- 297, 303, 310-315
  and Karma Yoga, 277
  eleventh chapter, 102
  teachings of the, 54
  twelfth chapter of the, 32

good
  to become, 16
  to look, 16
gudhvidya, 310
guna, 73, 150, 304
  rajo, 28, 105, 111, 150
  sattva, 28, 150
  tamo, 28, 111
Guru
  grace of, 26
  service of, 67
  tradition, 71
Guru-disciple
  Krishna and Arjuna, 280
Guru-seva, 67, 70, 86, 183, 184, 185,
  252, 254, 255
Guru-Shakti, 18, 27, 71, 169, 258, 328,
  348, 351
Guru-tattva, 339
Hanuman, 167
Haridasji, 229
idol worship, 32
ignorance, 14, 23, 76, 81, 102-105, 190,
  191, 209, 252, 255, 278, 279, 286. *See*
  ajnana
illusion, elimination of, 131
individual identity, 22, 85, 127
Indra, 123, 190
infatuation, 211
initiation, 21, 23, 66-72, 86, 154, 180-
  186, 195, 202, 206, 256, 261, 267,
  272, 280-282, 294, 296, 306, 315,
  319, 320, 321, 327-333, 338, 351
  as a service, 70
  formal, 23
  science of, 71
introspection, 21
  habit of, 27
invisible holy beings, 53
Jad Bharat, 212
James Crenshaw, 45, 54
Janah, 54
Janak, 233
japa, 62, 82-86, 92-97, 124, 128, 144,
  145, 162, 174, 179, 181, 192, 198,
  203, 225, 275
Jayadeva, 198
jiva, 14, 79, 80-85, 104, 122, 124, 127,
  128, 135, 136, 151, 189, 216, 288

About the Author

Swami Shivom Tirth was born in 1924, in a village in Punjab, with the name Om Prakash. He pursued university studies in Lahore, but was compelled by the partition of India to return to Punjab with his family. There, as a householder, he aspired to an ideal way of life, devoted to the pursuit of higher objectives. After coming to know about the spiritual attainments of Swami Vishnu Tirthji Maharaj, he sought permission to join him. He bid farewell to his family and was initiated in 1959.

Swami Vishnu Tirthji arranged for his disciple to be in the company of many distinguished spiritual personalities and to visit important religious centers. After receiving initiation into the order of renunciation (Sanyas), which he took in 1965, he was given the name of Swami Shivom Tirth. Swami Vishnu Tirthji afterwards authorized Swami Shivom Tirth to succeed him and propagate the system of Shaktipat for the welfare of all people. Since then, Swami Shivom Tirth has traveled to many countries of the world, including the United States. His works published in English are: *A Guide to Shaktipat; Rays of Ancient Wisdom; Sadhan Path, A Guide to Meditation; Shivom Vani, The Songs of Shivom*; and the three-volume *Churning of the Heart*.

For more information about Swami Shivom Tirth and Shaktipat, readers are invited to contact:

Sadhana Books
P. O. Box 9877
Berkeley, California 94709

Or email: sstirth@hotmail.com